MANCHESTER UNITED 2
BAYERN MUNICH 1
1999

LIVERPOOL 3
AC MILAN 3
2005

MANCHESTER CITY 3
QPR 2
2012

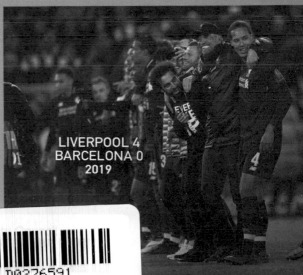

LIVERPOOL 4
BARCELONA 0
2019

THE GREATEST GAMES

www.penguin.co.uk

THE GREATEST GAMES

Jamie Carragher

BANTAM PRESS

TRANSWORLD PUBLISHERS
Penguin Random House, One Embassy Gardens,
8 Viaduct Gardens, London SW11 7BW
www.penguin.co.uk

Transworld is part of the Penguin Random House group of companies
whose addresses can be found at global.penguinrandomhouse.com

First published in Great Britain in 2020 by Bantam Press
an imprint of Transworld Publishers

A CIP catalogue record for this book
is available from the British Library.

ISBN 9781787634084 (hb)
9781787634091 (tpb)

Typeset in 11.5/15.5pt Minion Pro by Jouve (UK), Milton Keynes
Printed and bound in Great Britain by Clays Ltd, Elcograf S.p.A.

Penguin Random House is committed to a sustainable
future for our business, our readers and our planet. This book
is made from Forest Stewardship Council® certified paper.

CONTENTS

INTRODUCTION

Think about the greatest games you have seen.

Now ask yourself this: how often have you watched them again in full?

I do not mean edited highlights, or montages of clips reminding you of decisive actions. I am talking about frame by frame, so you can look beyond the elation, or perhaps despair, of the outcome.

It is surprising how few of us do so.

We can reel off a list of celebrated games that mean more to us than others, but we focus on our favourite sequences – the goals, the saves, the tackles, the final whistle and the trophy lifts. We savour the emotional impact. These sensations are impossible to recreate once the sporting battle is over and we know how a story ended. There is an adrenalin rush that comes with uncertainty.

I believe the general reluctance to sit through an entire match we have already seen is partially a psychological response to those experiences, in football or any sport, that we cherish the most.

When I was playing for Liverpool, I made a habit of re-examining our ninety-minute performance a couple of hours after the final whistle. I was often awake until the early hours, assessing what went well and where there was room for improvement. But that was all about preparation for the next match.

It is amazing how many players I have spoken to during the course of writing this book who say they are wary about rewatching their greatest games because it might challenge, or even undermine, their recollections.

When we win, we want to carefully preserve our preferred snapshots, our euphoric feelings guided by the instant post-match memories conveyed in the reports, broadcasts and pitchside interviews. Our reminiscences and anecdotes are influenced by these first drafts of history. In victory, even the worst performances are rendered meaningless. So often, we think the most illuminating recollections are shared by ex-players long after the event because in the midst of our professional careers we do not always get the chance to absorb the scale of an achievement. No sooner is the medal around the neck than the next fixture or competition is upon us.

In defeat, the reluctance to revisit a bad memory is easier to understand, even if you gave the performance of your career and suffered an unlucky or undeserved loss.

Many chronicles of the greatest games focus on the winners. I was keen wherever possible to see these games from a losers' perspective too, and discover what effects, if any, agonizing defeats had on players and their careers.

The starting point for this book was to reassess many of the games which left the deepest impression on me as a fan, player and pundit, and compare how my perception, and indeed that of those who featured so prominently, mirrored the reality.

I wanted to give other classic encounters my Sky Sports *Monday Night Football* treatment, offering a thorough tactical analysis of coaching set-ups and individual performances – some of which may have been overlooked or certainly underplayed at the time – and then discussing my observations with the players and coaches involved.

Many of the games are so famous they have had numerous books written about them, but by rewatching in full I wanted to bring a level of insight which may not have been available at the time, certainly in the 1980s when live televised football was infrequent.

The more games I examined, the more some of my preconceptions were challenged. Assumptions about fixtures such as the 1999 Champions League final, England's 5-1 win over Germany in 2001, and even my finest two hours – Istanbul in 2005 – demanded varying degrees of reassessment, in some cases prompting a U-turn.

One important point to emphasize is that the greatest games in this book have not been selected because I consider them the best ever played. Nor are they presented in order, to represent ascending quality or importance. I am aware there are notable omissions, especially some of the most celebrated international performances, which I would love to revisit in the future.

Some matches, like Everton's 1985 European Cup Winners' Cup semi-final victory over Bayern Munich, have been picked because of their personal meaning. Others were chosen because I consider them to be defining of a particular era, offering an opportunity to recognize innovative coaching methods and place them in their historical context.

Inevitably, there are more games featuring Liverpool than any other team as I have followed the trajectory of the club over the last thirty years. The Liverpool games selected thread Kenny Dalglish's classic side amid the trauma and shockwaves of the Hillsborough disaster in 1989 into the challenges of the 1990s, and on into the post-millennium European revival led by Gérard Houllier and Rafa Benítez, which laid the foundations for Jürgen Klopp's recent renaissance. For sixteen of those years I was a Liverpool player.

As with my accompanying *Greatest Game* podcast, discussions with contributors led to broader conversations about players' careers and how they and the side they are most associated with are remembered.

When sitting in my living room watching these games, the evolution of football punditry and commentary through the decades also became a source of fascination. How we view the sport has been revolutionized. Since football was first broadcast, the greatest games have become associated with the greatest single lines of commentary. I believe fans have more of an understanding of the game than ever since the Premier League began to be beamed into our homes on a weekly basis in 1992.

I started work on this book shortly before the Covid-19 pandemic paused the world as we knew it, football's brief absence collateral damage in the fight against the virus. I was among the millions with a sense of loss when the live action stopped, but while football and those who love the game tried to deal with unprecedented circumstances, there was one sector of our sport which thrived.

The nostalgia industry.

Fans, players and media found comfort in the past. Nothing could have been more demonstrative of how we cherish our shared football experiences, whether we were on the pitch, watching in the stands, spilling our pints viewing giant screens, or leaping around living rooms.

The greatest games reconnect us to signposts in our lives, whether the journey is from the German Black Forest to Anfield, a short tube ride from London's East End to Wembley, or from my childhood home in Bootle to the Atatürk Stadium in Turkey.

I would love readers to do as I did upon completing each chapter, to hunt down and rewatch my selections in their entirety to see if you agree with my conclusions and feel as immersed in the action when identifying the tactical evolutions over the last three decades.

My choices are so well known you will already be aware of the final scenes in these chapters. I hope my guide will offer greater clarity as to how and why they played out the way they did.

Jamie Carragher
November 2020

1

Tuesday, 7 May 2019

2018/19 UEFA CHAMPIONS LEAGUE
SEMI-FINAL, SECOND LEG
Anfield

LIVERPOOL 4 – 0 BARCELONA

Origi *7, 79*
Wijnaldum *54, 56*

'The Champions League victory gave us the
final proof we needed to be winners'

– Jürgen Klopp

LIVERPOOL'S RESTORATION TO THE PINNACLE of English and European football under Jürgen Klopp began on the aptly named Hope Street.

Directly opposite the city's prestigious Philharmonic Hall and within a well-directed set-play of the Everyman Theatre – the breeding ground for many of Merseyside's finest playwrights, poets and artists – lie the plush rooms and suites providing Klopp and his players with an HQ before Anfield fixtures.

The Hope Street Hotel is where Klopp signed the contract to become Liverpool's manager in 2015, and it offered him the stage from which in 2019 he delivered his most inspirational vocal performance yet. Only twice in European Cup history – Greece's Panathinaikos in 1971 and Barcelona in 1986 – had a team come from three or more goals down after the first leg of a semi-final to progress to the final. On the afternoon of the second leg of the Champions League semi-final against Barcelona, Klopp's impassioned speech in the pre-match team meeting convinced his players they could become the third side to do so, defy expectations and overturn their 3-0 deficit against Spain's newly crowned champions.

'Because it is you, it is not impossible,' Klopp assured his squad.

Listening attentively to the manager's persuasive address was captain Jordan Henderson. 'For me, the manager's team talk started everything for us that day,' he told me. 'He has the ability to say the right thing at the right time. The motivation, getting us in the right frame of mind, and the confidence he built by what he told us and how he said it is why we performed so well.'

Klopp's intention was to inject belief and fearlessness. 'The plan was to jump in Barcelona's face from the first second, so if we failed, we failed in our own way,' the manager explained during our discussion about the subsequent victory. 'We had nothing to lose that night. We wanted to make Barcelona uncomfortable from the first kick. And that is what we did.

'So far in my life, it is the greatest game I was ever part of, and one of the greatest ever, for sure. Maybe it was not against the Barcelona of Xavi [Hernández] and [Andrés] Iniesta, but they were good enough to win the competition and good enough to beat us. But not good enough to beat the team they faced at Anfield that night.'

When embarking on the venture to analyse this and the ten other acclaimed fixtures in this book, I thought it useful to ask Klopp how he defines a truly great game.

'Drama,' he replied. 'What stays longer in the memory of all the people involved is when the drama is there. The great games in history have a story. What is the situation before the game? What are the chances for both teams to win? You were part of a few as well. I am sure at least one is in this book!'

The drama we crave can have many themes.

There is nothing more thrilling than an unlikely comeback such as those enacted by Manchester United and Liverpool in the Champions League finals of 1999 and 2005.

There are those matches which become classics through flawless performance in the grandest sporting theatres, such as Barcelona winning the European Cup at Wembley in 2011.

Then there are games which supply an adrenalin rush like that which I experienced as a schoolboy Evertonian in 1985 watching Howard Kendall overcome Bayern Munich in the bearpit atmosphere of Goodison Park – an evening in which audience participation played a critical role.

Some games are memorable because of an almost comical imperfection, such as the slapstick defending when Liverpool defeated Newcastle United 4-3 in 1996.

And, perhaps most dramatically, there are the unforgettable twists, as was the case with Manchester City, fearing they had fluffed their lines until the final seconds of the 2011/12 title race – a modern revival of Arsenal's achievement in similar circumstances against Liverpool twenty-three years earlier.

Liverpool v. Barcelona in May 2019 absorbs elements of all of the above.

'A lot of what makes a game great has to do with expectation,' Klopp continued. 'In our case, no one thought we would have a chance. Playing against a team like Barcelona and being 3-0 down? Winning that is not easily done, eh? But most important of all in any great game comes the performance. You cannot have the drama without that. It will not be a great game if the players do not show up. The performance must be really good.'

A couple of sub-plots can help too, and Liverpool were grudgingly well supplied with those before this second leg, their defeat in the Nou Camp six days earlier one of many setbacks which made their triumph through adversity carry extra meaning.

Two of their feared three-man strike force, Mohamed Salah (suffering from concussion) and Roberto Firmino (in treatment for a groin strain), were unavailable. Two of Barcelona's, Luis Suárez and Philippe Coutinho, were former Liverpool players.

Liverpool's recent past was of being lauded runners-up. Klopp had already lost three finals with Liverpool, including the 2018 Champions League final, and his last six as a manager. Club owners Fenway Sports Group had celebrated one trophy since their buyout on 15 October 2010 – the 2012 League Cup under Kenny Dalglish – but lost a League Cup final, FA Cup final, Europa League final and Champions League final. They also narrowly missed out on the Premier League title under Brendan Rodgers in 2014 in excruciating circumstances, conceding advantage to Manchester City in game 36 of 38.

The nearly-men reputation was heading for a painful upgrade when, twenty-four hours before Barcelona's visit, Manchester City denied Liverpool again, defeating Leicester City 1-0 to go one point ahead of Klopp's side in the Premier League with one match remaining.

Despite amassing 97 points, Klopp's side would claim the most unwanted accolade in English football – a record-breaking second place having lost only one of their thirty-eight games.

'I was feeling angry,' said Henderson, wounded by all those close 'failures'. 'I don't know if that is the right feeling, but it was how I felt. It was because of what happened in the first leg in Spain, and then the night before the second leg. We all thought Leicester could get something against City and then [Vincent] Kompany scores from something like 40 yards and it is like, "fuckin' 'ell". But there was no sense of anyone around the squad feeling flat when we got together the next morning. Whatever happened we knew playing Barcelona at Anfield was a huge game which does not happen often, so we were ready to make the most of it. I thought our chance of getting through was more difficult than completely gone.'

What gave Liverpool confidence was the misfortune of that 3–0 reverse in Spain. 'We all felt we had played reasonably well in Barcelona and that the score did not really reflect the match,' Liverpool's chairman Tom Werner told me. 'You know football better than me, but it was a lopsided outcome to the play on the pitch. I remember hearing José Mourinho say he would not give a penny for Liverpool's chances going into that second leg, but the pace of our play was so relentless and determined. So, while I would not say I was feeling confident, I was not gloomy because of how well we were playing.'

That is why Klopp was adamant the situation was retrievable. 'After the first leg of a European tie, when you win 3–0 it is a great result and if you lose 3–0 it is an absolutely rubbish result,' the coach said. 'But each day you get closer to the next game, the 3–0 does not feel that good any more and the side losing does not feel it is so bad any more, because there is still a chance. So we took away two important things from the first game. We felt better and Barcelona knew it would have been better for them if they had scored a fourth goal. You could see it in their reaction when [Ousmane] Dembélé did not score the fourth at the very end.'

Klopp was referring to a critical final act in the Nou Camp in the sixth minute of injury-time when, in a frantic attempt to score an away goal, Liverpool goalkeeper Alisson Becker saw his manager encouraging him to run the length of the pitch to challenge for a corner-kick. This is what you normally expect in the closing seconds of a second leg or final. Fortunately, Alisson did not complete the trip, so when Barcelona broke clear and Dembélé had the easiest chance to make it 4-0, he still had a keeper to beat, shooting tamely at the Brazilian.

'Yeah, it was good he did not listen,' said Klopp of his number 1. 'It was not a real idea. It was a reflex decision. We thought, "Shall we give it a try?" Because at 3-1, to score one more goal, all the negative feelings of a big margin are deleted.

'To be honest, that was not my biggest mistake of the night. It was using Bobby Firmino as a substitute [after 79 minutes]. All the information I had was he was fit, but he was not ready, so we lost him for the second game, and then lost Mo [Salah] in the next game at Newcastle.

'On top of that, our biggest problem before the second game was this was still Barcelona.'

With the title still at stake, Klopp could not preserve his players' energy during the weekend trip to the north-east which preceded Barça's visit. Barça, confirmed as Spanish champions ten days earlier, rested all eleven of their first-choice starting XI for their match with Celta Vigo three days before the second leg.

But as kick-off neared for the return, there was one measure of influence Barça could not control. Liverpool rallying cries inspire the fans as much as the players.

'You never know with Anfield,' said Henderson. 'With our crowd, there is always the sense something big will happen.'

I have heard many attempts to downplay the relevance of Anfield's support. There are often sneering suggestions it is a myth sustained by Liverpool fans' self-adulation more than a reality, especially when away supporters occasionally out-sing The Kop during low-key, early-afternoon Premier League fixtures.

If the level between the two sides is vast, or the crowd is not 'up for it', the famed Anfield atmosphere can be neutralized. There are countless examples of teams outplaying Liverpool at Anfield. But when the skill level is equal or not so big, and The Kop brings its 'A' game, the environment undoubtedly affects outcomes.

You only have to see the results when the quality and vigour on and off the pitch are coordinated to realize where the hype comes from.

'People in America ask me what the Anfield experience is like on nights like that [against Barcelona]. I say there is nothing like it,' said Tom Werner. 'I had been to a few matches in London, but not Anfield [before becoming Liverpool chairman]. When I was there in our first year of ownership for games against Wigan and West Bromwich Albion, people would say to me, "Wait until you have a big midweek game in European football."'

English rivals can cover their eyes and ears as much as they wish, but this is true.

Is it the greatest atmosphere in world football? I could not impartially declare that. I am sure there are stadiums across Europe and in South America where supporters are as noisy or intimidating. But they cannot be more influential.

Independent of the noise level, I always felt we had an often overlooked but immediate and obvious advantage. Anfield is quite small. Although the stadium has been regularly upgraded since its construction in 1884 and hosts 55,000 fans, its compactness has never been compromised. The layout lends itself to a cage fight, with supporters so close to the action they can stare into the players' eyes, unlike the Nou Camp, Old Trafford or the San Siro which seem vast in comparison. Lengthwise, the pitch dimensions of Anfield (110 yards by 75 yards) make it as confined as any elite stadium. The Nou Camp measures in at 115 yards by 74 yards according to the official statistics, although when I played there in the 2001 UEFA Cup semi-final, our manager Gérard Houllier told us it had been widened to suit Barça's playing style. Manchester United used to make the same observation when at the Nou Camp for Champions League ties.

Whatever the precise measurements, Anfield seems much tighter compared to most top Premier League and European settings.

Even when being driven to the ground, there is a feeling of enclosure as the team coach carefully manoeuvres down the narrow streets and past the rows of terraced housing to the entrance. For those seeing it for the first time it must look like such an anomaly, as if a futuristic, otherworldly mothership has landed in the neighbourhood. Visually, the contrast is striking and stirring, somehow simultaneously contemporary and vintage.

Psychologically, that makes as big a difference as the crowd's partisanship, creating a sense of claustrophobia which those unfamiliar with the arena struggle with. Even the greatest players.

Wayne Rooney used to tell me he never felt he had any time on the ball when playing at Anfield, the combination of an oppressive, baying crowd, motivated opponents and little space to play having a smothering effect.

As a Liverpool player, we deliberately set out to make our pitch feel squeezed for visitors unaccustomed to the venue's quirkiness. They could be a couple of goals down before they adjusted. In the 2019 semifinal, fourteen minutes had passed before Barça settled, pieced together a meaningful passing sequence and started to threaten Alisson's goal. I have seen that so often and it was definitely due to them tuning in to the surroundings.

The longer I played at Anfield, the more I started to develop muscle memory on the pitch. By the last few seasons of my career I could remember my positioning from games years earlier, so it was as if I reacted to different situations through habit, familiar with every blade of grass and where each of my teammates would, or at least should, be.

'There is something to that,' Henderson, who became my Liverpool teammate in 2012, agreed. 'When you are used to playing there, if you close your eyes you can know exactly where you are. Whenever I visualize a game now, I am always on the Anfield pitch. Maybe it is because of the size. Maybe it is because it is so enclosed. But when I play at

Wembley it feels different – bigger and harder to close the space. Anfield is unlike anywhere else.'

I loved hearing former Arsenal manager Arsène Wenger describe the complications whenever he brought his side to Anfield. 'It's the hardest place in Europe,' he said in 2019. 'It's the only place now you can take a corner and shake hands with supporters! You can say "Hello, my brother, how are you?" and continue to play football. That's a real football field, you know. Today we build sophisticated stadiums, but that is a stadium with soul, with pressure really on the opponent. The atmosphere – everything – is special there.'

The weaponizing of the most famous stand of all, 'The Kop', began under Bill Shankly in the sixties. The buzz of the club's early forays into Europe under him and Bob Paisley culminated in the status-forming midweek nights such as the 1965 European Cup semi-final against Inter Milan, which Liverpool won 3-1 (though they later went out 4-3 on aggregate), and the rousing comeback against St Etienne in 1977, a 3-1 win completed by David Fairclough to take Liverpool into the semi-final 3-2 on aggregate. The first of Liverpool's six European Cups soon followed. In August 2020 Bayern Munich equalled that tally, but only Real Madrid and AC Milan have won the Champions League more times.

By the time I retired in 2013, Liverpool supporters considered us more of a European than an English football club. Like the team, they tended to show their best in the presence of overseas guests.

I believe it is reflective of priorities that Liverpool have just one fewer European Cup than FA Cups. Real Madrid have won their domestic knockout cup nineteen times, Barcelona have done so thirty times, and Bayern Munich on twenty occasions.

There developed a clear distinction between Anfield's character on a European night when compared to domestic cup tournaments. I have no hesitation on behalf of the managers I played for, and teammates I shared a dressing room with, in proudly acknowledging our contribution to that. As much as my medals, I cherish the fact that I played 150

European games for the club – more than any other Liverpool or English player at the time of writing.

Between 2001 and 2010 we appeared in three European finals, winning two, and also won two UEFA Super Cups. We reached another Champions League semi-final in 2008, and the quarter-final in 2002 and 2009. The decade ended with a Europa League semi-final in 2010. That's seven seasons in ten in which we were at least a European quarter-finalist.

Some of the veteran players openly admit that European fixtures at Anfield in the mid-1980s were not always so vibrant as in my or today's era. The significant rise in attendance figures reflects that. Watch the old footage from Liverpool's European Cup semi-finals in 1984 and 1985, and fewer turned up than for league games. On 20 March 1985, Liverpool played their home leg with Austria Vienna in the European Cup quarter-final. The attendance was 32,761. Even when accounting for the mid-eighties being an especially rough time in the city with poverty and unemployment, that figure was just under 11,000 fewer than for the FA Cup fifth round replay with York City two months earlier. Even more eye-catching is the home leg in the first round of Liverpool's victorious 1984 European Cup campaign, against Denmark's Odense BK, watched by just 14,985 fans.

The pining to be back among Europe's best and appreciation for what was lost – and might genuinely have never returned – grew during sixteen years of exile from the European Cup between 1985 and 2001. Today, there is a passion for UEFA competition which goes beyond the increased revenues.

Part of it relates to identity, Liverpool a pioneer on the Continent. The club became globally popular in the 1970s because of European success, and during less successful or troubled times, certainly in the nineties, history was the main source of hope for the future.

That European heritage first hit me as a player in 2001 when we were drawn to play Roma in the fourth round of the UEFA Cup. Our team coach was heading towards the Stadio Olimpico, the sacred ground on which Liverpool won their first European Cup in 1977 and fourth in 1984. The floodlights seemed to illuminate the city as we drew nearer. I felt myself absorbing the history. Those emotions returned when I played in the cathedrals of the Nou Camp, San Siro and Bernabéu.

I know foreign players and fans feel similarly about visits to Anfield. Ours justifiably see themselves as peers of Real, Barça, Bayern and the Milan clubs, relishing the challenge of justifying a glowing reputation.

There are more games to savour now, too, the change to the Champions League format since 1992 meaning there is a guarantee of at least three home matches. By the time the knockout stages come around there is a belief anyone can be beaten at Anfield.

Could we have defeated the world-class sides we did to win the 2001 UEFA Cup and 2005 Champions League without the Anfield crowd? No way. The supporters made themselves principal characters in those stories to such an extent, utilizing The Kop's power will always be a calculated ploy of Liverpool managers and players. Sometimes calls to arms are unnecessary, as when José Mourinho made himself a pantomime villain and first succumbed to Anfield in the 2005 Champions League semi-final. When he claimed our winner by Luis García was scored by the crowd, influencing Slovakian linesman Roman Slysko to adjudge his shot to have crossed the line at the Kop end, José thought he was being disparaging. The Kop fans still wear it as a badge of honour, the perfect riposte to anyone who maintains Anfield's atmosphere is not *that* inspirational.

Whether The Kop's clout provokes resentment, respect or reverence, it feeds the self-esteem of Liverpool supporters.

Such tales resonate with Jürgen Klopp's romanticism and he made fan engagement a priority from day one. 'When you have never experienced the Anfield atmosphere, you can never understand it,' he told me. 'I heard about it before I came to Liverpool, of course. But it is a completely different level to anything I expected. You always think it is a rumour before you come here. Actually, it is the opposite of that. Of all the stadiums in the world I would say if you play under the floodlights here and your team is good, and the other is good as well, it creates a special atmosphere. When you hear it and walk into it, it feels different, and when it is dark outside you feel even closer. I particularly like that time of the day. That is when we are all awake and we are all full of energy.

'We have a real football crowd. I would say in England the atmosphere is different to Germany. In Germany, when the game is not that exciting you still have the fans singing. Some sing for the whole game so there is a constant level. In Liverpool, when it is a shit game it can be quiet. Then people say, "I thought the atmosphere would be better." The fans react more to the action on the pitch. Sometimes I do wish that when we are not playing so well and we need it the fans would push us more, but it only needs a block, or a challenge, and they are there again. They are back in the game. Now I hear people celebrate challenges. When Milly [James Milner] makes a tackle, I can identify the noise. It is a cheer like a goal but not quite as long as a goal. Different. I like that a lot.'

Klopp has occasionally been described as The Kop's ultimate cheer-leader, which sounds belittling, neglecting his qualities as coach, tactician and man-manager. Nevertheless, his relationship with the Anfield crowd is part of what makes him perfect for Liverpool, ensuring he follows the ancestral trail which began with Shankly.

'Obviously I do not know what it was like when Shankly and Paisley were leading the club, but I do feel there is a bond between this manager, these players and our fans which is unlike anything I have ever witnessed,' said Tom Werner. 'When John Henry [principal owner], Mike Gordon [FSG president] and I met Jürgen in New York before he took the job, the first thing we thought was he would make a great executive in any organization. If he sold soap, he would be the best around at that! He is empathetic. He is smart. He is humble. He is compassionate. We also felt he was well suited to Liverpool. If he had gone to another club it would not have been so good a match.

'The last thing I want to do is diminish relationships with other managers. That is not fair or productive. But at the highest level, every-thing has to be excellent and we have that excellence with Jürgen.'

No Liverpool managerial appointment has been so gleefully received in my lifetime. Klopp was already a star at Borussia Dortmund, where he won two Bundesliga titles. As the images filtered through to England of him connecting with fans on the South Stand of Dortmund's Signal Iduna Park, what is known in Germany as the 'Yellow Wall', there was a sense of inevitability he would one day become Liverpool manager which went beyond the quality of his team's football

Recruiting Klopp was also reassuring to The Kop, proof that Liver-pool remained enticing to in-demand coaches after the previous three appointments since 2010   and I mean this with all due respect – had come from Swansea, Fulham and the Liverpool legends lounge.

After leaving Dortmund for a planned year's break, Klopp could have waited for any job in Europe. Manchester United spoke to him when Sir Alex Ferguson retired, but Klopp intuitively sensed Liverpool would come too. Once he was in place, the football world asked what the com-bination of the game's most emotional manager and Europe's most emotional football club would bring.

Liverpool 4 Barcelona 0 was the spectacular answer.

My first observation upon rewatching the game is that Barcelona did not play badly. And while Liverpool were fantastic, they were not so mind-blowingly great that they outplayed their opponents from first to last minute. I have seen more complete performances under Klopp in which his side did not score so many, and worse displays than Barça's which yielded a positive result. But as an execution of a premeditated game plan, and an exercise in utilizing every weapon available against a formidable opponent armed with a sizeable lead, it could not be bettered.

The match-defining pattern can be reduced to the first forty-nine sec-onds. Within five seconds of kick-off, Henderson and the understudies for Salah and Firmino, Divock Origi and Xherdan Shaqiri, surrounded Barcelona left-back Jordi Alba and midfielder Ivan Rakitić. Crucially,

Liverpool's three were against Barça's two, with the visiting full-back under incessant pressure.

This ability to outnumber Barça, especially in wide areas, was a theme of the night, instantly demonstrating where the tactical battle would be won. Alba and right-back Sergi Roberto had a torrid evening in their full-back zones, unnerved by Liverpool's determination to overcrowd them with Henderson, Shaqiri and Trent Alexander-Arnold on the right, and Milner, Sadio Mané and Andy Robertson on the left. Both Barcelona full-backs were forced into mistakes in the first ten minutes, one of which led directly to Origi's first goal.

Part of Klopp's tactical plan is to win possession in the opponent's defensive third. Liverpool did this on eight occasions over two games, compared to Barça's three. This was the consequence of the high press and counter-press – or *gegenpress* to give it its popular German translation – which Klopp is most associated with: ensuring the ball is won high up the pitch within seconds of losing it.

While his three forwards were the trigger for much of that, it also required the central three to be in prime physical shape against Barcelona's, Henderson, Milner and Fabinho excelling in both legs against Rakitić, Sergio Busquets and Arturo Vidal.

The contrasting approach between Liverpool and Barcelona here, or any meeting between Klopp and a side with the traits of former Barcelona coach Pep Guardiola, makes it a feast for tactical connoisseurs. It was a battle between a side famed for being the best in the world with the ball and one that was the best in the world without it.

According to UEFA's data, Barcelona ended the night with 55 per cent of possession, completing 512 successful passes compared to Liverpool's 358. But this information creates a mirage of Barça control because there were certain areas of the pitch where Liverpool wanted their opponent to attempt or complete short passes to teammates under siege. There was no sustained spell in which Ernesto Valverde's Barça players looked at ease on the ball.

Fabinho and Milner were particularly prominent in patrolling the central zone because of their ability to keep reclaiming possession. Fabinho won a total of twenty-three tackles, recoveries, interceptions or one-on-one challenges in this second leg. Milner retrieved the ball more than any player on the pitch (thirteen times). Right-back Alexander-Arnold was second with eleven recoveries. One was especially important in the second half.

Accordingly, Liverpool ran 6.7 kilometres more as a team.

Klopp has never aspired to copy the slower, patient passing game of Barcelona, seeing football as more about the consistent release of energy to sustain attacks. He once famously and colourfully described it as the difference between loud, heavy-metal football and the 'silent song of an orchestra'. This groove has visibly modified in recent years. Liverpool are now more capable of turning down the volume, lowering the tempo and making elaborate chord changes as necessary. On this night it had to be, and was, a wall of sound.

'I think you coach in a way that suits your personality,' Klopp explained. 'Obviously I am not as much of an artist as Pep Guardiola was as a player, or others who were world-class. I had to work hard, and that is what I expect from my team.'

While Guardiola absorbed the teachings of Johan Cruyff and cites Marcelo Bielsa as an influence, Klopp was infatuated by the other guru of the age and a manager you will see namechecked in this book more than any other – AC Milan's Arrigo Sacchi.

'Sacchi completely changed how we think about football,' said Klopp. 'He is one of the most influential coaches in the history of the game and a complete game-changer for me. Because of him we had to judge the size of the pitch in a new way. I am sure you remember playing with man-marking tactics where you pretty much followed the opponent you were marking to the toilet. The pitch always felt incredibly big. Nobody played a high [defensive] line because many teams played the libero [sweeper]. Before him I was told who to mark and that was it. Too often the team with the better individuals won the game because it was all one-versus-one challenges all over the pitch, so if the other player was better than you, how could you win? Sacchi's organization made it completely different.

'I did not learn it from Sacchi, but it was my manager at Mainz, Wolf-gang Frank, who brought it to us, which meant as a player I watched five hundred videos of AC Milan. I saw how whenever Franco Baresi raised his arms to play offside, everyone else in the team was waiting. Ball-orientated defending became a real tool, and of course on top of that Milan were a sensational team with Ruud Gullit, Marco van Basten and Baresi. They were some of the best players ever.

'So that was all part of my tactical training. From then on we had four sessions a week where we did not see the ball. That was maybe too much! But pretty much overnight we became a successful football team. We were not easy to deal with. We defended really well and it opened my mind. That was the basis for me when I became a manager, and still is. Organization is the basis for football.'

Rather like Gérard Houllier in 1998 and Rafa Benítez in 2004, Klopp had a blank canvas in terms of tactical set-up when he moved to Anfield. All were under instructions to win, not strictly adhere to a football bible. Yes, it was preferable to do so in the style of Kenny Dalglish's 1980s side, but there was an acknowledgement the game was modern-izing so there was no insistence on how they went about it.

Klopp's predecessor, Rodgers, was influenced more by the Barça way.

I see certain elements of Houllier's and Benítez's set-up in Klopp's system with defensive organization when the opposition have the ball, but the massive, fundamental difference (aside from much more strength in depth and technical prowess throughout the squad) is that everything Liverpool do today compared to when I played is 20 or 30 yards higher up the pitch.

The change is between counter-attacking and counter-pressing. Our game was generally about the former, which meant when we lost the ball, our outfield players tended to retreat back into our own half, reas-semble and wait for the chance to win it back and use our dynamic midfielders and pacey strikers to move us quickly from defence into attack. Klopp's side still has that counter-attacking threat when they are forced back, but they are more courageous at retaining forward positions when they lose the ball. They rarely, if ever, retreat. That means you will more often see at least eight, possibly even nine or ten Liverpool players in the opposition half, compressing the playing area and making it impossible for a defending team to escape. Often, it is more dangerous for the opponent to have the ball near their own penalty area as they are surrounded by Liverpool's attackers and midfielders and conceding possession can directly lead to a goalscoring opportunity. Sometimes, the only defensive option is to kick it far and high into Liverpool's half, where the centre-back, or goalkeeper Alisson, will collect and start another attack.

For a team such as Barça, which prizes playing out from the goalkeeper with a religious devotion, that makes Liverpool particularly hazardous opposition.

From the opening moments of Liverpool v. Barcelona, Klopp saw his modern interpretation of Sacchi's methods at its most stunningly effective. Under pressure from Liverpool's high-pressing forwards, Barcelona were forced into three hurried long balls within five minutes. The first was by centre-half Clément Lenglet after seven seconds, conceding possession. Keeper Marc-André ter Stegen and centre-back Gerard Piqué were compelled to do likewise as Origi, Mané and an assortment of attacking midfielders hounded them. From minute one the visitors understood how awkward it would be to impose their preferred style and rhythm.

'I loved the start of the game,' said Klopp. 'We just kept going without hesitation. I saw that in the first moment. What we developed was bravery. In a lot of games we pressed the other left-back with our right-back. It is all about timing and I loved that each mistake and misjudgement can lead to a football catastrophe. Against Barcelona you can look ridiculous if they pass through. They had their moments, but we were immediately there.'

Here is the key to nullifying Barcelona's passing game: deny them space because they love operating in the pockets of midfield, trying to bypass opponents with accurate 6- or 10-yard passes, especially when seeking to create space for Lionel Messi.

Liverpool's problem was that when Messi has the ball, tactics and formations can be rendered irrelevant. With him, anything is possible. His first dribble at the heart of Liverpool's defence was after twenty-seven seconds, halted by an exquisite Fabinho tackle.

From that came Liverpool's first chance.

Virgil van Dijk cleared and his teammates pounced on a poor pass by Arturo Vidal. Milner, Mané and Shaqiri found space beyond Barça's midfield, and Henderson could have tapped in at the back post from the Swiss winger's cross, denied by a toe poke clear by Alba. Meanwhile, 70 yards behind, left-back Andy Robertson was casually ensuring he made no attempt to avoid colliding with the back of Messi's head, giving it a rub as the Argentine picked himself off the floor following Fabinho's tackle. Messi complained to the Turkish referee Cüneyt Çakir.

Less than a minute had been played and the crowd was fully engaged and loving it, chanting Robertson's name.

This is Anfield.

The breathless start Klopp yearned for was helped by Henderson thriving in an attacking midfield role to the right of the central three, setting the tempo by pressuring Rakitić and Alba. 'My job in that position was to create space,' Henderson explained. 'It was not specific for this game or to target Alba, especially. Whether it was Mo [Salah] or Shaq [Shaqiri] there, I felt I could help free him up from his marker.'

Henderson had made a request to assume this position two months earlier, speaking to Klopp about a desire to move from being a number 6 – a defensive midfielder where he was the shield prior to Fabinho's signing from Monaco in 2018 – to a more attacking number 8. 'It was a really important conversation,' Jordan told me. 'Fair play to the gaffer. A lot of managers would have said, "No, this is where I see you." He was open to seeing me in both positions. I have learned the number 6 role and have improved to play at a level I could not when I was first there.

But I like using my energy as a number 8. I scored in a league game against Southampton [on 5 April] and my confidence was up.'

It was still a risk given the competition, with Georginio Wijnaldum, Milner, Naby Keïta and Adam Lallana vying for the same spot. Wijnaldum was named on the bench for the second leg. Henderson had been a sub at the Nou Camp.

'Obviously I wasn't happy about it,' he said. 'I was disappointed not to be playing in such a big game, especially in a stadium like the Nou Camp. I knew we had big games coming up in the Premier League and the home leg, but I felt good and thought I could play in them all. The manager wanted to rotate a bit. As it turned out Naby was injured early in the first game so I had to be ready.'

The switch was vindicated when Henderson's forward surge led to the first goal in the 7th minute, assisted by Alba's lack of match awareness so soon into a game in which avoiding an early setback was imperative.

Not for the last time on the night, it began with an Alexander-Arnold corner.

Rather than have all their defenders in the penalty area, Barça kept their shortest, Alba, on the edge of it. Aside from keeping him away from headed challenges, this was to utilize his pace should an opportunity arise for a counter-attack. Rakitić made a headed clearance to Henderson near the halfway line, which should have been the signal for Alba to assume his orthodox defensive position, especially as Mané had drifted to Liverpool's right for the set-piece and had the awareness to hang around in the left-back's absence. Henderson's forward pass was ricocheted back into Liverpool's half by Rakitić, so Alba sprinted to follow the ball and press Milner, who was covering for corner-taker Alexander-Arnold in the Liverpool right-back role. Alba's decision was misjudged because he had no chance of pressuring Milner, who comfortably exchanged passes with Alisson and then Shaqiri, before centre-half Joël Matip received the ball.

With Alba so high up the pitch – Suárez was the only Barça player further forward than him at that point – the left-back had to sprint back into his own half as Matip sent a high diagonal pass towards Mané. Having completed two 70-yard sprints in less than thirty seconds, Alba managed to recover his post, but when he headed back towards Piqué it was tired, timid, and expertly anticipated and intercepted by Mané. Mané's control and pass were brilliant as he supplied the captain making a forward gallop in that right-central role he had fancied.

'When I saw the pass from Joël and how it was being dealt with, I anticipated Sadio going and picking up the second ball,' said Jordan.

Henderson darted into the penalty area between three defenders, comfortably evading Piqué and shooting at Ter Stegen from close range. The goalkeeper could only parry to Origi, who slotted in.

'I should have scored but thankfully Divock was there,' Henderson added.

Barça's susceptibility was already exposed. There is no escaping the fact that the side led by Valverde in 2019 was not like that which won the Champions League under Guardiola in 2009 and 2011. Busquets and Piqué were still there with Messi, but Barça's threat was more individual than collective, Suárez also capable of moments of unparalleled genius.

I spoke to Xavi Hernández about Barcelona's 2011 Champions League win over Manchester United, which has a chapter of its own in this book in which I discuss in greater depth the traditional Barça style, but I was interested in his take on how the club tried to maintain the standards of that golden era.

'After Pep, Luis Enrique took over a team that had an attacking trident of Messi, Suárez and Neymar,' he explained. 'Those three were decisive and made all the difference compared with other teams. With that trident you didn't need high ball circulation or position changes, as once the ball reached any one of them they would create a piece of play to make the difference. Our game was a bit more vertical thanks to those three players. We could start in midfield and attack in transitions with Messi, Neymar and Suárez and they were unstoppable.

'That was a tremendous team, but yes, different to Guardiola's Barça.

With the current Barça I can only comment on what I see on television because I am not there. They are regularly changing coaches from one year to another. I see they want possession of the ball, but they are still not achieving results. It is a shame because I believe they have the competitive teams and players to win.'

Valverde was Barça's fourth coach since Guardiola's departure in 2012. They would have another two within twelve months.

For all that, it is worth reminding ourselves of Barça's amazing credentials upon their arrival on Merseyside. As well as being La Liga champions, they were unbeaten in their previous eleven Champions League games, winning eight and keeping six clean sheets in the process. They had failed to score just five times in their previous fifty-six games. The only defeat in their previous twenty-two European games was to Roma in the 2017/18 quarter-final, although the 3-0 reverse in the second leg was a source of encouragement for Liverpool who were seeking a similar scoreline, especially as Alisson was Roma's keeper that night.

Most of all, they had Messi, who had again surpassed the fifty-goal mark for the season. Barça needed only one to ensure Liverpool would need five to qualify – a point their social media editor, running the club's official Twitter page, may regret pointing out during the game. 'We're going to get at least one . . . agreed?' the post read.

With the world's best player in their side, you can't blame them for feeling confident.

As a unit, Liverpool were more cohesive than Barça, but Messi was still the difference in the first leg, his 82nd-minute free-kick in the Nou Camp to make it 3-0 a measure of his genius.

'That was just unbelievable,' Henderson recalled. 'When he was about to take it, I was not sure he could shoot because it was so far out. I thought he might have been thinking of chipping it towards the far post.'

Rather than allocate a man-marker to Messi in both games, Klopp acknowledged an element of playing the odds against such talent, calculating that dedicating a single player to shadow him is counter-productive because his level is such that he is bound to succeed in a dribble or create shooting opportunities eventually.

'There are certain things like Messi's free-kick you cannot defend,' Klopp said. 'To be honest, you cannot defend many situations against Messi because he has such individual quality. The way they pass it around and what they do means you have to be really brave. Against Barcelona it is possible to play the best game of your life and Messi will still score three goals. That was a little bit the case in the first leg. They had good moments in the second game, too, but when they did Ali [Alisson] was there.'

Alisson made five saves at Anfield, and was at his most alert in the first half when Barça carried the greater attacking threat of the teams despite the early setback. Once Vidal and Coutinho had cleverly combined to present Messi with his first opportunity in the 15th minute – a snap shot from the edge of the area which Alisson pushed over – Barça grew stronger as the first half progressed, with Ter Stegen less occupied than Klopp might have hoped.

Like Liverpool, Barça were set up in a 4-3-3 in possession, but they switched to 4-4-2 whenever Klopp's side tried to build attacks from the back, with Coutinho and Vidal withdrawing to protect their full-backs. After the initial intensity, the visitors' defence looked more secure before half-time, while Messi's influence grew.

The Spanish side created three chances between minutes 15 and 20, the second of which was due to another hopeful long ball from Piqué. Matip headed clear to the centre circle but Vidal was ahead of Milner to the second ball, freeing Messi where he prospers most in front of a retreating back four. He picked out Coutinho whose shot was too close to Alisson, who saved comfortably.

Messi then dragged a shot wide two minutes later as there were signs of Barcelona's rising confidence.

That spell was not prolonged, although some of Shaqiri's sloppy passing just before half-time was almost costly as Messi again shot wide from the number 10 position just outside the penalty area. The last action of the first half saw the Argentine superstar make his presence felt again with his superb pass to send Alba one-on-one with Alisson. The keeper made his best save of all, making his body big enough to block the goal attempt.

Liverpool's lead meant the tenacity and optimism of The Kop were maintained, their eagerness to interact helped along in quieter action periods by the inflammatory presence of two members of Barça's line-up.

Of my two former Liverpool teammates trying to kill the dreams of their old club, one in particular was showing all the desire, enthusiasm and menace his ex-fans were accustomed to. Suárez played like he was on a mission to burn anything that remained of his Anfield bridges.

Not since the outspoken Mourinho ahead of the 2005 and 2007 Champions League semi-finals had an adversary made himself such an easy target for a crowd seeking ways to ensure there was no let-up in the roars. Some Liverpool supporters were taken aback by Suárez's first-leg display which gave no clue that he was an ex-player, especially when he vigorously but unsuccessfully pleaded with Dutch referee Bjorn Kuipers to send off Milner for an innocuous, accidental barge into Messi.

It did not surprise me. I would be hypocritical to criticize Luis for the qualities I loved seeing in him in a red shirt just because he was wearing Barcelona's. What I loved about Luis as a teammate is, to put it bluntly, he could not give a fuck what anyone thought about him when it came to winning football matches. He never saw a line, let alone fretted about whether it could be crossed. It is a joy to have someone that good and determined in your dressing room. Prior to the arrival of Klopp and his recruits, Suárez was the best Liverpool signing since John Barnes in 1987. He is second only to Steven Gerrard as the best Liverpool player I worked with. He was a warrior for us.

That is why there was a natural inclination, no matter how misguided or wrong in retrospect, to defend him whenever controversies arose. We live and work in a bubble where everything is about 'team first', so when one of your colleagues is being hammered from the outside, the siege mentality takes over and judgement can become blinkered. I know we were guilty of that with Luis.

When such a player is against you, of course, there are no qualms about depicting him as a rogue who will use any dark art available to succeed.

In a way, Suárez's personality helped Liverpool in the second leg. His burying of any lingering Anfield loyalty meant The Kop had no hesitation doing likewise. Sentiment could be suspended until the legends games in a few years' time, when I am sure Suárez will be greeted like the hero he once was.

The Uruguayan was booed as he waited to kick off in 2019. I timed the first 'fuck off, Suárez' chant at 23 minutes and 30 seconds, shortly after he had exaggerated a fall under the challenge of Van Dijk. The chorus was repeated when he tried to console Robertson, who needed treatment after a tangle with the striker. Robertson would have to go off at half-time because of the resulting ankle injury, which meant Wijnaldum came off the bench into midfield and Milner moved to left-back.

Van Dijk, Milner and, most regularly, Fabinho were all involved in altercations with Suárez in the first half, the Brazilian midfielder showing most dissent towards him after being wrongly booked following another perfect tackle. Naturally, Luis made it look like it was the worst challenge he had ever endured.

His big chance to add to his Anfield goal tally came in the 51st minute, when Messi sent him between Milner and Van Dijk and Alisson was called upon again, making what, for him, looked a routine save diving to his right. The Barça technical staff studying the game could not have been critical of their side's performance at that point.

I knew Suárez would shrug off the crowd's reaction. So did Henderson. 'My feelings for Luis will never change,' he said. 'I know what Luis is like. A winner. He would do anything to win. I know the fans were angry with him, but I had no animosity towards him or Phil.'

Philippe Coutinho is a more sensitive character. I am not sure there was any circumstance in which he could have played well that night. Where Suárez will have no regrets leaving Anfield given his Champions League and La Liga victories at Barça, Coutinho's move to Spain helped Liverpool more than him. Having been destined to be remembered as the catalyst for Liverpool's rejuvenation with his goals and assists, he will now be regarded as facilitating it through the proceeds of his £142 million transfer in January 2018.

Hindsight leads us to that conclusion. Liverpool's chairman admitted to me that, at the time, there were no such positives taken from his exit. 'That was a temporary blow,' said Werner. 'I do not think I am saying anything that is a secret when I say we very much wanted Coutinho to stay. We were very disappointed because we felt that everyone wanted trophies and medals and we wanted him to accomplish that at Liverpool, and he told us he wanted to leave. You want people who will fight until the end of their career for Liverpool, not to be thinking of doing so for Barcelona, Real Madrid or Bayern Munich.'

When Suárez and Coutinho pushed to leave Liverpool, it confirmed fears that to many leading players the club was a stepping stone rather than a final destination, for they followed a trend. Raheem Sterling asked for a transfer to Manchester City in the summer of 2015. Fernando Torres did so and went to Chelsea in 2011. Shortly before that, in 2010, Javier Mascherano moved to Barcelona, and Xabi Alonso had gone to Real Madrid in 2009. The transfers of Suárez and Coutinho did not provoke the same venom as those of Sterling and Torres because there was a shred of understanding of the attraction of playing at the Nou Camp every week when compared to Stamford Bridge or the Etihad.

In different circumstances, I suspect Suárez and Coutinho would have been granted an ambivalent welcome for their first competitive return to Anfield in a Barça jersey. Some supporters may even have wrestled with their feelings had the reunion been in a group game. Instead, what Suárez and Coutinho suffered was the ferocious backlash of a crowd intent on showing them how much the team had grown without them.

Werner believes the Coutinho sale was a landmark, signalling the end of players seeing Anfield as a pitstop. 'It is an extraordinary quality of Jürgen's leadership that players now want to play for Liverpool, not look for a transfer to another club,' he said. I hope that is right, although I suspect South American players will always be drawn to La Liga.

The trajectory of Coutinho's career since his Anfield exit may itself serve as a warning as to the perils of sacrificing being The Kop's idol to risk being lost amid a group of established, senior superstars elsewhere. In the 2019 semi-final, Coutinho was a shadow of the player who had left sixteen months earlier. The contrast with his previous Champions League display under Klopp – his last European performance for Liverpool – makes for sobering reading.

The Brazilian was Liverpool's man of the match in a 7-0 victory over Spartak Moscow on 6 December 2017, a game Klopp's side had to win to reach the round of sixteen. Coutinho's productivity that night was world-class. As well as three goals, he enjoyed a hundred touches of the ball, fifty-seven of which were successful passes. Eleven of those were in the final third.

Against Liverpool at Anfield in 2019, Coutinho touched the ball thirty-seven times. Only eighteen passes found a teammate, of which just two were in the final third. He was subbed, replaced by Nélson Semedo, after 60 minutes.

Coutinho is a classic example of a player being enhanced by the trust of a coach who built the team around his assets. At Barça, he was never going to be indulged in that way while Messi and Suárez were so established. Although the Brazilian's sale was not planned, Klopp brought out the best in others once he no longer had to accommodate what the English press called Liverpool's new 'fab four' of attackers – Salah, Firmino, Mané and Coutinho – in the same line-up. At that time, Liverpool were brilliant to watch in attack but susceptible defensively. Rather than replace Coutinho with an attacking midfielder with the same profile, Klopp started to favour more tactically aware, defensive, workmanlike midfielders better equipped for the high pressing game, which then enabled him to give Robertson and Alexander-Arnold the chance to resemble wingers, or certainly wing-backs, more than full-backs. The balance of the side was perfected without a number 10, proving Klopp's theory that 'no playmaker in the world can be as good as a good counter-pressing situation'.

When Coutinho made his exit from this game, he cut a sad figure. Watching the replay, I genuinely felt sorry for him.

'Maybe that night Phil was not the player we saw at Liverpool,' said Henderson. 'But Anfield did not just affect him. It affected every Barça player. It can do that to anyone. Afterwards I spoke to Luis and Phil and even though they were down they wished us all the best for the final.'

Liverpool's response to Coutinho's sale is proof that the construction of a high-class team is 80 per cent by design and 20 per cent good fortune. The spending reached a new level when Van Dijk arrived from Southampton for £75 million in January 2018, and Alisson from Roma six months later for £65 million. Without the Coutinho funds, I am not certain the Alisson price would have been affordable. That is where an element of luck comes in, even if there is expertise and wisdom in taking advantage of an unwanted or unexpected change in circumstances. Liverpool have often spent big. They have never spent so wisely in the last thirty years.

There is a skill in identifying or making the right footballers fit the system, which Liverpool have become more adept at since I was at the club. 'When I think of some of the players you had to play with . . . let's just say now we look at a team with excellence in every position,' Tom Werner sympathized. Unlike in recent years, I cannot think of too many Liverpool signings during my time at the club who started poorly and got unrecognizably better.

There is a risk to any transfer, of course. Even established international players can fail to adapt to a new environment, so no one joins with a cast-iron guarantee. That makes Klopp's recruitment record since 2015 extraordinarily impressive, the club's sporting director Michael Edwards and his scouting team assuming much of that credit.

Every significant first-team purchase has thrived. Mané, Salah, Wijnal-dum, Matip and Robertson were not blockbuster, budget-breaking transfers when compared to the inflated fees common around Europe. Two of those players, Robertson and Wijnaldum, joined from clubs that had just been relegated (Hull City and Newcastle United respectively), while Salah had been considered a failure during his previous stint in English football at Chelsea.

All the great teams can point to deals which could never have been planned exactly as they materialized but proved to be game-changers. Think of Leeds United selling Manchester United Eric Cantona in 1992. That probably altered the course of the next two decades of English football.

You could make a case for half a dozen Klopp signings being his most important. 'It is not just the strikers,' said Werner. 'I think everyone is in agreement Virgil's transfer was a key element, but wherever you look on the pitch there is excellence. Sometimes a player of Milner's quality does not even start.'

For all those smart purchases, when Klopp arrived at Anfield, he could not have envisioned that a Liverpool-born-and-bred teenager of Alexander-Arnold's quality would be on the threshold of breaking into his first team. Such academy products are priceless. Trent was a central midfielder in the youth side, but since becoming a right-back he has become a symbol of Liverpool's athleticism and high pressing as much as any player. He plays the role exactly as Dani Alves did for Barcelona under Guardiola – a creative force as much as a defender – spending so much time trying (and generally succeeding) to win the ball in the attacking third and creating chances. Alexander-Arnold was responsi-ble for most Liverpool assists during their run to becoming European and later Premier League champions.

Given the Alves comparison, Barça must have felt they were being beaten at their own game when they conceded the second goal in the 54th minute.

It was a perfect illustration of *gegenpress*ing. Alexander-Arnold initially lost the ball with a sloppy header to Rakitić midway inside Barcelona's half. Rather than see that as a signal to retreat, the response of Trent and his teammates was to keep advancing to win it back. Surrounded by Henderson and Origi, Rakitić gave left-back Alba the same short, sideways ball he had given him in the first five seconds of the match.

Rakitić's was the archetypal 'hospital pass', putting Alba in immediate risk of a fifty-fifty tackle which, even if it did not result in physical injury, inflicted a football accident courtesy of the serious wound on Barcelona's defensive structure.

Trent was high up the pitch and tenacious enough in the challenge to recover his error, continuing his run down the right wing with the balance and poise of an attacking midfielder. He whipped in a cross where Wijnaldum was quicker and stronger to see off a lame attempt to block from Vidal and connect to beat Ter Stegen.

Anfield's energy was fully unleashed. This is when playing there becomes insufferable for opponents, as the home players kicking towards The Kop are energized by their own and the crowd's performance. Visitors feel blitzed, their emotional state affected by the realization the game is slipping away and there is nothing they can do to halt the irrepressible momentum.

All Barça could do to pause the assault was thank the video assistant referee for checking the validity of Trent's tackle. Henderson was involved in a quizzical chat with the referee as he waited for the all-clear. 'I was asking what the problem was,' said Jordan. 'There was no reason not to get on with the game.'

There was more time between Wijnaldum scoring and the game resuming (ninety-one seconds) than between kick-off and the third goal.

Liverpool's urgency ensured that nine seconds after the restart Fabinho had pressed Busquets, and Van Dijk had won the ball from Messi on the halfway line. Liverpool were 3-0 up twenty-two seconds later, nine touches of the ball involving Van Dijk, Henderson, Fabinho, Origi,

Milner and Shaqiri culminating in the Swiss winger's cross for Wijnal-dum. The Dutchman was unmarked between Barça's centre-backs, who were displaying all the symptoms of being casualties of shock and awe. Their composure gone, they were no longer completing basic tasks such as closing down attackers or keeping tabs on those in the penalty area.

'Once the second goal was scored I said, "Oh my God!"' Tom Werner, who was watching in John W. Henry's home in Boston, told me. 'People asked if it could happen and spoke about it being a dream. And then of course the third goal. Once it was 3-0, God was not going to let us down.'

Messi's and Suárez's look of deflation was compounded by memories of the Roma result a year earlier. Barça's reputation for going anywhere in the world and dictating a game was in tatters.

Messi continued to threaten, but even his set-piece excellence deserted him on 67 minutes when in an identical situation to the one in which he'd scored against Liverpool in Barcelona. This time the wall jumped high enough and Matip's head blocked the attempt. A minute later Alisson made his final save from the magician, at his near post.

Liverpool still needed the fourth to win the tie. By then it seemed inevitable. The manner of the winning goal underlined the sharpness of mind of Liverpool's players while Barcelona's were disorientated. It also demonstrated how the most inventive and instinctive moments in a game owe a debt to forward planning.

During the European run, Klopp had sent a message to the club's academy staff stressing the importance of the ball boys recruited from the youth team being alert and actively maintaining the game's pace, thus maximizing the advantage of UEFA's multi-ball system.

Among those receiving the briefing prior to Barcelona's visit was Oakley Cannonier, a Leeds-born Under-16 player, who was dispatched to sit by the right corner flag at the Kop end. His swift thinking ensured there was no let-up for Barça's defenders when the ball went into touch, so he could claim a key role in one of the most important goals of Klopp's reign.

'Before the game, Phil Roscoe [player care manager at Liverpool's academy] took us into a meeting to watch video clips from lots of European games, showing us how well the ball boys worked,' Oakley explained to me.

'Pep Lijnders [Klopp's assistant manager] told Phil the manager needed us to help keep the ball in play as much as possible. Everyone said it was especially important with us being 3-0 down.

'I had been a ball boy a few times before at Anfield, so I knew what was expected. And I always like to sit in front of The Kop, because that is where it is the best atmosphere, so I asked to be there.'

Eleven minutes were left when Cannonier and Alexander-Arnold combined to enable the right-back to claim his fourteenth assist of the season, and probably the most memorable of his career.

The twenty-year-old won the corner off Roberto and watched as the ball bounced off the advertising board into the penalty area. As Origi ambled to side-foot it away, Barça's players languidly ignored the set-piece taker, five of them standing by Mané – one of only two Liverpool players in the penalty area – because they presumed Alexander-Arnold would wait for Van Dijk and Matip to arrive to challenge for a header.

Cannonier swiftly supplied Alexander-Arnold with another ball, enabling him to catch Barça off guard.

'Barca kicked the ball out, and when it bounced back onto the pitch I think they thought that was the one that was going to go back to Trent,' Oakley recalled. 'Obviously it didn't happen like that. I noticed the ball on the pitch, so, with the one I had, there were two balls around. As soon as I could, I just gave the one I had to Trent and then picked the other one up.'

Having feigned to walk away from the corner flag to allow Shaqiri to take the set-play, Alexander-Arnold rushed back to pick out Origi who was standing alone while four of the eight Barcelona players in the penalty area had their backs turned. Origi's finish was not straightforward, connecting first time on the half-volley before Ter Stegen could get close.

Sometimes goals activate a temporary pause as spectators digest what actually happened. In this case, it was so unusual many wondered if it would be allowed to stand.

'I was thinking, "What's just happened?"' said Henderson. 'I looked back as the ball was coming in, just as Divock was going to put it into the top corner. When the ball was in, I thought, "Let's celebrate." The referee wasn't looking at it and I saw the Barcelona players walking back with their heads down. That was when I knew there was no problem with it.

'What Trent did was so instinctive. Most people in that situation would be thinking, "Let's take a bit of time, get the big men up from the back and concentrate on getting a quality ball into the box." But at this point in the match, Trent was thinking we wanted the ball in play all the time. It was such a big moment to do that.'

In Boston, Trent's ingenuity had his club's executives on their feet. 'The fourth goal was so spectacular – no one will ever forget it,' Werner said. 'The pass by Trent was brilliant enough, but it is the idea that makes the goal. The creativity of it reminds me of a schoolboy team trying to get the ball back into play quickly. It caught Barcelona on their heels, but by then the pace of play was so relentless and determined. When you watch it back it looks like Barcelona were moving into positions for a set-piece and there are nine of them [including the keeper] in the penalty area who are not prepared. That is the genius of Trent, that he not only saw that but still had the ability to pick out Origi unmarked.'

Having played themselves into a winning position, Liverpool's maturity and experience to see out the final eleven minutes and additional five minutes of injury-time were impressive.

The ball boys' work was not done. Having been in sixth gear for seventy-nine minutes, the academy youngsters were as adept as the players in changing tempo to suit the situation.

'When the fourth went in we were all told to slow it right down,' said Oakley, now sixteen years old and dreaming of one day participating on the pitch as much he did from the sidelines. 'That message came through to us from the bench, but with experience from previous games we already knew what to do in that situation. When I look back at it all now, it is nice to have had some involvement, although I never expected it to be mentioned as much as it was the morning after. I received an email from the club's chief executive [Peter Moore] thanking me for the job I did.'

For the first time in the tie, it was Liverpool with everything to lose, and yet Alisson was not required to make another save. Liverpool changed their system to three centre-backs for the last six minutes, Joe Gomez replacing Origi. Barça's last attempt to salvage the tie was to send centre-back Piqué forward as an emergency striker.

I especially enjoyed rewatching Liverpool negotiate injury-time, a virtuoso example of game management.

The final touch by a Barcelona player in open play was by substitute Arthur on 93 minutes and 14 seconds. Fabinho intercepted a rushed pass to Messi, sprinting forward and forcing the Argentine to chase him back and make a frustrated, clumsy foul. That summed up what I believe to be the finest individual Liverpool performance of the evening, the free-kick Fabinho earned greeted by The Kop as if it was a fifth goal. The last sixty seconds were dealt with by Milner after Van Dijk delivered the free-kick to the left wing and the ball was protected near Barça's corner flag. The noise from The Kop on the final whistle still induces goosebumps.

Milner fell to his knees when the referee blew for time. He broke into tears through exhaustion. So did Henderson. 'It was because of the way it happened,' explained the captain, who had recovered from the pain of a first-half knee injury to help his side across the line. 'I felt so drained. It was surreal. Huge. Just an incredible feeling. My body felt it could not go any more. What is strange is after eighty-seven minutes I thought I could keep running for as long as anyone asked. I was ready to keep pressing as if it was the first minute. Then the final whistle went a few minutes later and I had nothing left. The first thing you think of is all the effort you have needed to defend against a team of their quality. Then there is the realization you are going to another final after losing it a year before. Then there is a release with the final whistle. Yeah, it was a bit emotional.'

One of the enduring post-match images as the players and staff celebrated was Salah wearing a T-shirt with the message 'Never Give Up' – a slogan every Liverpool fan in the city wanted to publicize the next day.

In Boston, there was one regret. The owners were not in the stadium to experience the full-time celebrations. 'You must have heard our whooping from across the pond,' said Werner. 'To see the manager, coaching staff and team form the wall in front of The Kop and sing "You'll Never Walk Alone" . . . words like magical and spectacular do not do it justice. Those are the nights which have always marked this club as different. You know, Jamie, we all feel it like the fans. I know we all have a responsibility to guide the club, but we suffer with every fan when the results do not go our way, and we celebrate when the team is playing well.

'I hope in my lifetime I see a game half as exciting as that, but if I don't I think I can still be satisfied. I could watch it again and again in my sleep. I think it showed when you come here you are not playing for any club. With all the history and the shoulders of legends upon which the current players stand, you are playing for Liverpool Football Club. That is unique.'

My final question to Henderson referred to another classic Liverpool comeback in this book.

'So how does it feel to be part of the second-greatest Liverpool performance of all time, after Istanbul?' I asked.

'We will both be biased judging that!' laughed Jordan.

'I suppose we had longer to score our three goals. You only had forty-five minutes!'

'I think we can agree this has to be the greatest Anfield night, especially when you are playing against a Barcelona team with the best player in the world in its side. But yeah, that AC Milan team was not too bad either!'

I agree this is Anfield's greatest night. And I am ecstatic we can compare and share our experiences for the rest of our lives.

The difference with the Barcelona victory is that it directly led to three trophies, Liverpool winning the Champions League final against

Tottenham Hotspur on 1 June, and therefore qualifying for the Super Cup final and FIFA Club World Cup, which they also won the following August and December respectively.

Klopp says the Champions League win spurred the players on for the fourth trophy which meant most of all, his side spectacularly shrugging off the disappointment of losing the 2018/19 Premier League to Manchester City to win by eighteen points in 2020, ending Liverpool's thirty-year wait to become English champions. 'We won the other things because of the Barcelona game,' he said. 'The Champions League victory gave us the final proof we needed to be winners.

'My favourite moment after we won [the final] in Madrid, after seeing all my family, was when all the coaches were sitting together with a beer. We were looking at each other and thinking how lucky we are to come to a club like Liverpool and have these players. It is so difficult to win anything in football. You need luck, but you need to force the luck like crazy as well, which is what these boys did, especially after all the knocks going so close before.'

Prior to 2019, the club had gone seven years without any major trophy. No Liverpool team had gone eight years since Shankly's arrival in 1959. Now, instead of talking about cup and title famines, the discussion around the club is about creating dynasties.

As I reflect on that, I am often reminded of an interview I gave to Sky Sports shortly after Rafa Benítez's appointment as Liverpool manager in 2004. Michael Owen had recently been sold to Real Madrid, Chelsea were making no secret of their pursuit of our captain, Steven Gerrard, and the club was at a crossroads, desperately seeking overseas investment to challenge for the biggest honours again. My future Sky colleague, Geoff Shreeves, wanted to know if I would ever consider leaving 'for somewhere bigger'.

'Bigger?' I replied. 'Who is bigger than Liverpool? Bigger how? More money?'

Geoff suggested my hopes of winning the Premier League and Champions League would be more realistic at another English club.

'No, I am not having that,' I replied. 'If we get it right at this club we will be right up there.'

By the time I retired as a player, I must admit the confidence expressed during that interview had waned. Our Champions League victory in 2005 was not a stimulus for more honours. A club takeover by Americans George Gillett Jr and Tom Hicks in 2007 threatened financial disaster with bank debts exceeding £280 million, and although the second takeover by FSG promised and eventually delivered a more considered, gradual rebuilding of the club, I knew it would not bear fruit until I had left – though I did worry I had gone a year too early when Rodgers' side almost won the Premier League.

By then a media pundit, after Suárez's sale in 2014 and Steven Gerrard's departure in 2015, whenever I took a more dispassionate look at my club I saw no prospect of Liverpool becoming Premier League champions in the near future. Not with Manchester City so financially powerful, Manchester United able to break world record transfer fees, and at that time Chelsea, Arsenal and Tottenham Hotspur obstacles to Champions League qualification, let alone a title challenge.

For the owners, 2019 was the start of a period where they saw tangible reward for nine years of steady progress in which they had been tantalizingly close to every honour.

'In my wildest dreams I would never have imagined we would get to a point at which we were simultaneously champions of Europe and the Premier League,' said Werner. 'What made winning the Premier League so special is we were within a whisker – the length of a football – from winning in 2019. I thought it would be tough to come back from that. I thought a step back might be as likely as a step forward. But the players were so focused there was no let-up at all.'

The Barcelona victory and all that has followed demonstrated how two key decisions by FSG changed everything.

The first is obviously Jürgen Klopp's appointment.

The second was the announcement in October 2012 that the club was staying at Anfield rather than building a new arena on the neighbouring Stanley Park.

Reliving this game and looking ahead to future European campaigns, it seems inconceivable that Liverpool ever considered leaving. To me, it is telling that such a proposal was formed with minimum opposition as a response to where the club found itself at the end of the 1990s, before the European renaissance. That reinforces my view that Anfield's famed UEFA nights are as much a consequence of my generation as the legacy of the sixties, seventies and eighties. FSG's ditching of relocation plans and finding a means to renovate Anfield must be regarded as one of the most important Liverpool decisions ever. The club would not be what it is without the stadium rightly credited with an assist in each major trophy on the honours board, and in every one of Anfield's greatest games.

'The Barcelona win would not have happened without the supporters,' said Klopp. 'That is not possible. It is a real inspiration. How I felt before the game, how I felt during the game and how I felt after the game – it is special. We still had the final to play, but this was the moment we won the Champions League.'

2

Wednesday, 24 April 1985

1984/85 EUROPEAN CUP WINNERS' CUP SEMI-FINAL, SECOND LEG
Goodison Park

EVERTON 3 – 1 BAYERN MUNICH

Sharp *48*   Hoeness *38*
Gray *73*
Steven *86*

'They were the crème de la crème. There was a perception that we were Rag-arse Rovers.'

Andy Gray

I HAVE NEVER FORGIVEN BAYERN Munich for stealing my Everton bobble hat.

I was seven years old at the time, balanced on my dad's shoulders as we made our way from Munich's Olympic Stadium, when the prized possession I had been wearing with such pride was cruelly snatched. Surrounded by home fans, I used my elevated view to try to find the culprit and saw my dad's friend, Tommy, grab a German by the throat and demand the thief's identity. To no avail.

We had been 'welcomed' by the locals at Munich airport a day earlier with the question, 'Have you come for a fight?' Now it felt like we were being provoked into meeting expectations.

I had just watched Howard Kendall's side secure a commendable goalless draw in the first leg of the European Cup Winners' Cup semi-final. Now I was consumed by one, vengeful thought: 'I hope we batter these at Goodison.'

Welcome to European football in the 1980s.

I would love to believe the rally cry 'Let's do it for Carragher's hat!' bounced off the changing-room walls before the players emerged into the Merseyside inferno for the return encounter a fortnight later, but I am prepared to accept that retribution for this heartless heist did not occur to Kendall when delivering his final, inspirational address.

No matter. Everyone inside Goodison Park that night has a personal account of the magnificence of the occasion. Each will testify to the sound of fury, the belligerence and brutality of a full-blooded ninety minutes – the greatest in the stadium's history.

Everton outfought and outplayed Bayern Munich on that April day in 1985 with a template performance against which every Toffees side has since been judged. No Evertonian has ever felt prouder or more connected to the players and everything they represented as the club finally emerged from the shadow of their neighbours.

Of the eleven games I selected for this book, this is the first I was drawn to. It was one of the most important days of my football education.

Revisiting the sights and sounds on hazy old footage took me back to being that seven-year-old Evertonian, sitting in the Upper Gwladys Street with my dad, Philly, and his two close friends who were with us for both legs, Tommy Valence and Davy Mulholland.

'The streets were swarming with fans and the stadium was packed an hour before kick-off,' the former Everton striker Graeme Sharp reminded me, reigniting the fires in my belly. 'We all turned up with this belief we would not get beat.'

The assault on my senses guaranteed that football would be my life, whatever the future had in store. The game gripped me as a kid and never let go. Obviously I had no idea I would become a professional player. Had I not, I would still be travelling home and away with my mates from Bootle, craving the day the modern Everton is worthy of comparison with 1985.

That may shock those who do not already know my background. It is well documented that I shifted allegiance when becoming a Liverpool player, but there are two Evertons in my life: the Everton I know as 'us' and the Everton I know as 'them'. There is the Everton I supported before I made my Liverpool debut in 1997 and the Everton who became my greatest rivals after that.

My career is defined by my attachment to Anfield, the club I have loved throughout my adult life and which I make no apology for caring about more than any other. I have no mixed feelings. Liverpool is my club now.

That was not always the case, however, and my affection for the

Everton players of the eighties is as great now as it was then. I idolized them on the Marsh Lane pitches near my Bootle home, where I was rarely out of my Le Coq Sportif blue kit. To me it will always be the smartest, trendiest and most iconic Everton ever wore because it is forever associated with that triumphant team.

Just say the numbers '84/85' and it will send a shiver down the spine of every Evertonian who had the privilege to watch them. They won the league championship with ease, added the European Cup Winners' Cup on 15 May and narrowly missed out on what was then an unprecedented treble as they ran out of steam in extra-time against Manchester United in the FA Cup final three days later. I attended every game I could during those nine months, regardless of whether or not I should be at school. I had my dad's permission. That was enough.

My dad, his friends and I became recognizable characters among the hardcore travelling supporters, well regarded for our determination to follow the side at home and in Europe. In Munich, I was able to get to the team hotel and collect the autographs of all the squad. As I chased the team bus as it left for the airport, the coach driver was ordered to hit the brakes so that left-back John Bailey could give me a can of Coke. It was some consolation for losing that hat.

This was the era of Neville Southall, Peter Reid, Kevin Ratcliffe, Andy Gray and Pat Van Den Hauwe, ensuring that if anyone wanted a physical battle with Everton they were as good as beaten before kick-off. Bayern will testify to that, although the biggest bruising they suffered at Goodison was to their egos.

'Bayern were the European elite,' Gray recalled. 'They were the crème de la crème. There was a perception that we were Rag-arse Rovers.'

My dad used to tell me to study Huyton-born Reid and be like him. What a central midfielder. He was Player of the Year in 1985, an embodiment of Everton's dual personality – proactive with and without the ball.

Even if you had the attributes needed to scrap against that Everton team, they possessed the technical excellence to pick through you, Kevin Sheedy and Trevor Steven their midfield artists. Everton's third goal against Bayern in this second leg is as slick as anything you will see today.

As a developing centre-forward for Bootle Boys, I loved Graeme Sharp. The Scot was a complete centre-forward, dominant in the air, touch-perfect with his feet and capable of unselfishly combining with any strike partner. In consecutive seasons he was paired with Adrian Heath, Gray and later Gary Lineker and Wayne Clarke, all possessing different traits. They became better players when alongside Sharp. I worshipped him so much I alternated wearing an Everton and Scotland jersey during schoolboy training sessions at Liverpool's School of Excellence at Melwood at the start of the 1990s. When manager Kenny Dalglish spotted this cheeky young blue invading Anfield territory he gave me the nickname 'Sharpy', which stuck for years.

The Bayern game was the epicentre of a Goodison earthquake which had started to tremor the previous season. Kendall's emerging side reached both domestic finals in 1984, losing the League Cup to Liverpool after a replay before beating Watford in the FA Cup – the club's first trophy for fourteen years. But there was little to indicate what was coming that year and beyond when Everton won only six of their first twenty-one league games and Kendall was close to the sack. Then everything clicked.

'We'd all come through the bad times together,' Ratcliffe, the skipper in 1985, told me. 'You know how close we were to losing Howard. If we had, that team's success would not have happened. He brought the right players in. When he signed Andy Gray we were asking, "Is he still fit enough to play, or have we just bought a crock?" Well, he could still play, and he was still a crock! Reidy came into the side quite late and then suddenly it all gelled.'

By the time of the Bayern second leg, Everton were on a twenty-three-match unbeaten run going back to December 1984, the team everyone was talking about.

Live domestic games on television were rare and video recorders only just fashionable, so whenever Everton were first up on *Match of the Day*, which was an increasingly frequent occurrence, the tapes circulated around Bootle like they were a precious Hollywood release. When they reached our house, I played them on a loop. I memorized the TV and radio commentaries of Everton's games so that I could recite them in the school playground.

Receiving a copy of the ninety minutes of the second leg against Bayern Munich for this book was my first opportunity since 1985 to compare my and every Evertonian's romanticized view of the match with the unvarnished reality. 'Did it really happen like that, or is my mind playing tricks and I've just convinced myself it was that good?' is a question many fans ask themselves years after an event. Strangely, it can make you hesitant about retreading steps. There is a danger of corrupting a pure memory.

The game was not screened live in the UK. It was filmed by the north-west's regional TV crew from Granada, a young Martin Tyler providing solo commentary in the knowledge that at least sixty minutes would be cut for that evening's highlights package on ITV's *Midweek Sports Special*.

Before I rewatched it I made notes so that I would know how many reminiscences were based on truth, and how many had been distorted by the stories reproduced since. The official records say 49,476 were in attendance. You can find witness statements from another 200,000 claiming they were there. I really was.

My perception was of a bloody, bruising battle. I recalled a game played in a toxic atmosphere, in which Everton played combative, direct football and, to use a well-worn Scouse phrase, 'tried to kick the shit out of Bayern'. Two goals came from long throw-ins, and when the game was under control Everton had the chance to counter-attack, and the poets came to the party with the third. That was the Everton I remembered. Half steel, half silk.

Was this a view seen through blue-tinted spectacles?

Here are a couple of lines from Tyler's commentary:

'There is more aggression than football out there.'

'This is no place for the faint-hearted. Both teams are slugging it out. You can't hear the referee's whistle.'

'Yes,' I thought to myself, as the footage continued. 'This is how I remember it.'

With one significant exception.

I had become accustomed to the idea of Everton battering Bayern into submission, the traumatized Germans ill-equipped for what hit them inside a Goodison cauldron.

Forget it.

'They could look after themselves all right,' said Reid. 'You do not need me to tell you what German sides are like. They were not shrinking violets. We knew they would be lively. They gave as good as they took.'

This was a game of such unyielding power, the teams could have been introduced on to the pitch by a master of ceremonies telling the crowd to 'get ready to rumble', and there is one German name etched into the memory of every Everton player.

'Hans Pflügler,' said Gray, sounding like a man who could point to every scar received and inflicted that evening. Pflügler, Bayern's central defender and chief agitator, spent the first ten minutes sending a series of 'greetings' to the backs of Sharp's and Gray's heads. 'Let's just say he let me have a couple early on, and I think Reidy's leg was already pouring with blood by then.'

There is no disguising the savagery of the challenges. There were nineteen free-kicks in the first half, amounting to a stoppage nearly every two minutes. That's not including pauses for long throw-ins, corners and goal-kicks. To put that into perspective, in 2019/20 Everton averaged twelve fouls a game. Both teams were uncompromising and unapologetic in their ferocity to the point where there's not much to re-evaluate in terms of refinement. That does not make it any less thrilling.

Bayern were not at all submissive; they were well up for the duel. Full-back Wolfgang Dremmler and Danish midfielder Søren Lerby accompanied Pflügler as the German side's weapons of choice and they picked their targets, although not particularly wisely.

Lerby's first meaningful contribution was to introduce his studs to the side of Reid's Achilles tendon.

Not clever.

Lerby was unmistakable with his socks around his ankles and lack of shin pads, contrary to today's rules.

Even less clever.

Playing at Goodison without shin pads was the 1980s football equivalent of going into bat without a helmet against the West Indies fast bowlers of that era.

In what might be seen as a regrettable coincidence, the early skirmishes proved especially painful for Pflügler and Lerby's teammate Norbert Eder, who developed an unfortunate habit of picking up an injury seconds after every foul on an Everton player. Eder felt Reid's wrath immediately after Lerby's first indiscretion when the Everton man delivered what on the surface looked like a mistimed lunge, potentially taking out the centre-back a second after he had released the ball. I suspect the challenge was actually executed with military precision.

A minute after Gray and Pflügler were booked following an altercation in the centre circle midway through the first half, Eder temporarily left the pitch with what looked like a broken nose after the first of several rendezvous with the Everton number 9. The incident was caught on camera from distance, evidence inconclusive regarding its accidental nature. 'Eder got the back of Gray's head in his face,' says Martin Tyler, generously judging the innocence of his future Sky Sports analyst.

'In the early days of your career you could get away with one or two things like that,' Gray told me. You can imagine him winking as he said this.

I re-analysed the game in detail with Gray. His performance reminded me why he was so loved by Evertonians, his personality carved into the game thanks to a potent combination of courage and ability. Alongside Sharp, there is no finer example of a couple of strikers wearing down defensive markers who took to the pitch fired up and motivated for the task at hand, but were harassed into defeat by the end.

For me, Reid and Gray represent the true heart and soul of that Everton side, setting the tone and relishing every scuffle. When I suggest no punches were pulled in order to resist Bayern's early strong-arm tactics, I mean it literally. Fortunately, one directed at Pflügler by Gray did not connect.

'When Pflügler tackled me for about the third or fourth time, I just turned round and had a wild swing at him on the halfway line and missed him. Thank God I was hopeless. I was a bit stupid and I have no idea why I did it, and to this day I'm so glad I missed because if I'd caught him, I think I'd have been sent off and who knows then what would've happened for Everton and all of the things they went on to win. It might just have changed everything. So every time I look at it and every time I see it I cringe. I just think, "You idiot, what the hell were you thinking?" Anyway, Reidy grabbed me, got me out the way. The referee thankfully saw there was no contact and was more concerned with him because he started rolling about on the ground. But that was madness.'

While Pflügler prepared for the next rounds of the bout, Eder would not go the distance, his night ending in the second half after receiving treatment flat on his back from the renowned Bayern doctor Hans Müller-Wohlfahrt.

The more Bayern asked the provocative question about the home side being up for the fight, the more determined the Everton players were to hunt them down and get them by the throat. Watching a couple of bone-rattling exchanges between Reid and Lerby within a minute on the stroke of half-time put me back in my blue seat, recalling how these challenges made seven-year-old me enthusiastically jump out of it. They are classic examples of adversaries sending each other a message – one of the many personal 'communications' delivered around the pitch that night.

The statement is timeless: win your private battle and win the game. There was no hiding place.

Bayern possessed one of the finest central midfielders of his generation, Lothar Matthäus, but their most potent attacking threat was nineteen-year-old left-winger Ludwig Kögl. Kögl was a more fragile, technical footballer, blessed with pace and dribbling ability. That probably explains why any blue shirt within kicking distance seemed under orders to take him down. There was an especially ugly challenge by Ratcliffe on Kögl in the second half, catching him on the tibia as he sped past. It would be an instant red card today. Swedish referee Erik Fredriksson, who had officiated the previous season's European Cup final between Roma and Liverpool, thought a stern warning was more than adequate.

'A rash challenge,' Ratcliffe admitted to me thirty-five years on, with more than a hint of understatement. 'I never even got booked. I would have missed the final if I had. The game was more aggressive then.'

By full time, two of Bayern's defenders were off injured, others were hobbling around nursing a variety of wounds, and goalkeeper Jean-Marie Pfaff seemed to be playing on one leg.

'Mr Kendall, this is not football,' Bayern's legendary manager Udo Lattek is famously quoted as having protested to the Everton dugout, while suggesting Gray take up rugby.

Kendall's response was forthright: 'Fuck off and sit down.'

I used to laugh at that story. Now I see irony in it given Bayern's equally forceful approach. This was not, as many have depicted since, a culture clash between suave Europeans and ultra-aggressive Brits. Bayern tried to do everything Everton did, taking long throw-ins whenever they were close to the penalty box and attempting to win second balls off their powerhouse striker Dieter Hoeness. Everton just did it better.

We would never see a game like this today, certainly not at the highest level. Not with twenty-two men still on the pitch or without a month of disciplinary hearings anyway. I make no apology for saying how much it puts a smile on my face: I admire the character displayed by both teams. Given the gladiatorial environment, Bayern's attitude was more courageous than foolish.

Obviously I am not advocating punches and cynical late tackles risking injury, or 'reducers' as they tend to be described. But I am a firm believer in players instantly marking their territory with hostile, confrontational but fair attempts to get possession. What you might call 'earning the right to play'.

Spectators still love nothing more than a thunderous fifty-fifty that puts the opposition's star man on his backside. How many times have you been at a game that is tediously meandering along before being ignited by a home player ferociously sliding in and emerging unscathed with the ball? It can change the mood of a stadium and shift momentum. You only have to see the response of the Goodison crowd that night whenever Reid and Lerby clashed. The fans were so involved and influential, Tyler occasionally sounded hoarse as he needed to shout into the microphone to be heard.

We too casually describe this as 'old school'. I hate that phrase because it implies there is a superior 'new school'. 'The game is less physical than when you or I played, that is fair to say, but I am with you,' said Reid. 'A good tackle is massively important. I am not talking about "topping" people, where you skim the top of the ball and know you will get the man. The game has changed in that way.

'I can remember playing against players like Peter Barnes and later John Barnes, and they were so good you pretty much had to "lay one on them". You had to, to even get close to them. It had to be done. Obviously it is a different game now.

'But a team needs all components. You need players who sit, fill holes, and protect the back four. There are great examples of those players. They are not always the sexiest, but when it comes to the big moments you will always find they have done a job for you.

'What you have now is players who can read it more. John Terry and Rio Ferdinand had that ability. So did you. But what is even more important is when you get the ball, you must take care of it. It is hard to win it, and when you have it you need to keep it.'

I can imagine plenty of people rolling their eyes reading a celebration of this or any game in the eighties which gives the impression of lamenting a lost age of wincing tackles and casual elbows to the ribs beyond the eyeline of the referee. 'Here we go again. This is the attitude which held English football back for years.'

Do not misinterpret the argument. Football has correctly evolved so that skilful players receive greater protection, and tackles deemed the wrong side of crude rightly meet with appropriate punishment. Equally, let's not get too holier-than-thou about how the game can and should be played.

One of the side effects of stricter disciplinary measures is that hard tackling is no longer recognized as an art, as if it is a remnant of a prehistoric age. I can remember my friend and former teammate Xabi Alonso being bemused by English players listing tackling as a quality, arguing it should be the last resort for those who are unable to keep possession. His comments were warmly received by those who argue our game is too obsessed with physical attributes.

Many modern players would be appalled by some of the incidents in that Everton v. Bayern match. Reid had a chuckle when I mentioned my regular discussions with Xabi on the subject. 'He must not have seen much of that Spanish lad [Andoni] Goikoetxea when he was growing up,' he said. Goikoetxea was known as the Butcher of Bilbao for his uncompromising style. Check out Athletic Bilbao's assaults on Diego Maradona during their fixtures with Barcelona in the early 1980s if you want to know how he earned the nickname.

I agree that technique and ball retention are and always must be the number one priority when coaching youngsters. Where I take exception is with the idea that tackling cannot or should not be encouraged – or worse, that it reflects limited talent. That is not a 'typically British' view, even if it is embedded in our football culture. During my playing career, it was the overseas managers like France's Gérard Houllier, Spain's Rafael Benítez, Sweden's Sven-Göran Eriksson and Italy's Fabio Capello who were most keen to ensure we made the first tackle and demanded a physical base to their line-up. It was my British coaches at Liverpool, Kenny Dalglish and Brendan Rodgers, whose training was more possession-led. We should be wary of pigeonholing coaches and players based on nationalities, but I hear or read such things all the time.

Show me the most technically adept teams of the last ten or twenty years from any continent and they will have world-class players who relish 'putting a foot in'. Physical engagement is as important as ever. You cannot have a successful team without fearless competitors who make and withstand tackles. The difference today is players are more cunning.

Real Madrid legend Sergio Ramos, Spain's most capped player, did not become one of the best defenders of his generation solely because he can pass. Manchester City would not have been the team they have been over the last decade without Vincent Kompany and Fernandinho. Jürgen Klopp's Liverpool rose a level when they introduced Virgil van Dijk and Fabinho, men who win the ball as well as they use it.

Look at the best South American players and teams. Would anyone seriously argue that Argentina's defenders do not prepare for and enjoy physical games? Each country has its specialism. I love watching Diego Simeone's Atlético Madrid. They are not a beautiful side and are often criticized, unfairly in my opinion. I have never seen them come off the pitch without ensuring their opponents had to match their warrior spirit to beat them, and whenever I see them I think they are a modern incarnation of the Everton team in 1985. They are exactly what Everton should aspire to be today.

'Do you know the worst phrase in modern football, Carra?' Andy Gray asked me. '"They play football the right way". What's the right way? Howard wanted us to physically test Bayern that night. We were going to try and play when we got the ball down in the last third and go from there, but we were not going to mess about in getting it there. It was a night that required that sort of game. It did not require us rolling it to the full-back, back to the goalie and across to the full-back. That was not us. We wanted to get it from back to front fairly quickly. We had two strikers, Sharpy and me, who could deal with it and bring people in to play and work it. So there was no point in us messing about in midfield. It was a case of keeping the tempo of the game high.'

That pattern meant neither Everton nor Munich were able to keep the ball for long periods in that April 1985 game, defenders sending the ball forward and skyward as soon as they received it.

Despite the multiple stoppages, the game was played at an amazing speed. You often hear modern pundits talk about football being much quicker now. Anyone looking at a match like this might ask if that is true. The game resembled pinball.

Here is the crucial difference: in that Everton v. Bayern Munich match it is the ball that is moving speedily from back to front, not necessarily those trying to get it.

When we talk about a faster game, it is the natural pace of the players and their technical ability to control the ball under pressure, run with it and make decisions that contrasts with previous generations. Moments of technical excellence stand out in older games because they are rarer over ninety minutes.

This match was especially rapid because Gray and Sharp were under orders to stop Bayern's defenders passing back to their goalkeeper, closing the angle to Pfaff. That prevented a classic time-wasting ploy. At the opposite end, every time Southall picked up the ball he hit it long. Over the course of ninety minutes I counted thirty-two occasions when Southall kicked out of his hands deep towards the edge of Bayern's penalty area. Each time, certainly until Everton led late in the game, he did so with the haste of a goalkeeper whose side is chasing an equalizer in the final minutes. It stands in stark contrast to modern keepers under orders to pass to centre-halves so that attacks can be built from the back.

'That was a deliberate ploy at half-time,' Ratcliffe told me. 'If you see it, Neville kicks more in the second half than the first.'

I disagree. It was the same in both halves.

'Howard [Kendall] told me and [fellow centre-back] Derek Mountfield not to get the ball off Nev,' Ratcliffe explained. 'His thinking was, if we could not get the ball to either of our full-backs early, we had to kick long and push up. They had a couple of great footballers in midfield, Lothar

Matthäus especially. We could not let them have time and space. So we made the pitch smaller and won the battle.'

Gray says the plan was perfectly implemented from the first whistle. 'Howard was very keen to test them physically,' he said. 'We never allowed the pace of the game to drop. If Neville got it he didn't take ten or fifteen seconds trying to get it out. He just got rid quickly. We were non-stop, incessant, pressure, pressure, pressure, and that's what Howard wanted.'

Bayern knew what was coming. Coach Lattek played a defensive line-up, dropping striker Michael Rummenigge (younger brother of German legend Karl-Heinz) to play an extra midfielder in a 5-4-1 formation. He trusted Hoeness, a target man who would have been at home in the English First Division in the 1980s, to stand up to Everton's defenders. Hoeness scored but the game was played almost entirely in Bayern's half. Unlike Sharp and Gray working in tandem, the Bayern striker was largely unsuccessful in holding up the ball to relieve pressure on his defence.

Klaus Augenthaler, the Bayern skipper, played as the sweeper behind two orthodox centre-backs. Gray and Sharp focused on pulling their markers into unfamiliar, uncomfortable areas. Everton's efforts to limit the influence of Augenthaler is a key feature of the first half.

'In those days if the ball was with our right-back, the sweeper would be at that side of the pitch, behind their left-sided centre-back,' Gray explained. 'If Gary Stevens got it on the right side, the sweeper would immediately go and patrol behind their left centre-back because they thought it was coming straight that way. So what we were trying to do was hit big diagonals to nullify the sweeper. I would isolate myself on the other centre-back and have people coming running off me from that side. It was the same idea when Pat Van Den Hauwe had it at left-back, Sharpy dragging their centre-back wide to the right. It meant there was a 30- or 40-yard gap between their centre-backs and because we were half decent in the air there was always a fair chance one of us would win it. Then we could get our wide midfielders making runs on to the second ball.'

The ineptitude of Bayern's plan to neutralize Everton's diagonal long-ball plan is exposed with the most extraordinary sight of their high-line offside trap. From the start of the game when Ratcliffe played his first direct pass into the opposition half, Bayern's defensive shape was comically poor. Rather than the symmetry of, say, the AC Milan back four choreographed by Franco Baresi, Bayern's efforts are best described as a ragged ten-man cavalry charge. They tried to squeeze the play so far up the park they might have caught half of Everton's midfield and even a couple of defenders offside. It did not work, and Everton regularly bypassed the expanded defensive line.

So poorly rehearsed and implemented was the manoeuvre it had to have been designed for that night – a sign that Bayern carried as many scars into the game as they would be nursing by the end.

It is worth noting that the German club had suffered at the hands of British opponents for four consecutive years before they arrived at Goodison. They'd lost to Liverpool in the 1981 European Cup semi-final, Aston Villa in the 1982 European Cup final, Aberdeen in the 1983 European Cup Winners' Cup and Tottenham Hotspur in the 1984 UEFA Cup, each time beaten by the tournament winners. Lattek was also Borussia Mönchengladbach's coach in the 1977 European Cup final and 1978 European Cup semi-final, losing to Liverpool on both occasions.

Lattek was a fabled figure in German and European football by 1985, still the only manager to win the European Cup, European Cup Winners' Cup and UEFA Cup with three different teams, Bayern Munich, Barcelona and Borussia Mönchengladbach. But English clubs were his nemesis and his losing streak was about to continue – as was this country's spectacular run of European success. In the nine years preceding the enforced exile which followed the Heysel Stadium disaster in 1985, English clubs accounted for eleven European trophies, seven of which were the greatest prize of all, what is now called the Champions League.

There was more to this success than a confrontational brand of football. Prior to the ban, English teams possessed a quality and streetwise savviness which the national team lacked. When paired with boisterous home venues they were a seemingly unstoppable force. 'The ambience and atmosphere of the crowd was crazy,' recalled Dieter Hoeness, who played in all of Bayern's defeats to British sides between 1981 and 1985. 'Our team was very impressed by that at Goodison Park. The pressure was coming more and more from the Everton team.'

Reid and Ratcliffe feel Everton's immediate European success was partially down to tactical flexibility, which may not have been so obvious in the second leg but was critical in setting up the tie in front of a home crowd which, cliché or not, spurred the side on as twelfth man.

'Howard was so clever in that first leg in Munich,' said Reid. 'With Kevin Sheedy and Andy Gray out, he used Alan Harper and Kevin Richardson in the wide areas and Trevor [Steven] in the hole behind Sharpy. In those days no one made such a big deal about tactics like that. Now, that would have been analysed and everyone would have said how brilliant Howard was to change the shape. To be honest, I take the piss when I hear people talking about playing "between the lines", "transitions" and "recycling" as if it is something new. It was there then.

'People call it the "full press" in football now. We did not call it that then, but when I was at Everton, that was all we did, asking our forwards to make it as difficult as possible for their defence. Ian Rush led that for Liverpool. It was what the best sides were built on. The great AC Milan team of the late eighties was built on getting on the front foot, Baresi getting his defence on the halfway line. It is just a different way of going about it.'

Ratcliffe agreed. 'All our sessions on the training field were closing-down sessions to make sure that people get pegged down so that they can't pick the pass or make the cross,' he said. 'The amount of times I see people letting the ball come into the box from wide positions now, and not working hard enough to get close to the ball, is unreal. You have a little bit of a smile on your face to think that it's just been invented. It's just been reinvented – that's all.'

The first leg was about withstanding pressure and tweaking the line-up due to Gray's and Sheedy's injuries. 'A boring game in which Everton played very narrow,' Hoeness told me. The Goodison game plan was based entirely on the first-choice starting XI in a rigid 4-4-2, winning second balls from the long diagonals Gray referenced and feeding off intimidation on and off the pitch. There are no extended passing combinations from back to front. When wide players drift inside, they do so facing goal in the final third to collect or compete for the lay-offs or flicked headers of their strikers, never to receive a pass from their full-back or centre-half as is commonplace today. The coaching manual has been drastically updated since.

'Get it wide and get it in the box,' as Sharp summed it up. 'We knew they were not comfortable with aerial balls.'

Bayern's inability to withstand Everton's bombardment was increasingly obvious despite them taking the lead. The Germans' first shot on target came on 36 minutes, a result of a long throw which fell to Matthäus at the edge of the penalty area. Southall gathered easily.

By now Kendall was alongside his backroom team in the dugout having started the match watching from the directors' box, which many of the top managers did during that era. His decision to get to the touchline so early in the match was not a positive sign and shows that Kendall was concerned. In the first half, his side had not made their superiority count.

Against the run of play, the visitors scored seven minutes before half-time, proving how quick-footed and penetrating they could be in midfield when given the chance. Kögl played a one-two with Matthäus on the halfway line and was sent towards a one-on-one with Southall. He saved, but the rebound dropped kindly to Hoeness who, according to Tyler, 'ponderously but effectively' scored the away goal.

This was the only occasion the high defensive line Everton used throughout their eighties success was breached all night, Ratcliffe's pace usually the means to get them out of trouble if the offside flag did not. There was no faster centre-back in the division than the Everton captain that year.

Suffice to say, I felt calmer watching this in my forties than as a seven-year-old. In 1985, my dad's mate, Tommy, reassured me, 'Don't worry, we will win this 3-1.' His word was gospel after that.

I could not understand his confidence at the time, but it is easy to recognize now why the fans were not panicking. By the time Bayern managed another shot on target they were 2-1 down.

Kendall's half-time talk has become part of Everton's folklore, particularly his famous observation to keep going long and 'the Goodison crowd will suck it on to their net'.

An obvious change after the interval was the rotating roles of Sharp and Gray. Although their first-half starting position against the two orthodox central defenders was effective in stretching the back three, the distance between them meant they did not benefit from each other's flicks, despite dominating aerially. They worked closer, more centrally, and started to combine after the break. Gary Stevens' succession of long throws early in the game also tended to be directed at Sharp at the near post for Gray to run on to. For Everton's equalizer early in the second half, the positions are reversed. Gray beats Augenthaler and Sharp's glancing header is perfectly placed beyond Pfaff.

The noise level inside the stadium hit a decibel level I doubt it had ever reached before, eclipsed only when Gray scored the second twenty-five minutes later.

Here is where the game was won.

There are two critical moments before Gray's goal which I had forgotten. A minute earlier, Bayern were beyond the Everton defence, Dremmler's chance to rush clear halted by Southall's handball outside the penalty area. This would lead to a red card now because it illegally denied a goalscoring opportunity. There was not even an appeal for punishment.

What followed was rank amateurism from Bayern as they self-destructed within sixty seconds.

The exertions of the evening had finally taken their toll on centre-back Eder, who was once more having a facial injury treated by the

Bayern doctor. With his side down to ten men, Lerby decided to smash the resulting free-kick over the bar rather than wait for his teammate to recover or be substituted. Southall again wasted no time, kicking the ball back into Bayern's half before a change could be made. Bayern still had not replaced their defender when Everton won the throw-in which led to the second goal. This time Stevens' delivery was horrifically misjudged by Pfaff, and Gray guided into an empty net.

Pfaff did not look fit all night. He had been given a painkilling injection in the thigh before kick-off and stepped aside to allow Augenthaler to take every goal-kick. Where possible, Pfaff threw rather than kicked out of his hands, something he had to stop doing when the Everton strikers closed down defenders.

That said, his error for Gray's goal was mental rather than physical, colliding with his centre-halves, looking in vain for a free-kick that never came. Cue Goodison bedlam as Bayern finally had eleven men on the pitch again.

Despite ditching their sweeper when substitute Rummenigge replaced the stricken Eder, Bayern never came close to equalizing.

Everton could have had a couple more before Steven beautifully guided the ball past Pfaff after the game's shining moment of technical quality four minutes from the end, Sheedy and Gray perfectly weighting passes so that the winger could pause, pick his spot and lift it over the Belgian number 1.

'It would have been easy for Kevin Sheedy to have just dumped it in the corner and say, "Go on, Andy, just chase that into the corner and waste some time,"' said Gray. 'He just waited, waited, waited. And the quality of that goal? I think it said everything about us.'

The Gwladys Street sang 'Are you watching, Manchester?' – evidence of where the most venomous rivalry lay in 1985. 'We're the pride of Merseyside' soon followed.

The Germans were furious. In their haste to escape their torment, their coach driver forgot to wait for Lerby as he was conducting a pitchside interview with Tyler. 'I had to give him a lift back to the team hotel in Liverpool city centre,' Tyler told me. Maybe it was the Dane's punishment for that awful free-kick.

I must admit I have few memories of the criticism of how Everton won the game at the time, or of the team's style of play. Looking at it now, it just looks like what I would describe as a typical 1980s football match, where both sides are implementing similar tactics but one is more adept than the other.

Hoeness was more charitable than his manager with those graceless post-match remarks. 'I do not exactly remember what he said, but sometimes the disappointment immediately after a game means you are not so clear in your head,' he said. 'For me, it was a pleasure to play in those games. It was a tough game and very physical, sometimes a little bit over the limit, but Everton deserved the win because they were more determined on that night.'

For Gray, some of the negativity still stings. 'I hear people criticize the team and say we beat Bayern Munich with two long throws. My response to that is if you know you have defenders who do not like playing against me and Sharpy, and they are worried, and you have a guy who can throw it right into the near post . . . It's like a corner – are you saying we shouldn't take a corner? Why wouldn't you?

'There is this snobbiness about long throw-ins. I don't get it. Isn't a long throw part of football? There is this idea now that unless you play four hundred passes and then score a goal at the end of it, then it's not a good goal. We never believed that, and I never watched football or played football to be involved in that sort of stuff. We played football to get it in the box, get people round it and find their weak point. Isn't that good football? Isn't that good tactics from the coach? Isn't that what tactics are about?'

So assured was that Everton team, it did not matter how a game developed. Once ahead, they felt the surge of inevitable victory. 'I'm sure you've been in games where you're thinking "we're gonna win this game, it's a matter of how many we're gonna win it by",' said Ratcliffe. 'It's a great feeling. It's not being big-headed. We knew if we played to our maximum we would win. As a team, you knew if there was one guy off then the other guys covered him. If we had eight lads showing up on the day, giving it their all, the other three that weren't doing it would put a shift in anyway. That was just an unbelievable feeling.'

That confidence extended to the final, which Everton had initially believed would be against Celtic. The Scots had beaten Rapid Vienna 4-3 on aggregate only to be ordered to replay at a neutral venue, Old Trafford, because of crowd trouble at Parkhead.

Reid, Gray, Steven and Heath went along to scout the opponents, hoping for a Celtic victory. 'I could not believe it when the Austrians won,' said Reid. 'I do not mean disrespect, but I knew we would beat them. I have never been so confident going into any game.'

Kendall had to tell Reid to keep his thoughts to himself to prevent complacency spreading. He had no cause for concern, Everton easing to a 3-1 win in Rotterdam. That felt like a formality; the Bayern match is recalled more fondly and regularly than the final. No English manager has won a European club trophy since Howard Kendall.

The legacy of the Bayern match is bittersweet. It is a celebration of what was and a requiem for what might have been. This should have been the first chapter in a volume of memorable European nights at Goodison Park. Supporters were reluctant to leave the stadium, savouring the moment, blissfully unaware of how long it would be before they could feel that way again. I left believing it was going to be this way for at least the next five years, the cream of Germany, Spain and Italy sent packing. Everton had not played in Europe since 1980 and here they were, winning a UEFA competition with a young team at the first attempt.

Sadly, the core of that Everton side played only one season in European competition. Fourteen days after that Rotterdam final, fighting between Liverpool and Juventus fans at Belgium's Heysel Stadium caused the death of thirty-nine Italian fans. After repeated incidents of hooliganism involving English fans, English clubs were banned from UEFA competition for ten years, later reduced to five.

'They wanted to make an example of us and there was nothing we could do about it,' said Sharp. 'Hooliganism was a European problem but there was a feeling the Football Association and the prime minister, Margaret Thatcher, just wanted us all out.'

Many of the players came to reflect upon this void in their careers years later.

'We all just wanted a little bit more and we were denied it,' said Ratcliffe. 'I was playing my best football in the mid-eighties. We were all at our peak. I'd come up against world-class strikers for Wales, you know? Players like [Jürgen] Klinsmann and Rudi Völler, when I still had the pace I had in 1985. They were always that little bit cuter at international level. Once you have that taste for it you just want to be tested and tested and tested, and that was not to be.'

Although Andy Gray was informed he was to be replaced by Gary Lineker the following season, he says the European ban hastened his departure. 'If we'd have been in the European Cup the following season I'd have stayed because I'd still have felt part of it and because I played a part in us getting there. It would have been my one chance to play against the elite. It definitely influenced my decision. I would have quite fancied a few trips and maybe getting the odd game here and there.'

You will often hear Evertonians say that, having easily won the English championship, they would have won the European Cup in 1986. There is no guarantee of that, but the argument cannot be dismissed. They would have been one of the best sides in the competition.

The 1986 European Cup final was played between Barcelona and winners Steaua Bucharest. The 1987 European Cup final was between Bayern Munich and winners Porto. All four clubs were in the European Cup Winners' Cup in 1984/85, like Everton on the verge of becoming domestic champions.

'I had not even realized that,' said Gray. 'That's amazing. We obviously felt we were better than Steaua Bucharest, and it wasn't the Barcelona we know now, so there was obviously a chance. We had shown we could take on the best. It was just a pity, Jamie. It really was.'

Everton remained strong for the next three years, narrowly beaten to the double in 1986 and regaining the English title in 1987. Regardless of whether they would have added to their honours list, they would have been European contenders, and none of their rivals would have fancied a trip to Goodison Park.

Instead, key players departed before the end of the decade. Gary Stevens and Trevor Steven headed to Glasgow Rangers and Howard Kendall joined Athletic Bilbao. Speak to many Everton supporters and ex-players and they'll attribute Everton's subsequent deterioration to these departures, and suggest that the lack of European competition was a major factor. 'I actually thought it led to the demise of our side, losing players. I honestly think the club has never recovered,' said Ratcliffe.

As an Evertonian of that generation who lived through the decline of the late 1980s and into the 1990s with the club in his heart, I think that is debatable. I can honestly say that when I was in my early teens my despair at Everton's loss of form was directed solely at my club.

Kendall left the English champions in 1987 to join a side that finished thirteenth in La Liga, so competing for the European Cup, or any UEFA trophy, was not his motivation.

Stevens left for Ibrox in the summer of 1988, and Steven a year later. By the time English clubs were allowed back in Europe in the summer of 1990, they had played one European Cup tie with Rangers, ironically enough against Bayern Munich in 1989. The competition was a knockout rather than the prolonged and lucrative group stages of the modern Champions League.

As for the other high-profile transfer of the period, Lineker, he joined Everton after the ban was imposed in 1985 and stayed for a year before joining Barcelona. I never believed his ambition to play at the Nou Camp was because of European exile. I always thought he saw Everton as a stepping stone, and he was one of the world's most wanted strikers after winning the Golden Boot in the 1986 World Cup. That is why I never felt the same love for him in a blue shirt as for the man he replaced, Andy Gray.

Everton spent big in order to retain their position as title challengers at the end of the decade, breaking the British transfer record for Tony Cottee and signing Pat Nevin, Stuart McCall and Neil McDonald for considerable fees. Across Stanley Park, Liverpool bought John Barnes, Peter Beardsley and John Aldridge with the proceeds of Ian Rush's sale to Juventus (the Welshman was sold in 1986 and moved to Italy in 1987). Despite losing the best number 9 in the world at the time, Kenny Dalglish revitalized the Liverpool team with great players who made the club even stronger.

Everton's new signings were not as good as their predecessors, while stalwarts Reid, Ratcliffe and midfielder Paul Bracewell were getting older and suffering more injuries. That is why Everton faded away. Poor recruitment was nothing to do with Heysel.

Something more valuable than great players, and even the most successful manager still in his prime, was lost with the European ban. Players and coaches leave to broaden their experiences all the time. What really hurt a generation of Everton fans was missing out on the chance to do likewise, denied visits to the greatest venues where they could collect precious football memories. As a young Everton fan I could not have foreseen or understood that, especially as we won the league again and made annual trips to Wembley until 1989. We all thought we would be back in Europe eventually. I was seventeen and in Liverpool's FA Youth Cup squad when Everton next played in a UEFA competition.

For five years, at least, that was beyond Everton's control, and the fact that some Liverpool fans were responsible at Heysel would have longer-term, undesirable consequences for the relationship between supporters which, as a boyhood blue, were not so noticeable at the time. The blame game has become more spiteful, but there was no logical reason for other English clubs to be more prepared for the European return in the 1990s than Everton.

Kendall returned as manager in 1990 but could not recapture the magic of his golden era. Everton fans' yearning for the feeling his eighties team inspired has grown in the three decades since.

That is the enduring legacy of the Bayern night, impacting on the psyche of the supporters and the club today. Every managerial appointment will be told about the game and will be expected to study it. The architects of Everton's new stadium on Liverpool's dockside are under orders to ensure that an atmosphere comparable to 1985 can be recreated.

Recent Everton coaches have no way of truly understanding from the footage what the Bayern game meant to those there that night. Some may have privately rewatched it with a sense of bemusement, believing the game has moved on so much there is no way they would try or even want to replicate the style of football. Certainly Roberto Martínez tried to take Everton in a vastly different direction during his tenure. He was viewed with suspicion from day one as he encouraged his centre-backs to exchange passes rather than pump forward long diagonal balls to a bustling number 9.

What the supporters expect as a minimum is that their manager senses and captures the spirit of that night. The Bayern game defines how Evertonians of my age perceive their team, or at least what it should aspire to. When I think of Everton, I look to the 1985 team rather than the title-winning side of Harry Catterick who coined the phrase 'the School of Science' to celebrate a more technical approach in the 1960s.

The ideal Everton coach favours a finely tuned combination of aggressive, front-foot football with a dash of skill. They match Reid's combativeness with Steven's wizardry; Dave Watson's competitiveness and Duncan Ferguson's aerial power with a sprinkling of Gary Speed and Andrei Kanchelskis's class; they relish being described as Joe Royle's 'Dogs of War', while having a winger of Anders Limpar's skill to create the winning goal in the 1995 FA Cup final; and they have Mikel Arteta's cultured passing in a side led from the back by Phil Jagielka.

At their best, David Moyes's Everton team had that, and Martínez's most successful spell was when he added Romelu Lukaku to the side he inherited and was close to finishing in the top four.

The most effective Everton teams will never be shy of playing long and direct from defence to attack and bullying the opposition into surrender. In the last thirty-five years, I believe the downfall of many Goodison managers has been their failure to grasp that.

Those who argue that this does not fit modern sensibilities are being too narrow-minded about what football can or should be. One of the most enjoyable interviews I have conducted recently was with Carlo Ancelotti, shortly after he joined Everton. We discussed how the greatest coaches are prepared to play in a variety of ways to get results. After years hearing about the traditional 4-4-2 being outdated, I sat with one of the most successful Champions League coaches and he looked bewildered at the suggestion. 'If you want to play long balls and fight for the second ball, that is football,' said Ancelotti.

To me, this idea epitomizes Everton. Any side that comes to Goodison looking for a fight, no matter how esteemed their reputation, should expect to suffer the same fate as Bayern Munich in 1985.

3

Friday, 26 May 1989

1988/89 FOOTBALL LEAGUE, FIRST DIVISION
Anfield

LIVERPOOL 0 – 2 ARSENAL

Smith *52*
Thomas *90+1*

'Bloody 'ell, I'm near the penalty box'
– Michael Thomas

EVERYONE KNOWS THE STORY OF the Scottish manager who knocked Liverpool off their perch. How he rejuvenated a flagging institution in the mid-eighties, studied the Anfield template and wrested away the league championship to end a glorious Merseyside era.

If the name Sir Alex Ferguson springs to mind, congratulations. You are one of those who has swallowed a regurgitated myth in English football.

Those with a fuller grasp of our history in the late 1980s and early 1990s understand that it is misleading to say Ferguson is the man who stopped Liverpool. The knockout punches had been thrown. By the time Manchester United took the Anfield crown they were marching into a conquered empire.

When Ferguson built his first title-winning team seven years into his Old Trafford reign, in 1993, Liverpool were no longer contenders for the newly created Premier League. Kenny Dalglish had resigned in 1991, followed by Graeme Souness's unsuccessful attempts to replicate the previous decade of domestic dominance.

It was another Scot, whose two titles in three years came when Dalglish's side was at its peak, who made the first significant contribution to Liverpool having to wait thirty years to return to the summit of English football. That was George Graham. The team was Arsenal. And the greatest game in the Gunners' history, the most spectacular climax to any league season, came at Anfield on the evening of Friday, 26 May 1989.

The story of Arsenal's title has been the subject of several books; it inspired Nick Hornby's novel *Fever Pitch*, which was turned into a successful film, and has been an enduring fascination for documentary makers. The script was worthy of its eventual cinema premiere. Game 38 in the First Division. Liverpool were three points ahead, with the luxury of being able to lose 1-0 at Anfield and still become champions on goal difference. Arsenal took the lead through striker Alan Smith on 52 minutes, and as full time approached, Liverpool midfielder Steve McMahon nervously walked around the pitch informing teammates they had one more minute to survive and the FA Cup and league double was theirs.

Enter Michael Thomas, breaking from midfield, scurrying towards the Anfield Road end and evading the challenges of Steve Nicol and Ray Houghton. The celebrated commentary of Brian Moore, 'It's up for grabs now', echoed around twelve million living rooms, the edge of every seat occupied.

Everything about the game screams history, not only because of how the title was won and lost, but also the context behind why it was played on this date, and its broader legacy.

As football journalist Amy Lawrence, whose work on the book and film 89 chronicled the oral history of that season, told me, 'It was the only time in English football a game was the league title decider and FA Cup final rolled into one.'

Rewatching the conclusion, as with many of the games in this book, feels like accessing a time capsule, going back into a world where players wear numbers 1 to 11 without their names and every pair of football boots is old-school black. I am transported to an age when coverage of a fixture of such stature was unprecedented, highlights shows the norm, the BBC and ITV having only recently increased live output previously limited to cup finals and internationals. This was a transitional period for broadcasters, this game a glimpse into a future where domestic league football is extensively beamed into homes.

Before the late eighties, the scheduling of Friday night football on primetime TV was as unlikely as two title challengers meeting in an all-or-nothing game.

I am not going to shy away from saying the television coverage looks primitive compared to the lavish production values of today. It is like seeing pioneers taking their first tentative steps into a new age of live league football. I could not help but smile when Brian Moore referenced the appearance of a clock in the corner of the screen in the 86th minute, counting down the seconds to what looked like being Liverpool's eighteenth league title, as if it was a grand technological feat. At 90 minutes and 45 seconds, the clock mysteriously disappears, thus failing to accurately record how deep into injury-time Thomas strikes.

Even when Thomas's iconic goal brought the amazing climax, I cannot help but mention that the broadcasters failed to capture and project the magnitude of it. I understand why Moore's line means so much to Arsenal fans, but it compares unfavourably with Martin Tyler's emotional summing up of Manchester City's last-gasp win over QPR in 2012: 'Agüero! I swear you'll never see anything like this ever again.'

Sorry, Martin, we already had.

The difference in 1989 was there were no cameras to focus on the players bouncing towards the euphoric Arsenal fans. We were told by Moore that the Liverpool players had sunk to their knees before kicking off again in a frantic last attempt to score. We never saw it.

Co-commentator David Pleat's knowledge and understanding of the game were obvious throughout and he spoke well, but only occasionally. He did not get the chance to evaluate the enormity of what he had witnessed.

The end of the broadcast was rushed and slightly chaotic. A surprisingly restrained Tony Adams was ushered to pitchside reporter Jim Rosenthal for a flash onfield interview before he methodically collected the trophy, and we returned to the studio where Bobby Robson, whose presence as England manager was obviously a coup, offered the bland observation, 'Nothing surprises you in football.'

With that, the greatest finish to any season ended with none of the merited fanfare. There was no lengthy analysis of how or why the game evolved as it did. Today, we would milk such a seismic moment for several weeks with a series of debate shows and rapidly commissioned specials.

Why was it like this in 1989? Mainly because investment in such live events was incomparable to today. After enquiries to the producer on that evening, Trevor East, I was informed the broadcasters were under strict instructions not to overrun before the start of the ten o'clock news. A delay in the kick-off due to traffic congestion as Arsenal fans travelled to Anfield added to the pressure on the hosts to squeeze in the trophy presentation before going off air.

I am wary that this sounds unfairly disparaging. It is harsh because it is easy to sit here and pick holes as a modern pundit, with all the benefits of the vast resources, digital equipment and touchscreens my employers at Sky TV provide me with. To those who worked on those broadcasts, I must sound like one of those precocious footballers criticizing the lack of pace and technical deficiencies of the game thirty years before my debut. I have only respect and admiration for the trailblazers of sports broadcasting, football especially, and recognize the different landscape in which they operated. The voice of Brian Moore takes me back to my youth; his ultra-professionalism oozes throughout the commentary. Moore has the gravitas and comforting familiarity of a veteran news anchor as he casually wishes ex-Manchester United manager (and former Liverpool player) Sir Matt Busby a happy eightieth birthday before switching to a more solemn tone to send condolences to the family of legendary Leeds manager Don Revie, who died on the afternoon of the game. Today's broadcasters and pundits operate in a more opinionated, excitable and consequently provocative social media age.

I understand why Arsenal's joy was not portrayed in a way a modern viewer is accustomed to. The moderation of commentator Moore and anchorman Elton Welsby echoed the sentiments of the victorious Arsenal players, guarded against over-zealous celebrations in front of the home fans. It is a point Alan Smith emphasized when discussing what, in retrospect and relative to the achievement, looked like muted jubilation at full time. 'Our gaffer asked for respect rather than too much jumping around,' said Smith. This was caught on camera. As the final whistle blew and his backroom team bounced out of the tiny dugout, Graham visibly urged restraint. The Arsenal manager, meticulous in his club blazer, was class personified.

Before I offer my analysis of the match, it is necessary to emphasize why Graham told his players it would be wrong to go overboard until they were in a more private setting. This game took place forty-one days after the Hillsborough disaster on 15 April 1989. It was played at a time when fans, players and media were struggling to deal with what happened, amid a countrywide debate on how appropriate it was to be so enthusiastic about football. In the weeks before the games resumed, there had been question marks about whether the season could go on.

It is striking how little the events in Sheffield were referenced during the coverage, save for Welsby indicating, 'If you believe in happy endings, the championship trophy will stay at Anfield for another year.' He did not linger on why. The hypersensitivity of the broadcasters was obvious, the shadow of Hillsborough inescapable.

Arsenal's players emerged from the tunnel before the game carrying bunches of flowers to place at the Kop end. Liverpool's were accompanied on to the pitch by mascot Paul Dalglish, the manager's twelve-year-old son, and wore black armbands in tribute to the ninety-six Hillsborough victims.

There was another, chillingly graphic clue which many viewers would not have noticed at Anfield before. The red metal barriers on the Kop terrace, so prominent through the 1970s and 1980s, had just been removed, in keeping with the permanent shift in attitude across English football in Hillsborough's aftermath. No longer were thousands of supporters caged in. The catastrophe in Sheffield would lead to the Taylor Report, the beginning of the end of squalid, unsafe stadiums in favour of all-seater arenas in England, setting football on its course to be a more spectator-friendly sport.

Today, the impact of the tragedy on the players and supporters would dominate the agenda heading into this game and following it. Not then.

No one felt comfortable approaching the subject. I am sure this was a symptom of the post-traumatic stress so many experienced at that time. 'The game has to move on' was the message, albeit with a whisper. The consequences of that were endured by many of the leading characters in this drama.

Lest we forget, this game would not have been played when it was, two weeks after the planned conclusion of the league season, but for Hillsborough. Originally scheduled for April, it was postponed because of the suspension of fixtures. A canny ITV executive recognized the possibility of a final-day shoot-out and deliberately manipulated the schedule. As Arsenal's faltering form created the perfect set-up, the evening was more than simply a football match. It was a cultural event. The two best teams in the country were in a gunfight with English football itself at a crossroads, on the threshold of emerging from catastrophe and crisis to become the commercial beast it is today.

I had little sense of the history about to unfold as an eleven-year-old Evertonian watching with my dad, expecting and fearing another Liverpool league and cup double. I was so thrilled when Liverpool blew it that the following day when we headed to the local pub, the Chaucer in Bootle, I laughed as a diehard blue friend of ours, John 'Conch' Connolly, scribbled 'Thank You, Arsenal'. I revelled in my rivals' failure.

In 2020, I sat alongside my son James – now a youth player at Wigan Athletic – with vastly different emotions. I had the foreboding of an ex-Liverpool player and fan knowing what was coming, but still scarcely believing it possible.

Although Thomas's goal is often replayed, I had never before felt the urge to rewatch the full game so was genuinely curious as I scribbled notes and hunted for those moments of tactical and technical excellence that I would usually pick out on *Monday Night Football*.

I have to say, as the first half progressed, worthwhile incidents being so notorious by their absence, James offered a cheeky teenager's observation: 'How can you tell which of these players are any good? This is like watching a League One game.'

I could have stopped the tape and handed him a stern lecture about showing more reverence for past stars, but his remarks fairly reflected the quality on show.

'This is what happens when there is so much at stake, playing the occasion as much as the ball,' I told him.

John Aldridge, the Liverpool striker who was pursuing a second successive league title, put it to me more bluntly. 'Let's face it, it was a shit game,' he said, although he admitted he had never watched it. 'And I never will,' he stressed.

Naturally, the Arsenal players I spoke to were more enthusiastic, while acknowledging it was not a thrilling spectacle. 'The game in general was more direct, then,' said Alan Smith. 'Liverpool were probably an exception because they tried to play through the pitch. I remember it being quick, even by today's standards. It felt 100mph. But it helped us because Liverpool didn't quite know how to approach it.'

The most diplomatic way to describe the opening exchanges is 'tactical'. What is instantly obvious is that the team expected to sprint out of the traps to win by two was as cautious as the one happy with a goalless draw. This was not what the country tuned in for, or what the producers wanted.

On the ITV coverage, Bobby Robson had summed up the prevailing view of Arsenal's chances prior to kick-off. 'They have to take a positive approach,' he said. 'They won't sit back. They have to attack and to some degree leave themselves wide open.' George Graham intuitively saw it differently, his foresight about to be spectacularly vindicated.

I have to say, the more I have studied this game and all that preceded and followed it, the more fascinated I have become by Graham's place in Arsenal and English football history.

When we think of that 1989 Arsenal team, we have images of set-piece excellence and defensive resilience rather than the 'sexy football' of Patrick Vieira and Thierry Henry at the turn of the millennium. We think of fans in the Clock End singing 'One-nil to the Arsenal' and rival fans mocking their pragmatic approach with 'Boring, boring Arsenal'.

We may even think of that famous scene from the film *The Full Monty* where the trainee dancers led by Robert Carlyle choreograph moves in the dole office by mimicking Tony Adams and Steve Bould moving in tandem and raising their arms to catch a striker offside.

A reputation developed for what is incorrectly derided as 'percentage football'. After speaking to those he managed and the man himself, I think Graham deserves better. He was a sophisticated, forward-thinking coach when many were pursuing formulaic, outdated methods. When we discussed the game, I was impressed by the broadness of his influences. He was a man of his time in some ways, and ahead of it in others.

Graham explained to me why he was an avid reader and student of NFL coaching, American footballers naturally making the rigorous practising of dead-ball situations the cornerstone of their training routines. Graham wanted to apply this more diligently to football, particularly corners and free-kicks. 'What I could not believe – and I still feel this way today – is how so many clubs did not practise set-pieces. I was like, "You have to be kidding me!" It is such a massive part of the game and if you could get it right you would score plenty.'

He set challenging goal targets for his defenders, which seem ambitious even by today's standards, telling Adams he could get double figures and Bould 'to target between six and eight' a season. For the record, they managed seven between them that year, although their presence contributed many more.

Graham mined one of his biggest confidants, Terry Venables, for information. By then, Venables had enjoyed a successful stint managing Barcelona, where he won La Liga. As for the famous offside routine, that was born in Italy. 'I was a big fan of AC Milan when they played offside to perfection,' said Graham. 'I copied a lot of what we did at Arsenal from [Milan manager] Arrigo Sacchi. When I left Millwall to join Arsenal I knew the system I was going to go with. I looked at the Arsenal squad and saw we had the players to do it.'

By the start of the 1988/89 campaign Graham had built an energetic team led by an inspirational young skipper, packed with dead-ball specialists and with one of the best, possibly most underrated strikers in the country in Smith.

Arsenal's players no longer had cause for an inferiority complex when facing Liverpool, the reigning champions. The teams met five times during 1988/89 before the Anfield decider and there was nothing between them, drawing three times and sharing a win apiece. 'There was a general view Liverpool were invincible at Anfield,' said Thomas. 'No one ever went there expecting to win. But as a group, we had confidence we could do it. We drew a League Cup game at Anfield that season and we were the much better side. And we beat them in something called the Football Centenary Cup.'

That said, Arsenal's long-term record at Anfield was dismal. They had not won there since November 1974, losing ten of their previous thirteen league visits. They had not kept a clean sheet at the stadium for fifteen years.

A Wembley date two years earlier was fresher in the memory of the squad, proving that this was a different Arsenal, an emerging force to take on the best. 'Beating Liverpool in the 1987 League Cup final was a starting point for us under George,' said Thomas. 'Liverpool never used to lose finals. We were on the bus to Wembley and there was a flag, "Liverpool, Annual Wembley Trip 1987". We felt how massive it was. I remember George putting the Liverpool team sheet up before that final, 1 to 11. He said, "Right then, Grobbelaar. He is average. A clown. Don't worry about him. Nicol. Average. Hansen. He has quality, but nothing to worry about." He just kept going until he got to Ian Rush, and then said, "Rush is world-class." We were looking at each other thinking, "What the hell is going on here?" It is the kind of thing you might expect from José Mourinho now. He gave us belief we could beat Liverpool. To do that on such a big occasion as Wembley was a big deal.'

For all the books on NFL visionaries, it was another American influence on Graham which enabled him to get into the heads of his players.

'John Wayne,' Thomas told me.

'George loved his westerns and loved quoting them,' he explained. 'His message before every away game was "Get in there, do the job, and get out". That's what he said when we went to Anfield that night.'

On the coach north, Graham inspired his players by playing the video of Arsenal's 1971 double winners beating Liverpool at Wembley, a game in which he played.

Surprisingly, Arsenal only travelled to Liverpool on the day of the game to keep the players away from the Merseyside 'bubble', as the manager saw it. Graham reasoned his squad would endure a more nervous night's sleep, and no doubt a disrupted one, if they made the trip twenty-four hours earlier and Liverpool fans found their hotel.

That strikes me as a big decision and a massive risk that paid off.

In my career, aside from derby matches, there were only two away days in a season when I recall an overnight stay being unnecessary. They were short journeys to Manchester and Wigan Athletic. To spend three or four hours on a coach from London to Liverpool for a game of such importance sounds as crazy now as it was then. As a fan, the coach from Bootle to Wembley would tire me out. The idea of playing the most important ninety minutes of my life after such a journey is incomprehensible.

Graham's demeanour and attitude sent a message of calm and confidence through his squad. Ahead of his greatest night in management, he shrewdly second-guessed Liverpool's looming tactical dilemma. He had designed his Anfield plan months earlier and the influence of the league table on both managers' approach had the unexpected bonus of making it more effective.

Arsenal's back four of Adams, Bould, Nigel Winterburn and Lee Dixon is legendary. By the time they reached Anfield they had a fifth member. Graham had decided well in advance that he was going to play David O'Leary as an extra centre-back against Liverpool, changing the defensive system in early April for a trip to Old Trafford, a 1-1 draw. 'It was specifically prepared for the upcoming Liverpool game – I wanted three at the back to deal with their wide men,' George explained to me.

'John Barnes was on a high for Liverpool, their biggest threat, outstanding on the ball and the best player, probably, in England at the time. That was a massive problem for any side playing Liverpool. On the right side they had someone I tried to buy, Ray Houghton. I was a big admirer and met him when he left Oxford, but I must not have said the right things. I thought if we contain the wide players, use David [O'Leary] as a sweeper with Adams and Bould, it would help the other boys, particularly the full-backs. It was designed to stop the passing options and make Liverpool do what they never wanted to, which was hit longer balls and compromise their usual style.'

Again, without wishing to sound too critical, there was minimal discussion about this major tactical change on the ITV coverage except for commentator Moore, when naming the teams, suggesting that O'Leary's inclusion was 'surprising'.

In England at that time, a sweeper was radical and generally misinterpreted as a defensive measure. Kenny Dalglish occasionally used a similar system upon becoming player-manager in 1985, utilizing the benefits of his usual central midfield playmaker, Jan Molby, finding space in a deeper role and connecting to midfielders and attackers. Like Graham in 1989, Dalglish made the same reshuffle with the title at stake in the final game of a season. In 1986, Liverpool travelled to Chelsea needing a win to fend off Everton's title challenge. Dalglish selected three centre-backs who were all comfortable in possession: Mark Lawrenson, Alan Hansen and Gary Gillespie. Liverpool won 1-0 to complete the first stage of the double.

Bobby Robson would also successfully go down this route halfway through the 1990 World Cup, Mark Wright the spare man at the back alongside Terry Butcher and Des Walker.

The difference in 1989 is that Arsenal spent weeks rehearsing it, so it was no impromptu change. The intention was to ensure the starting position of Dixon and Winterburn was 10 yards higher up the pitch. That is the difference between playing full-back and wing-back. The effect was to get the Arsenal pair closer and tighter to the dangermen

Graham was most concerned about, Barnes and Houghton. Smith, an exceptional target man with a magnificent first touch, was fundamental to the formula's success, holding the ball and linking play for midfield runners.

While Arsenal arrived at Anfield having worked on their 5-4-1 strategy for two months, Liverpool tried something alien to their instincts. They faced an unexpected, unfamiliar and ultimately undermining problem which Graham preyed on: how does a team bred to win adjust to the idea they can lose? This is something you rarely deal with and was particularly unusual for players of Liverpool's class, accustomed to the demand of winning every week and generally succeeding.

Let's remind ourselves what Liverpool represented in 1989. The club was a winning machine. Between 1972 and 1989, there were only three years in which Liverpool failed to win at least one major trophy – 1975, 1985 and 1987. They had just beaten Everton 3-2 in the FA Cup final a week before the Arsenal decider, playing their usual brand of dominant, possession-based football. Their players were programmed to score, score and score some more.

Although I never played in a team so attacking or so successful, or in a game exactly like this, I can relate a little to the situation Liverpool faced protecting a comfortable lead from my experience of two-legged European ties.

In 2001, I played a UEFA Cup round of sixteen match against Roma in similar circumstances. We won the away leg 2-0 so knew we could afford a narrow defeat at Anfield and still progress into the quarter-final on aggregate. The transformation in the approach I experienced was psychological more than tactical. Without realizing it is happening, you find yourself playing 'no risk' football. You become less inclined to attempt ambitious passes or make overlapping forward runs that might leave your teammates vulnerable to a counter-attack. Attacking players who usually feel free to be creative and flexible will opt for safer, easy passes because they are more worried about losing possession.

The overall effect is you overthink everything and end up defending more.

It is a rare kind of challenge and one you can never really anticipate or fully prepare for, even in a side that was generally built for defence and counter-attack as it was under Gérard Houllier. Against Roma we lost 1-0 and needed a controversial refereeing decision (a penalty was awarded and then the officials changed their minds) to prevent the Italians forcing extra-time.

Had we needed to win the second leg, I have no doubt the game would have been very different.

Early in my career I played in a youth match and we were 2-0 up at half-time. Ronnie Moran, a Liverpool boot-room legend who was by then the club's assistant manager, came from the stands into the dressing room and told us we now faced a challenge. 'We will see how good you are now,' he said, interested to see how evolved our game management skills were.

We drew 2-2.

There is an art to seeing out a game. There are many teams who excel at working themselves into the lead but who suddenly look vulnerable when it comes to protecting it. The greatest teams are adept at both, switching gears and styles as the circumstances dictate.

The Liverpool team of 1989 had little cause or opportunity to consider or practise that because they were so much better than most. They were rarely in a situation where they felt compelled to stop attacking. I believe that distinguishes some of the 1989 side from the triumphant Anfield teams of the past who had the added and vital experience of European competition and were masters of scoring early and killing the game.

Dalglish's Liverpool blew teams away. Their unbeaten run went back to 1 January, winning fifteen out of eighteen games. In one particularly blistering spell in March that season they scored sixteen goals in four games, conceding two. On 23 May, West Ham had become the third visitors in six to concede five at Anfield. Even though club captain Alan

Hansen made only six league appearances all season (he would not have been eligible for a title winners' medal), they conceded only two goals in fifteen hours at Anfield before the finale, although their last – to West Ham's Leroy Rosenior – was the difference between Arsenal needing a two- or three-goal winning margin.

'Leroy always claims he was just as important to us winning the league,' said Smith.

Despite the trauma of Hillsborough, Liverpool somehow settled back into what, on the surface at least, resembled sporting normality, albeit with a congested fixture schedule. Even by the standards of the time, it is amazing that they played seven games in sixteen days prior to Arsenal's visit, winning six. Try explaining that to a modern coach the next time they mention the demands on players. Nobody at Anfield complained.

'Seriously, I only noticed how busy that schedule was when I looked four years ago,' admitted John Barnes. 'I can see now it looks like a game too far. But I never felt tired on that night. None of us looked for excuses.'

The hectic run-in included the FA Cup final against Everton on 20 May, won after extra-time, and the 5-1 win over West Ham, just three days before the Arsenal game. With goal difference on the agenda as Dalglish's side sought a layer of security, the philosophy against the Hammers could not have contrasted more with what followed, Liverpool scoring three in the last ten minutes to swing the maths in their favour. Attending the Professional Footballers' Association dinner in London, Alan Smith was receiving regular updates from the West Ham game with increasing dread. 'Journalists kept coming up to me and saying, "Now it's 3-1, now it's four . . . now it's five." By the end we worked out we needed to win by two at Anfield.'

Yet while Arsenal were coming to terms with the scale of their challenge, Aldridge told me 'battering' West Ham was the worst preparation. 'If we had gone into the Arsenal game needing a result, we would have done it,' he said. 'I know that is easy to say now but because we had the cushion of those two goals, the message was all "don't do anything stupid, be careful". If we'd had to play our normal game it would have been different. But we didn't. It was like we played for 0-0. We didn't go for it in the flamboyant way we had played for two seasons. The wingers were tucking in and doing the right things. But it was an unnatural game.'

It still seemed Liverpool were heading towards the finish with a sprint, Arsenal with a stumble. Graham's side had been twelve points ahead on 2 January. When they returned to action on 1 May after the suspension of games following Hillsborough, they beat Norwich 5-0 and followed that up with an away win at Middlesbrough. The title was in their grasp with home games against Derby and Wimbledon before their Anfield trip.

'We'd had it all worked out a few weeks earlier,' recalled Michael Thomas. 'We were looking through the fixtures and saying to ourselves, "We'll win it in front of our own fans." Then we had the wobbles, Dean Saunders had one of those games for Derby to beat us at Highbury, and then . . .' Thomas pauses as if he has momentarily forgotten that it worked out fine in the end. 'Fuckin' Wimbledon.'

An equalizer on debut by Wimbledon's Paul McGee meant although Arsenal moved level with Liverpool, they had played a game more.

'There was a general sense we had fucked it up,' said Smith. 'We did a lap of honour in the last home game and it was like we were saying sorry we could not quite manage it, but we had a good go. The chairman came into the dressing room to congratulate us on a great season. No one was thinking of giving up, but it felt like it was over. But the day after in training, talking with the lads it was like, "You know what, it is not over." It was a shot to nothing. A free hit.'

The psychological role reversal was extreme, Arsenal going from the side with the title in their hands to the side with nothing to lose within four games, Liverpool fretting over whether to finish the job with adventure or pragmatism.

During the early moments of the decider, it was obvious how Graham's plan was working, albeit at the expense of entertainment.

'We knew in the first fifteen minutes Liverpool were not themselves,' said Smith. 'The longer it went on, the more we were thinking, "It's on."'

Dalglish opted for Ian Rush and John Aldridge up front but they were unable to get their usual service from creative midfielders. Rush looked sharp but was subbed early because of the groin injury that had been bothering him for weeks. Barnes was increasingly forced to move inside for possession – something which had serious consequences later in the game.

Both teams were holding back. Liverpool's compromising was understandable, albeit ultimately calamitous. They were caught in Graham's trap. 'While everyone was saying we would have to go there and attack, I was telling the players the opposite,' said Graham. 'I told them to take it easy, do not concede, and let's see how Liverpool approach it. In the first half, to be honest with you neither side was trying to win. It was very unlike Liverpool. Liverpool were always outstanding at home and always trying to win games as quickly as possible. They went at teams to get the game won in the first twenty minutes. That was their philosophy.'

Arsenal's main threat came from the persistent long goal-kicks of keeper John Lukic and the set-plays they had so meticulously rehearsed. When an inswinging Winterburn free-kick on the right was headed wide by Smith at the Kop end, it was a preview of what was coming in the second half.

At half-time both sides looked content, the viewing public enthralled by the tension more than the spectacle.

It was Smith's goal, an unnecessarily controversial moment seven minutes into the second half, which changed the atmosphere and fully exposed Liverpool's vulnerabilities and anxieties.

The sequence leading to it is typical eighties football containing a mini game of head tennis between opposing centre-backs. Lukic kicks long, Gary Ablett heads it clear, Adams heads it back, and in the fight for the second ball Ronnie Whelan fouls David Rocastle. All those months of set-piece preparation came to fruition when Winterburn's free-kick was glanced in by Smith.

'We practised set-pieces in training all the time and the one from which I scored we always tried,' he said. 'From the right, Nigel would inswing it with his left foot, and if Brian Marwood was playing he would inswing from the left with his right foot. The idea was for Bouldy or Tony to peel around the back and create the diversion so I could sneak in. Until then, that one never came off. In fact, it had reached the point where I was thinking, "Why are we doing this one again? This never bloody works." Finally it did.'

Liverpool's players pleaded with referee David Hutchinson to rule out Smith's goal, his twenty-third of the season. I kept rewinding the tape to work out what they were complaining about.

You see Liverpool's players crowding the referee claiming Smith did not touch it, with only O'Leary nearby to represent Arsenal's case. It is so obvious Smith headed it when you see the replay it left me confused as to why the referee decided to ask his linesman for clarification. There was no way the linesman could make that call, so what were the officials talking about? Surely it could only have been about a possible offside?

I decided to call the linesman on the night, Geoff Banwell, for some clarification and he kindly verified that there was no chance of the goal being ruled out. 'Everyone thought that was a dispute about offside. It wasn't. The argument was because Ronnie Whelan said it went straight in from an indirect free-kick. It did not. Alan Smith glanced it.'

'So the referee thought you had a better view than him?'

'He said he wanted my verbal confirmation,' he explained. 'After the game David gave a politician's answer saying he had no doubt Alan Smith had touched it and he was just going through the motions consulting me. I was relieved when I saw the replay that I had got it right, especially as when I got home my wife told me it was one of the incidents shown on the ten o'clock news.'

Arsenal's players were more concerned than they needed to be. 'I thought, "There is no way he's going to give this goal,"' said Smith. 'I kept asking, "What was wrong with it?" It was well onside.'

Had they disallowed it, the clamour for video assistant referees (VAR) would have begun thirty years early.

What followed cuts to the heart of my assessment of how and why Arsenal succeeded and Liverpool succumbed in those final moments.

Panic.

There is no greater threat to a football team. It is a rarity at elite level, but when it grips, it is contagious. The more there is at stake and the more you have to lose, the worse it gets.

Just as a perfectly coached side works in a chain reaction, so it can fall apart with a single malfunction. And whenever you see a well-drilled team of world-class footballers temporarily lose shape – and we see plenty of examples of this in the greatest games – you can be sure panic is near the scene.

Panic comes from the fear of losing, although fear itself can have positive and negative consequences. I played most of my career worried about the outcome and in the vast majority of situations it was a useful source of motivation. I would go into the week of a Merseyside derby, for example, not thinking so much about winning but apprehensive about losing or being the one whose mistake impacted on the result. That ensured I retained focus.

Cup finals or all-or-nothing Champions League games were the biggest source of stress. It sounds irrational. I would train hard all year to give myself an opportunity to fulfil my ambitions of collecting medals, and then be worried sick when the chances came. The more experienced I was, the worse it became. Winning means so much to family and friends as much as players, and if you have suffered once and felt that pain of being so close and failing, you know what is coming if it happens again. Weeks, maybe even months and years, of replaying the game in your head, or avoiding seeing the clips on television.

No player or team can ever be fully immune. I believe it is the most successful – those who have been to countless finals and experienced the torture of defeat and euphoria of victory – who suffer more than any because they know what they will go through if it goes wrong again.

When embraced as a source of motivation, fear can help, making you doubly determined to ensure you concentrate for every second. But panic is the unhealthy symptom of fear. What is so dangerous about it is that it creeps up on you when you should be at your calmest, such as when you have a significant lead but can sense a change in a game's momentum. You may not even be aware you are panicking as the instinct to chase the ball rather than stay disciplined takes hold. While the tactical intricacies of the winners contribute to their success on the biggest stages, so does the loss of emotional control of the defeated.

Elsewhere in this book, we can apply this to Barcelona losing at Anfield in 2019 after winning the first leg of their Champions League semi-final 3-0, and AC Milan in those six minutes of the second half in the 2005 Champions League final, both teams squandering a substantial lead. We could also mention Bayern Munich's reaction as Manchester United poured forward having just equalized at the end of the 1999 Champions League final.

But of all the games I have studied, the last twenty minutes of Liverpool v. Arsenal in 1989 stand out as the prime example of a side undone by its anxiety, players making decisions they would not have made in the previous thirty-seven games. That was the consequence of Liverpool players thinking about the outcome rather than the processes that took them so close to the finish.

The highest stakes can do that to the very best, scrambling your brain and rendering you powerless as you begin to feel you are fighting destiny.

What I recognize in the Liverpool v. Arsenal case three decades on is the difference between the team that should be chaotically searching for the winner, gambling by piling more men forward, and the side with the advantage with players pulled out of position.

It was Arsenal, feeling they had nothing more to lose, who demonstrated greater clarity of thought. Liverpool, protecting their fortress, looked confused and hesitant in the precariousness of their situation. The team generally regarded as one of the best in Liverpool history, famed for its possession-based, attacking football, could barely string a move together to get near the opposition penalty box. The Kop sang 'attack, attack, attack' every time their team was on the ball. But as the clock ticked on the Liverpool players were looking for clever passing angles back to Grobbelaar, who, three years before the change to the law preventing keepers from picking up a backpass, received the ball more than any Liverpool player. Grobbelaar regularly exchanged at least one more pass with a centre-back whenever he had it in those final minutes.

'Boring, boring Scousers' sang the Arsenal fans – an ironic twist on the insults they had fended off all season.

The encounter came to its epic conclusion in the 92nd minute. Barnes, as he did most of the evening because of Graham's formation, drifted into central midfield from his usual left wing. For three-quarters of the game this was logical. Arsenal's 5-4-1 limited his space out wide and he wanted to get on the ball. But by then Bould had been subbed for Perry Groves, Arsenal playing a back four since the 76th minute. There was no reason for Barnes to be so central.

He picked up possession and his pass was intercepted by Tony Adams. Barnes's natural inclination was to chase the ball and he was initially successful because he won a fifty-fifty tackle with the Arsenal captain. He continued to dribble forward. 'I was going to head to the corner flag but because I won the tackle and Tony had fallen over, I thought to myself there is going to be more space in the middle,' Barnes explained to me. 'When I looked up I saw I had only Kevin Richardson to beat.'

Because of that, safer options were ignored. As well as deciding not to head for the corner flag himself, Barnes had run past Peter Beardsley, who hesitated instead of running down the line as he normally would. Beardsley, a first-half substitute for Rush, was terrified of losing his position. In holding back to retain the team shape, he did the opposite of his teammates, who were beginning to spread all over the pitch.

'At any other time, Beardsley would have run forward and asked for a pass,' I suggested to Barnes.

'Absolutely,' he agreed.

Instead, Barnes attempted another run and lost the ball to Richardson, who gave it to Lukic.

Barnes was now on Liverpool's right, leaving a gap on the opposite wing. Lukic had the sharpness of mind to immediately throw the ball to Dixon. Dixon, the right-back, would usually be closed down by Barnes, the left-winger. Barnes is obviously not there.

In his absence, McMahon, who should have been holding his position in central midfield, sprinted towards Dixon. This decision tells me McMahon's heart was ruling his head. There is no way he would have done this under any other circumstances. He feels compelled to react and cover the ground, attracted towards the ball, because it is so late in the game.

During the course of every match, a player like Barnes will often drift around the pitch. You can find ten examples in this game. It is not a problem. What you would never expect is the central midfielder covering a left-winger by challenging a right-back so far up the pitch in injury-time. In this case, it means McMahon is no longer near Michael Thomas in the centre.

Liverpool's structural problems did not end there.

When Dixon passed down the right to Smith, Liverpool's defence retreated so deep that the Arsenal striker had enough space and time to control the ball and flick it in Thomas's direction. The centre-backs should have been further up the pitch, into Smith's back, ready to give him a kick up the backside if necessary.

Not for the first time that night, Smith's touch and pass were exquisite.

With no Liverpool players seeing or covering the midfield break of Thomas, he ran through and with the outside of his right boot changed the course of Arsenal, Liverpool and English football history. He benefited because the Liverpool players compromised their normal behaviour in the tension of that moment.

I discussed this analysis with Barnes, suggesting that the apprehension was obvious in the decision-making. I stressed that this was an explanation for Thomas's goal rather than criticism, although I sensed his discomfort that the season was being condensed to those pivotal thirty seconds.

'Look, in a thirty-eight-game season there are so many key moments where it could have been won and lost,' he said. 'It is never down to one decision. We could trace the move back to when I received the ball, or go further back into the game and find a moment where it could have been different. We could go back to games earlier in the season and find a game we drew or lost which we should have won. That is football.'

I agree, but there is no escaping the magnitude and significance of this goal, nor the structural mishap which I interpret as entirely due to the circumstances, allowing Arsenal one of their only chances on the night to string together a couple of passes and free Thomas.

There was still work to be done but destiny was the Arsenal mid-fielder's friend.

'At the time when the ball came to me my first thought was "I am still near the halfway line",' Thomas recalled. 'Then it hit me and I thought, "Bloody 'ell, I'm near the penalty box." When the ball hit Steve Nicol's shoulder I knew fate was on our side because it bounced exactly where I wanted it. Even then I could feel someone else near me – I saw later it was Ray Houghton – and even now when I think back it gives me the chills. As a kid I dreamed of winning the FA Cup in the last minute. When you were with your mates kicking the ball around, no one ever shouted, "This is for the league title!" It was always a last-minute chance to win the FA Cup final. The enormity of that goal was just weird, too much to even take in because you would never have imagined that situation to be possible.'

Aside from Thomas's memorable belly flops at the Anfield Road end of the stadium we did not see the full repertoire of Arsenal celebrations.

There was plenty of mutual goodwill after Liverpool's frenzied last attack fizzled out and the final whistle sent most of the stadium into a state of eerie silence. The Kop remained full, the fans putting aside their dejection to show appreciation for the players' efforts at the end of a distressing season.

O'Leary tried to console his Republic of Ireland teammate Aldridge. He was having none of it, shrugging him off. 'Yeah, I regret that, David is my mate,' said Aldridge. 'But my head was gone. I was in a trance. I could not believe it had happened and wanted the ground to swallow me up. I was thinking, "Did that happen? Am I dreaming?" It looked like sour grapes, but maybe people understand what we had gone through over those few weeks. Arsenal deserved it in the end and it was meant to be for them, but it was hard to take in that moment. It felt like a proper kick in the bollocks.'

Adams received the trophy and the broadcast swiftly concluded. In the absence of immediate thorough analysis, certainly on TV, the players would fill the insatiable appetite of supporters craving anecdotes for the next thirty-one years.

A boozy trip home was followed by an even boozier open-top bus tour in North London. 'Even the gaffer had a drink with us on the coach back from Liverpool, something which he never did before, so you knew it was special,' said Smith.

To his eternal regret, Lee Dixon stayed in the north-west because relatives from Australia were visiting his native Manchester. Stopping at a chip shop in Liverpool before heading down the M62, he was met with an enthusiastic ovation from a group of Evertonians.

Even the officials hit the bubbly after playing their part in a classic. 'Kenny Dalglish came into the officials' dressing room with a bottle of champagne and said, "You might as well have this,"' explained linesman Banwell. 'I had to drive back to Stafford, so the referee took it.'

The Arsenal players headed directly to the Winners snooker club in North London for pies and pints. Thomas was spotted leaving in the early hours with a fan, collecting the first editions of the morning papers. On Merseyside, another memorable first edition was rapidly redesigned, the original front page remaining in the *Liverpool Echo* editor's office for several years as a painful reminder of what might have been for the home team.

'Champions', it read.

For Thomas, there would be a further twist when he signed for Liverpool two years later. He made over a hundred appearances for the club, scored in the FA Cup win over Sunderland in 1992, and won the League Cup. 'At one point I think I was the only player on Merseyside who Liverpool and Everton fans wanted to buy a drink,' said Thomas.

Arsenal headed into an era where they would become regulars on the winners' podium. For those unconvinced by my opening submission, that of all their rivals it was Arsenal, not United, who have the more genuine claim of dethroning Liverpool, consider this. Graham took over at Arsenal in the same year as Ferguson arrived at Old Trafford, in 1986, and won a trophy in his first season, beating Liverpool at Wembley. Ferguson waited four years for his first, the FA Cup in 1990. Arsenal won the title again in 1991, and a further three major trophies under Graham. Having gone a decade without a major honour, Arsenal won six in eight years under Graham, including the European Cup Winners' Cup in 1994. It fits a convenient but incomplete timeline to see the eighties as the era of Liverpool, seamlessly followed by United in the nineties and noughties. The record books show that is not true.

I suspect Graham's legacy has suffered because of how he left the club in 1995, sacked after admitting accepting an 'unsolicited gift' from Norwegian agent Rune Hauge, and what followed when Arsène Wenger arrived in 1996, overseeing revolutions in style and sports science which took the standard of football at Highbury and in England to another level.

When Arsenal's official website held a vote in 2017 asking fans to state the greatest moment in their history, Thomas's golden goal was relegated to second place behind Wenger's season of 'The Invincibles'. As a neutral, I find this hard to believe. 'That is very much a generational decision,' says Amy Lawrence. 'To have engaged with the game in 1989 you would have to be in your forties. To younger fans it feels like ancient history, but for the rest of us it is like that "JFK" moment. Where were you when we won at Anfield in '89?'

Wenger's debt to Graham is indisputable. When he transformed the bulk of Graham's squad into double winners at the end of the 1990s, although different in football philosophy it was built on the defence he inherited and a back four institutionalized with the same principles that served Arsenal in 1989. Would Wenger have enjoyed his success without Graham's legacy? I will quote the Anfield hero on that. 'Without that defence, Wenger's team would not have won anything,' said Michael Thomas. 'They never won a title after the last of George's defenders, Martin Keown, finished, did they?'

Graham was an enlightened figure during a transformative period for English football yet he remains modest about his Arsenal team's place in history. 'When I look back it is not just about that particular day,' he said. 'When you're talking about the great teams, and their great performances, you can find a game where it all went to plan. We see that nowadays with the great Manchester City and Liverpool teams. But Pep Guardiola and Jürgen Klopp will tell you it is never just about the day. It is everything leading towards getting that performance, and that comes from understanding the philosophy of the coach.

'We played the same as all season and had a system we believed in. I always wanted to beat Liverpool because they had been the best team for so many years, so from day one it was always in my head that if we could get near them, we had a chance. I used to think of that "This is Anfield" sign which all the Liverpool boys touch. I thought to myself, "I want to be able to go there and be allowed to do that." It was a compliment. Liverpool were the team.'

Liverpool won another title in 1990 but by the time the Premier League kicked off Dalglish had left and Souness's toils meant his old club vacated their 'perch', finishing sixth in the inaugural season of the revamped top flight in 1993. Liverpool fans will always believe it was as much an abdication as being usurped. They lost their mentally exhausted young manager, saw their title-winning team dismantled, and failed to adapt to a new world of personalized numbers, revamped stadia and more widely distributed wealth among the elite clubs. Only then did Manchester United fill the vacuum. The frustration for English football is that the greatest of battles between the best Liverpool and United teams never materialized.

Liverpool's subsequent difficulties can be traced back to those six weeks in April and the wounds on and off the pitch.

Although the circumstances are incomparable, this title decider, allied to the following year's World Cup, Italia 90, had an impact on English football's future as profound and consequential as the tragic events at Hillsborough. Thomas's goal sits alongside Paul Gascoigne's tears in Turin after England's defeat to West Germany in the World Cup semi-final. Together they proved there was a public appetite, and an opportunity, to give football permanent residency in the UK's living rooms.

In 1987, the Football League negotiated its first significant contract for live football, a four-year deal worth £11 million a year, which enabled ITV to broadcast a live game every week. They could never have envisioned such a gem as Anfield '89 being part of that package.

With the considerable ammunition of the climax to that season and the public response to Italia 90 fresh in everyone's memory, London Weekend Television's managing director, Greg Dyke, held a dinner date with football's big five, Liverpool, Everton, Arsenal, Manchester United and Tottenham, to revive negotiations for a newly formed, more lucrative Premier League with more live games every week.

In the same year, an obscure television company called British Satellite Broadcasting merged with Sky, initially trying to lure viewers with the Leyland DAF Cup. Their eyes were on a bigger prize.

The revolution was set in motion.

When I see Michael Thomas come face to face with Bruce Grobbelaar in the 92nd minute at Anfield, I do not only see the title up for grabs. Little could I have known as an eleven-year-old giggling at that graffiti artist in Bootle that I had watched a key moment in a timeline leading me to a punditry seat on TV three decades later.

For that, at least, I say this.

Thank you, Arsenal.

4

Saturday, 1 September 2001

2002 FIFA WORLD CUP QUALIFIER, GROUP 9
Olympiastadion, Munich

GERMANY 1–5 ENGLAND

Jancker *6*

Owen *12, 48, 66*
Gerrard *45+4*
Heskey *74*

'I think the English did get carried away'
                    – Dietmar Hamann

MICHAEL OWEN RUSHED INTO THE dressing room like a man possessed, stared wide-eyed into the faces of his teammates and offered a damning verdict on the opposition.

'This lot are fucking shite!' he yelled.

It was half-time in Munich, and I was one of the substitutes for England's World Cup qualifier, keeping a discreet distance from the main group as Michael, usually so mild-mannered, channelled his inner Tony Adams.

'Let's keep going forward and attack them,' he continued.

Manager Sven-Göran Eriksson barely had a chance to speak as the future Ballon d'Or winner pleaded with teammates to seize a once-in-a-career opportunity. In the eight years I was Michael's roommate and colleague, I never saw him so animated.

'I remember the look on your face,' Michael said when I told him about just one of my abiding memories of that September night in the Olympic Stadium. 'You knew me better than anyone and I was pretty quiet in the dressing room in general. I wouldn't say anything. I don't know what it was that night. I felt confident, I felt as if we were going to beat them. I was feeling on top of the world at the time. It was a "just give me the ball" type of feeling.'

Michael's frankness was spectacularly vindicated. His hat-trick in England's 5-1 win was one of the highlights of his international career, the victory the pinnacle of Eriksson's reign, the emphatic and stylish nature of it raising expectations for the following summer's World Cup in Japan and South Korea.

The line-up contained the cream of English football, most of them yet to peak for their clubs. Rio Ferdinand was twenty-two; Owen and Steven Gerrard were twenty-one; Ashley Cole was twenty; captain David Beckham was one of the more experienced players at twenty-six. There were three Manchester United stars and a future Old Trafford legend, four players from Liverpool and three from Arsenal. Two of the three substitutes used played for Real Madrid and Bayern Munich, and the third played a cruelly overlooked but critical seven-minute cameo in centre midfield to protect the four-goal lead.

That was me, summoned thanks to Gary Neville when he pleaded with the bench to rest Paul Scholes before he picked up a yellow card and one-game ban.

England looked young and dynamic, Germany leggy and ragged. Seeing the promise of an emerging squad fulfilled in such breathtaking fashion, a flattering description was born. Here was England's 'Golden Generation'.

To the majority who witnessed it, Munich represents the England game of a lifetime.

'Whenever I meet Liverpool fans they want to talk about the Champions League final in Istanbul. Whenever I meet England fans, they want to talk about Germany in 2001,' Steven Gerrard told me.

If Scotland v. England is the closest to an international derby, Germany are considered the bitterest overseas rival. There are historic reasons on and off the pitch for that, the fixture appealing to the most nationalistic English fans.

Gerrard's first taste came in Euro 2000, when Alan Shearer scored the winner in a 1-0 win over Germany in Belgium. 'Until then I just thought they were another nation,' he said. 'It wasn't until I was around the likes of Paul Ince, Tony Adams and Alan Shearer that it really dawned on me. Their reaction in the build-up was different. It was all, "this is fuckin' England v. Germany". It is more than a normal international.'

The manner and scale of victory in September 2001 were worth more than three group points. Before Munich, England had not beaten

Germany in a World Cup fixture since the 1966 final. Germany had not lost any World Cup qualifier in their previous sixty and had not suffered defeat in Munich for twenty-eight years. Humiliating one of the world's strongest nations on their own soil was some retribution for the heartbreaking penalty shoot-out defeats of Italia 90 and Euro 96.

Now there was justifiable hope that exciting times lay ahead for the national team, with world-class young players and a sought-after manager.

Sitting on the bench for eighty-three minutes, I had the perfect view. It was my fifth cap, having been called up for the first time a year earlier with Kevin Keegan on the brink of quitting. I can testify to a changing, positive atmosphere. I was part of the squad for the last game beneath the old Wembley twin towers eleven months before Munich. Keegan's reign ended on a sodden Saturday afternoon after an ignominious 1-0 defeat against the same opponents, my Liverpool teammate Dietmar Hamann scoring the winner. I was a bemused onlooker as Keegan delivered his goodbye speech to the squad, having been earlier ushered into the changing-room toilets by FA executives where he ignored pleas to change his mind.

'So, this is what senior international football is like?' I thought.

Chaos.

Before Eriksson arrived, the man entrusted with sorting it out was the Football Association's chief executive Adam Crozier. He was among the first I thought I ought to speak to about this game because his decision to appoint Eriksson, hugely controversial at the time, defined the era.

Crozier joined the FA from advertising and marketing giants Saatchi & Saatchi in 2000 and is credited with the 'Golden Generation' branding. He laughed when I put that to him.

'The funny thing is, Jamie, I don't think I ever said that,' he said. 'I genuinely cannot ever remember saying it. It is just not the kind of thing I would say. Somehow it got attached to me. I do not know if someone else came up with it. I have no idea. It is one of those really strange things. I can remember being asked, "What can this team achieve?" I said, it depends. We knew that between 2002 and 2006 these players would be at their peak.'

What is a matter of record – and, I sensed, a genuine source of pride – is that Crozier was the architect of the FA's move for Eriksson, although he told me that was as much due to circumstance as design. 'You will remember as well as anyone that Kevin resigned in slightly unusual circumstances after the first Germany game. I loved working with Kevin. He was very popular with the players, was a great motivator and he always wanted to play attacking football. But the truth of it is, we had not had a great Euro 2000 and we did not play well. Somewhere around that time I remember speaking to him about bringing in a defensive coach, in the way Terry Venables had Don Howe alongside him. But Kevin was loyal to his backroom team.'

The onus was on Crozier to lead the headhunt, and he instantly confronted the philosophical divide with those who felt an English passport was more important than coaching ability. 'When I looked through the list of previous England managerial appointments there was a common theme,' he recalled. 'The FA had always gone for someone who had just won the cup or been second in the league, as opposed to a coach with a track record of success over a long period of time. I wanted someone who was a consistent winner, not someone with a one-off win. Part of the problem when we were looking was there were a lot of potentially good, young, very interesting England coaches coming through, but they did not have that experience or winning record.

'We didn't start the process looking abroad, but the reality was, in that moment of time, the only England coach with serious experience was Bobby Robson, who had done the job before. So we asked Bobby to come in as an interim measure with two young coaches. He was going to be supported by Steve McClaren and Peter Taylor. Bobby was keen, but – well within their rights and understandably, as they were doing well at the top end of the Premier League at the time – Newcastle would not let him do it.'

As an interim measure, Howard Wilkinson was put in charge for the next qualifier, in Finland in October 2000, a 0-0 draw best remembered for the caretaker manager's much-maligned decision to leave out Owen. The result left England bottom of the qualifying group, two points behind Albania and Greece. Japan was a distant hope.

Taylor, my former England Under-21 coach who was by then managing Leicester City, was given the interim role for the next international, a friendly in Italy. We performed well but lost 1-0. I played sixty-five minutes in Turin. Taylor appointed Beckham captain and the squad already had a fresh direction.

'I remember speaking to a few of the senior players,' said Crozier. 'You were all working with great coaches at your clubs. Sir Alex [Ferguson] was at Manchester United, Arsène Wenger at Arsenal, Gérard Houllier at Liverpool. I thought we simply had to make sure the England coach was of the same pedigree, or even better if that was possible. The general view of the players was they just wanted a brilliant coach. They all said, "We have to get the best person." So in the end, the shortlist was Sven, Fabio Capello and Johan Cruyff. There were also a lot of people pointing at Martin O'Neill, obviously from Northern Ireland.

'Capello did not speak English too well at that time, although I am not sure he did much better when he took the job later. Cruyff had not been well and, as I remember, we weren't quite sure if he would fit with that group of young players. Sven ticked all the boxes. He had a track record, improving the clubs he had joined and the players he worked with by playing with a specific system. He had won in Sweden, Portugal and Italy. He had won European trophies and he was used to working with big-name, high-profile players. Don't forget we took him from Lazio, who had just won the Italian league. He created an amazing team there and at the time he was one of the most coveted managers in the world. So we all got around the idea of Sven coming in, and he was also enthusiastic about having young England coaches work with him. The idea was this could be a one-off to bridge the gap, with Sven coaching up an English successor. Although it did not work out for Steve [McClaren], that is what happened. There was a succession plan there.'

Convincing a patriotic nation was a tougher sell for Scottish-born Crozier. 'I had plenty of death threats post the announcement,' he recalled. 'There were always going to be those dead set against it. Because my background was not in football, I had a straightforward view: let's get the best person for the job, irrespective of where he comes from. The 5-1 was where it all flipped. Germany were top of the group and only one team was going to qualify automatically. They had already arranged friendlies for the upcoming play-off dates. People started to take notice of the national team after that.'

While England flew to Germany believing they were sweeping away the remaining debris of recent disappointments, their opponents were dealing with their own crisis. There had been calls for wide scale reform of German football after they were knocked out at the group stage in Euro 2000. Bayer Leverkusen manager Christoph Daum was appointed Germany coach before the World Cup qualifiers but never managed the side, forced to quit because of allegations surrounding his private life. The details are sketchy. Let's just say it was the result of a sordid tabloid report involving cocaine and prostitutes. Former striker Rudi Völler took over a team in need of a new impetus as much as England, despite an encouraging start to the qualifying campaign.

Hamann explained to me that after prolonged success, German football was adjusting to a period of self-reflection, its sights set on grander ambitions than dealing with England. 'We had a disappointing Euros,' he said. 'We had a new manager and we hadn't beaten a big team in a competitive game for two or three years. After the 1998 World Cup all the winners from the 1990 World Cup had finished and we didn't really have too many players coming through. We were still trying to find enough players good enough to play at that level. A national team is probably always in transition to a certain extent, and we certainly were then.

'We didn't get carried away when we beat England at Wembley. Not really. I think England made a bigger thing out of it because it was the last game at Wembley. Obviously it was a big goal for me because I played in England. But personally, honestly? It wasn't a big thing. I wouldn't say it was the most important game whenever we played England. England hadn't really done anything since 1990. We thought more about Holland and Argentina. England was just another rivalry rather than *the* rivalry in Germany.'

Naturally, England players and fans felt differently then and still do, spurred on by patriotic calls to arms by our fans and media.

So began the fixture England supporters of my era savour more than any other, Germany aware that a win guaranteed qualification, England knowing that even victory would leave us struggling to avoid a play-off because of inferior goal difference going into the final two group games. Only a significant away triumph could be a game-changer. No one anticipated what Owen described as a 'result that sent shockwaves around the world'.

Approaching kick-off in 2020, I sensed an impending dilemma. There were two obvious angles. As one of the England players that night, did I really want this to become a tub-thumping celebration of our proudest moment in international football? Or must I balance the enthusiasm with a recognition of what followed over the rest of the decade?

I knew there had to be elements of both.

The players' view of this game is tarnished because of how the story of our international careers ended. We cannot escape the painful truth. The excellence of that night in Munich was never matched at the World Cup or European Championship. 'Having the team and the individuals we did, we should have dominated more in international football,' Beckham said. This game is therefore seen as the start of the ultimate false dawn and the 'Golden Generation' label intended as a compliment became a curse, as if the description itself were contaminated. That is why nobody wants to claim ownership of it.

What struck me most when watching the game again is how little effort was needed to find the clues about what materialized over the next decade under Eriksson, McClaren and Capello. No sooner had the game kicked off than I became aware of my notebook filling with reasons why we did not get to the next level, from being a very good

international team consistently reaching the knockout stages of compe-
titions to a world-class one that made semi-finals and finals, and lifted
trophies.

That is a provocative observation given that England won so convinc-
ingly. I advise anyone who disagrees to watch the first half, especially
the opening twenty minutes. Everything considered wrong in the aftermath of our knockout defeats in major tournaments is right there: the
ease and regularity with which the ball is lost, the number of times
opposition attackers position themselves unchecked between the England defence and midfield, and the lack of penetrating short passing
movements from back to front.

In the first five minutes Sebastian Deisler, an attacking midfielder
positioned behind two strikers, Oliver Neuville and Carsten Jancker, in
a 3-4-1-2, worked his way between England's midfield and defence three
times without being pursued or challenged. It was so easy for Germany
to create dangerous situations, England's defence under constant pressure as they did not cope with the German attackers' clever movement.

Germany's goal after 6 minutes was aided by England's imbalance. The home team's anchorman, Hamann, was running the game.
For the opening goal, he had no England player near him as he passed
15 yards forward to his midfield partner Michael Ballack. Ballack was
under less pressure when he clipped a clever ball to Neuville on the edge
of England's penalty area, and no one followed Jancker as he ran from
deep on to his strike partner's header and beat David Seaman.

So comfortable and confident were the German fans at that stage,
and over the next few minutes, that their fans broke into a chorus of
'Olé!' every time their players exchanged a pass, which was often as they
dominated the ball. There was no indication England would win, let
alone so easily.

Even when England settled, equalized and grew into the game,
Deisler missed an easy chance midway through the first half, miskick-
ing from 6 yards with only Seaman to beat.

Possession was squandered so carelessly. In the first twenty minutes

I counted twelve occasions when the midfielders Gerrard, Beckham or Scholes attempted an overly ambitious long ball, either over the top to Owen and Emile Heskey, or diagonally to advanced full-backs or wide midfielders. Only two of these passes found their intended target.

It was like watching an American football team with three quarter-backs. In a balanced team, that is at least one, possibly two too many. Pausing the match at that point, you would conclude Eriksson was guilty of a mistake with his selection. He picked the best eleven players available. That did not mean he picked the right or even the best team.

That would be a familiar criticism. Eriksson always found a place for Gerrard, Scholes and Beckham, ignoring the option of a specialist, sitting central midfielder. Frank Lampard would join that group and find himself the focal point of a debate which still shadows Eriksson.

There were several candidates in English football for a designated role you might associate with, say, Dunga when Brazil won the 1994 World Cup, or Didier Deschamps when France were victorious in 1998 – players who rarely moved from that zone protecting their defence, covering the opposition's deepest attackers, or advancing midfield runners.

Michael Carrick was in the travelling squad in 2001, and Owen Hargreaves on the bench, both players more suited to that holding role. I played in that position as a youngster and in the final seven minutes in Munich, patrolling the space in front of England's back four. In later squads, Nicky Butt was involved and did well, but he only played because of injuries.

The outstanding midfielders in the England squad were attacking and creative rather than defensive. At no point did I or anyone else imagine Eriksson would start without them. It would have been big news if he had.

So the line-up was generally predictable. The only dilemma which preoccupied Eriksson was who would play left midfield, Nick Barmby getting the vote on this occasion.

That meant Gerrard was the most defensively capable of the four across the middle. Having made his international breakthrough a year earlier, Gerrard was an all-round box-to-box midfielder and this game was typical of his broad repertoire in attack and defence. No sooner would you see him making a couple of vital tackles chasing back in his own half than he would be in the final third claiming a goal or an assist. Retaining a deep position and shielding his centre-backs was not his natural instinct as a youngster.

Against most teams, certainly during qualifying campaigns, this did not matter. Such was the quality of Gerrard, Beckham and Scholes, their inclusion was productive, not detrimental. Given time and space to showcase their talents, they were destructive.

Gerrard and Scholes were two of the most gifted passers this country has ever produced, players who could have partnered and kept the ball as well as any midfield partnership in Europe. I would go so far as to say Gerrard is the best passer I have ever played with. No one is ever going to convince me he could not retain possession as well as any of my Spanish or German teammates at Liverpool. Given the chance, he would have effortlessly slotted into the midfield of one of the La Liga giants, and could have played in midfield for the Spain and Germany teams that won the World Cup. That is why Real Madrid kept trying to sign him.

'Stevie gave one of the best performances you will see that night,' said Beckham. 'He could do everything. He was one of the best midfielders I played against or with, and also one of the toughest. When you are in the same team and see a performance of that level, you see up close how good a player is.' It goes without saying the United lads felt the same about Scholes.

Bearing that in mind, I made a point of counting how many times the central midfield pair directly exchanged passes in the 5-1 win.

It was six. Three in each half.

Gerrard and Scholes exchanged a one-two in the first half and repeated that in the second. There were two more successful passes between them before Gerrard's substitution on 78 minutes.

We can draw many conclusions from that even though the scoreline shows England did not unduly suffer from their lack of interplay. It had absolutely nothing to do with their passing ability.

In a 4-4-2, there was often a massive gap between them when each took the ball, and even when they were nearby neither felt inclined to pick the other out and start a patient build-up because they had the time and space to look up and pick out Owen's runs. Time and again the midfield trio made the same decisions, collecting the ball from a centre-back or full-back before hitting long to the strikers.

Any rival coach watching videos of our qualifiers could counter our style by ensuring their front men worked harder to deny our long passers space and time, or by ordering defenders to take up a deeper starting position than Germany's. Alternatively, a coach of a possession-based team would willingly allow England to play this way, knowing they would give the ball away more than find the rapid strikers.

Coming up against Gerrard, Beckham and Scholes, Hamann sensed he need only wait for the inevitable error. 'I always felt that because they had these players who always wanted to play that pass,' he said. 'They never passed it to one another because they thought, "I'm not going to get the ball back." That is how England played, and not only in this game. It may have worked that night, but more often than not, as you know, if you're not able to control the ball, if you're not able to control the game, it's hard to win games consistently. That was their downfall. Unfortunately, we couldn't take advantage in 2001 because we weren't as good as we would become later.'

This cuts to the heart of the debate about how and why England played like this. Was the players' mentality really dictated by their personal ambitions, or embedded into them by coaches?

Having spent most of his playing career in the Premier League, Hamann is qualified to offer his theory. He thinks it is rooted in our culture. 'When it comes to the national team, or in any team, I think our mentality in Germany is "it's not about yourself",' said Didi. 'Even though sometimes you may want to play that 50-yard pass, if the better pass is the 6-yard pass, you play it. People in Germany will not put up with losing the ball like that – teammates, coaches, the public. The mindset in England is different. We wouldn't accept anything less than doing the best for the team. I don't think that's always been the case with England.'

Naturally I am less inclined to criticize my teammates for this. In 2001 we were young players ready to be moulded for our country as successfully as we were for our clubs. We played as encouraged, and the combination of Gerrard's long passing and Owen's speed and razor sharpness was nurtured as a devastating partnership as schoolboys. They were thriving with an immediately successful transition to senior level for club and country.

'From the age of ten or eleven when we first started playing alongside each other, I just knew as soon as he got the ball Stevie had the bravery to try a hard pass and the ability to deliver it,' said Owen. 'There are certain players in your career that you just loved when they got the ball. Stevie was one of those. I knew exactly what he was capable of, and he knew where I was at my strongest.'

These onfield relationships flourished so soon into Eriksson's reign there was no incentive to change a winning formula.

But whatever happened over the next few years, in the Olympic Stadium everything went to plan. The ability of the midfield trio to penetrate the German defence with deep passes, paired with a striker at the peak of his powers, shifted the momentum irreversibly England's way.

As the first half progressed, the hit rate of those 'quarterback' deliveries massively increased. By half-time there were twenty-one long passes by the three creative midfielders, ten of them successful. England started to get more joy because Germany's back three was slow and their offside trap failed. You can see from Owen's body language that he fancies his chances every time he is in a race for the ball, which is why he was so animated at half-time. He had destroyed a German defence when Liverpool beat Bayern Munich in the Super Cup final in Monaco eight days earlier, so he knew he and Heskey had the beating of centre-back Thomas Linke and the measure of keeper Oliver Kahn, who featured in both games.

England's attacking plan was focused entirely on feeding Owen. He scored seven in his first five games that season, so the persistent testing of Germany's three centre-backs made sense. You can say it was astute of Eriksson and his coaching staff to play to Owen's strengths. At the time, Owen relished it. 'That's all I ever wanted then,' he said. 'You don't score a goal by just passing it sideways all the time. At some point, someone's got to take a risk. Stevie was a risk-taker. Then you go into the England team and there are two or three other players like that. David Beckham could put the ball on a sixpence, and Paul Scholes another one. As soon as certain players get the ball your eyes light up.

'There was also a lot of turnover play in the game then, where you're giving the ball away an awful lot and then winning it again and trying to score within one or two passes. Anyone that got the ball was looking for a Hollywood pass straight away. From my point of view I loved it. Whether it would work nowadays is hard to say.'

The equalizer came from a free-kick won after Gerrard located Owen with another 50-yard pass, Deisler committing a foul on the left of the penalty area. Germany's defence was poor. There was clever work from Gary Neville when Beckham's set-piece was cleared, his header finding the well-timed run of Barmby who took advantage of Kahn's erratic goalkeeping and picked out Owen, who calmly found the empty net.

'Germany are all over the place,' said commentator John Motson. His co-commentator Trevor Brooking was cautious, suggesting that defensive vulnerabilities meant none of the fancied nations would be worried about facing England or Germany at the World Cup.

He had a point as chances materialized at both ends, England still not dealing with attacking runners from deep, and the Germans increasingly fragile every time they were pressured by the improving accuracy of Gerrard's and Beckham's deliveries.

The decisive spell came in first-half injury-time, when Seaman made a critical save from Jörg Böhme and England rushed straight to the other end and took the lead with the last kick before the interval. Another Beckham free-kick, this time on the right, was cleared and Ferdinand cleverly diverted a header into the shooting range of Gerrard, 25 yards from goal.

It is the sweetest of hits, Kahn with no chance.

'What a half – fantastic performance,' says Brooking, now forgetting those defensive concerns.

Until then, it was encouraging more than fantastic.

I know my half-time conclusion does not sound overly enthusiastic, nor does it fit the idea of this being one of the greatest England performances. Fortunately, this review gets better. Much better. A more complete display of England brilliance came in the second half. That is when we saw what this group of players was capable of.

There was maturity and ruthlessness about England's approach once ahead. The long, diagonal passes were less frequent (there were only seven after the interval compared to the twenty-one in the first half), and when England had the chance to retain possession their quality on the ball was exceptional. Beckham often drifted from the right into a central position, a tactical tweak which ensured Germany were no longer outnumbering England in midfield, and although there were still occasional opportunities for the hosts, they did not test Seaman. Ashley Cole was world-class at left-back, and Neville barely needed to break into a sweat on the opposite side. Sol Campbell and Ferdinand were a formidable centre-back pairing.

Alongside Owen, Heskey terrorized the German defenders with his aerial dominance, the perfect foil for his nippy strike partner. Völler made a defensive change at half-time replacing centre-back Christian Wörns with midfielder Gerald Asamoah and switching right wing-back Marko Rehmer into the back three. It made things worse for the home team.

The game was defined by Owen's clinical finishing, although he owed Kahn as well as Heskey for the assist for his second three minutes after half-time.

'Oliver Can't', as Mark Lawrenson quipped on the BBC coverage.

Beckham crossed again from the right, Heskey guided his header to Owen, and his instant finish seemed to catch the keeper by surprise.

From there, England were in complete control. We were more intelligent on the ball, finally swapping passes in deeper positions so the team more methodically worked their way forward.

Owen's hat-trick goal is pure quality. Gerrard was at his best, winning the ball from Ballack deep into the German half and delivering a perfectly weighted assist to the striker. He was a killer in those positions.

Michael was still at the start of his senior career and he has often spoken of his regret that this proved to be his peak year, the treble in Munich swiftly following a season in which Liverpool won three trophies, his FA Cup final goals to beat Arsenal particularly memorable. He would be named European Footballer of the Year in 2001, an astonishing accolade he only came to fully appreciate much later. This was the performance that confirmed his superstar status after first rising to prominence as an eighteen-year-old, scoring the goal of the tournament – one of the best goals in any tournament – at the 1998 World Cup.

'If you ask people around the world, say whenever I was speaking to fans from South America or China, they only ever remember me playing for England and that goal against Argentina,' Michael said. 'It is because of my age and because of the type of goal that I scored, the quality of it, and against a side as good as Argentina. They gave me a nickname for it in China. The "wind-chasing kid".'

England's fifth was also beautifully constructed, Beckham exchanging passes with Scholes in central midfield, sending his Manchester United teammate forward, where he delicately fed Heskey to complete the rout.

These passages of play were brilliant to watch in 2001 and infuriating in 2020. They prove we had the players to do this for the next ten years, whatever the situation. What stopped us? It was nothing technical. It was tactical, psychological and cultural.

The way England played at that stage is how Spain, Brazil and all the other leading nations approach every tournament – relaxed, confident, patient and accurate with their passing, waiting for the moment to raise the tempo in the final third and strike, demoralizing the opposition, preying on mistakes, or pouncing for lightning counter-attacks. Spain are the modern maestros at this. Some call it keeping possession for possession's sake. There is much more to it. Their players intuitively understand what the right pass is and whether it is for creative or defensive purposes. The reason the classic Spanish midfield of Xavi, Iniesta and Alonso was so good is they played with their brains as well as their boots.

The most capable technical teams 'defend with the ball', recognizing the opponent cannot hurt them if they cannot get hold of it. No England squad I was a part of was instructed or inclined to play that way, at least not while the game was in the balance. We appeared to believe we could only play 'keep-ball' with the game won. The smarter nations played that way at 0-0, or even when a goal behind, not when easing to victory with a four-goal cushion. We are accustomed to seeing our players send the ball forward quickly.

As England teased Germany heading towards full time, the away fans indulged in the 'olés' they had heard in the home stands an hour earlier. You can see how deflated and beaten the Germans were on those occasions England prospered when hiding the ball from the opposition. That is what we should have fine-tuned in readiness for the knockout stages of major tournaments.

On the final whistle, Eriksson headed to the tunnel where he shared a touchline embrace with Crozier, the pair now able to plot England's march towards the World Cup and beyond.

Although they were shocked and appalled, the Germans dismissed it as a freak result. That is why they did not panic. 'Obviously we got a lot of stick, as you can imagine, but it was not as harsh as after Euro 2000,' said Hamann. 'It was also softened because during the game Rudi Völler's dad had a heart attack, so we only saw him briefly in the changing room. Fortunately he was OK, but we did not hear about it until later. At the same time, we're pretty pragmatic when it comes to these kinds of results. There was a feeling of "yeah, it was bad, but we're still in it and we can still be top of the group because there are games left". So the reaction wasn't good, but it wasn't over the top.'

In the commentary box, Motson asked the question, 'Where do the Germans go from here?' The answer was the World Cup final in Yokohama on 30 June 2002, their centre-forward Miroslav Klose rising to prominence as the second-highest scorer in the tournament alongside Brazil's Rivaldo, while Kahn was named goalkeeper of the tournament.

No wonder Didi Hamann offers a nonchalant shrug when I ask him about the impact of this thrashing. 'I still get calls now on the anniversary of the 5-1 game,' he said. 'I don't even know when it was and I say to these people, "Well, you know it was a qualifier, don't you? You know it was one game to qualify for a tournament?" And then I say to these people, "Do you know what happened in the World Cup the following summer?" The English were on holiday for two weeks when we were still in Japan getting ready for the final. So yeah, I think the English did get carried away.'

Germany beat Paraguay, the USA and South Korea in the knockout phase before being comfortably beaten by Brazil in the final, but the runners-up were wise enough to know their tournament performances papered over cracks. They were advancing with reforms.

After a poor Euro 2000, Bayern Munich legend Karl-Heinz Rummenigge chaired a task force consisting of representatives from seven Bundesliga clubs to investigate how to help the national team. They built fifty-two centres of excellence and 366 regional bases where 1,300 professional full-time coaches began to nurture the next generation.

England left Germany in September 2001 believing they were already on the right path, blissfully unaware of the stumbles ahead.

It was not my original intention to revisit such a popular and meaningful game and make it seem like it was obvious the era would proceed as it did. One of my pet hates with England is seeing or hearing history rewritten as though we gathered as a squad and complained about

Eriksson's tactics or his refusal to leave out star names. There is a danger of sounding wise after the event, even though discussions about the direction of English football recur during tournaments or in the immediate aftermath of being knocked out.

I have no recollection of negative conversations about Sven in the team hotels, on the training pitch or in the dressing room when I was part of qualifying campaigns. That is because we won so often. In the build-up to tournaments there was confidence and optimism more than trepidation. If anything, the country believed we were better than we were.

Sven was like an honorary Englishman after Munich and lost only one qualifier during his five years in charge, so he was doing more right than wrong. The only team to knock his England side out of a major tournament without the help of a penalty shoot-out was Brazil.

'If you look at Sven's record in terms of points won, with regard to competitive matches, his win rate is up there at 80 per cent,' said Crozier. 'He reached three successive quarter-finals in major tournaments, and in the latter two the matches themselves were not lost. It was the penalty shoot-outs that were lost. As we saw in the last World Cup in Russia, that little bit of luck can make all the difference.'

Such was Sven's soaring reputation, he agreed to join Manchester United after the 2002 World Cup, only to be denied the chance when Sir Alex Ferguson changed his mind about early retirement. 'It was a compliment that everyone else wanted to have him,' said Crozier. 'If great jobs come up you are inclined to listen, same as any industry. He was always upfront with me about any approaches. I am not sure that relationship with the FA was as strong later. You need good relationships with the people running things. That is no disrespect to anyone who followed me, it was just that a lot of people followed me very quickly.'

The senior players enjoyed working with Sven, a likeable character who created a relaxed atmosphere in the camp, and he can justifiably attribute England falling short under him to bad luck with injuries, red cards and penalty shoot-outs. He never had the chance to select the line-up that beat Germany by the time we reached the following summer's World Cup. Gerrard and Neville were injured. Beckham played after recovering from a broken foot, and Owen was also short of 100 per cent fitness.

But while there is no doubt Eriksson's overall record looks good on paper, I consider him an unremarkable England coach.

The finer details of his tournament defeats provide a fuller picture. In the 2002 World Cup quarter-final against Brazil in Shizuoka, England faced a team reduced to ten men for the final half-hour. They had less of the ball and could not trouble goalkeeper Marcos, losing 2-1. The only meaningful tactical change came with ten minutes remaining when left-back Cole was replaced by striker Teddy Sheringham. 'We needed Winston Churchill and got Iain Duncan Smith,' current England manager Gareth Southgate famously quipped, unimpressed by the lack of imagination and spark when the moment of truth arrived.

England's possession stats were below our opponents' in subsequent quarter-finals against Portugal at Euro 2004 and in the 2006 World Cup. Although we could point to the heartbreak of penalties, when did we ever leave a tournament feeling we had played to maximum potential? We always went out feeling we had more to give.

As games meandered towards extra-time or penalties, where were the tactical tweaks, the adventurous substitutions or changes that would give the opposition coach something to think about?

Given Eriksson's track record, especially with Lazio, I anticipated a visionary who would wow me in team meetings with insightful observations about the strengths and weaknesses of the opposition. My preconception was of an exotic coach who mastered a technical and tactically superior Italian league, handling some of Europe's biggest personalities. I wanted to absorb some of that experience and knowledge.

After playing for workaholics in Gérard Houllier and later Rafa Benítez at Liverpool, I was accustomed to managers with my passion for the game. They were meticulous to the point of obsession, constantly trying to second-guess opponents, assessing what was going on during a match and making tactical changes. Sometimes they were minor tweaks, at other times risky and radical shifts in team shape at half-time or after an hour to get us back into a match.

There was none of that when I joined the England squad. In my five years working with Sven, I did not have one conversation with him about football. It was a generally underwhelming experience.

Every squad, you turned up knowing what was going to happen: the same formation, the same favourites guaranteed to start, and the same like-for-like substitutions.

There is broad agreement between the players that Eriksson was a great guy. 'A good man-manager, he got on really well with the players,' Gerrard said. 'He was calm. He was balanced.' Equally, there is a frustration that we lacked tactical flexibility against the strongest teams in a World Cup or European Championship.

What generally dominates reviews of the Eriksson era, encompassing the debate about whether he got the most from the players at his disposal, is his fixation with 4-4-2. The system that helped us surpass expectations against Germany was also our greatest flaw. 'To go and win a tournament on the back of an English season, to expect to beat the best teams in the world with 4-4-2, is ambitious,' said Gerrard.

When you consider which teams were dominant in English football in September 2001, that might sound like strange reasoning. Manchester United were Premier League champions, in an annual tussle with Arsenal. Liverpool had just won three trophies in a season. All three English clubs played a version of 4-4-2, Arsenal and United with two wingers, Liverpool with a system very similar to England's. We were short of natural wingers so used wide midfielders who tucked in more centrally, with Owen and Heskey the focal point of our attack, and Gerrard's passing range responsible for many of our goals. Like England, Houllier's Liverpool were competitive but continually came up short where it mattered, in pursuit of the Premier League, although we had success in Europe. We relied on our toughness and physicality and lacked that 'X Factor' quality of champions. Ferguson played 4-4-2 for most of his career at Old Trafford, but his teams always had that extra layer of attacking skill and creativity and played more of a possession game. United had recently won the Champions League.

At club level, the weaknesses of playing 4-4-2 are less obvious. In a packed, vibrant English stadium, where possession is conceded frequently and a home side is generally dominant on the ball, stronger sides reap the rewards of effectively playing four, maybe five attackers.

Eriksson was a 4-4-2 man before he arrived in England, and after enjoying the success in Europe that earned him the job he was never inclined to change when here.

But at international level it is a different game. Tournament football is slower, more studious and methodical, with long periods where you must adjust to not having the ball. You must problem-solve to find the spaces in which to hurt your opponent. I cannot stress enough how demanding it was to play 4-4-2 when we came up against those countries in circumstances where we could not rely on our fitness or physicality to chase down and regularly turn over possession. On a damp night in Munich or at Wembley we had the energy to iron out the defects, but not after a gruelling English season in the heat-sapping conditions of the Far East or the Portuguese summer. We had fitness tests as an England squad at the start of the season and before the World Cup, and all the measures showed our energy levels were down after eight months of demanding club football. We could not play the 100mph style required to make 4-4-2 work.

The ball needed protecting with more care than England could get away with in qualifying campaigns.

'We might have been very old-fashioned in our system,' Owen conceded. 'Playing 4-4-2 is very difficult. There are not that many options in the centre of midfield. When Beckham got the ball it was three-against-two in the centre of midfield. Same with Stevie. It dictated how we played. We thought we had to go direct to Heskey or to me over the top because there were no other options. To say we were "backwards" in our approach is probably the wrong word, but I think we were quite slow to adapt to the game around us. We certainly had the players that could pass the ball but 4-4-2 shuffled us away from that.

'There was a real sort of change out there, wasn't there? Spain were keeping the ball better than anyone else by outnumbering everybody in midfield. Half the time they wouldn't even have a centre-forward. They would have so many midfield type of players and they'd just almost pass you to death and keep the ball from you.'

It is no coincidence it is those England coaches who moved away from 4-4-2, such as Bobby Robson in the middle of Italia 90, who were able to inspire more complete performances at a World Cup, their sides viewed more fondly even after defeats.

'I would always say we should have played 3-5-2,' said Owen. 'If we had then we could have had our hands on a big trophy. If you look at England over the last twenty to thirty years, whenever we've played 3-5-2 we've always had our best results. I am looking at Euro 96 and the France World Cup [in 1998]. We were a very good team under Terry Venables, and under Glenn Hoddle we were a brilliant team. Then we went through a generation of having great players but nobody could understand why these players played better for their clubs than they did for the national team. That coincided with us playing 4-4-2 most of the time.

'Now you look again at recent times: Gareth Southgate took us to the semis of the World Cup in 2018 with 3-5-2. I often think to myself, "If only we had played 3-5-2 when we had all these great players." That system has always suited England. We had brilliant left wing-backs like Ashley Cole. We have always had amazing centre-midfielders. Imagine Scholes, Lampard and Gerrard as a three. We always had strong centre-halves. Instead, we would put players like Scholes out on the left wing and different things like that. It never really worked.'

Having watched Barcelona evolve the game and Spain take on board the Nou Camp methods, and then Germany radically change their youth set-up after Euro 2000, we see clearly how, where and when we went wrong.

Spain benefited from a specific style of coaching and graduates from Barça's La Masia youth academy.

Germany revamped their academy system and refined the 4-3-3 that would bring them another World Cup.

England were still comfortably qualifying for major tournaments with 4-4-2 and Eriksson's reign became an exercise in making his best players fit his system rather than working out a system that most suited the players.

At club level, knowing exactly how you want to play and broadly sticking to your principles makes sense. You can work with your players on a daily basis and train them to execute your methods or buy new ones more tailored to it. As an international manager, you have to accept the hand dealt, and if necessary rethink as and when better options are available.

Southgate has changed formation two or three times during his first few years as England coach, starting with three centre-backs, and then recognizing the skills of wingers Raheem Sterling and Jadon Sancho, making 4-3-3 more attractive. He is letting the availability of players dictate.

Sven's faith in the formation that guided England into major tournaments governed his major decisions. That is why Scholes ended up left midfield. If the system was never going to change, he had to play there because Lampard and Gerrard were the two best central midfielders in England. It was not radical using Scholes in a position where he could drift infield, just as Beckham did from the right. Zinedine Zidane played from the left in Real Madrid's midfield. World-class midfielders adapt. Scholes had to ask himself if he wanted to be on the left, or if he wanted to be on the bench. He eventually chose neither and retired from international football aged twenty-eight.

I look at the players in the squad at that time and agree with Michael Owen that 3-5-2 would have suited us. Sven has been retrospectively criticized for not encouraging Ferdinand to step out from defence and provide more of a link into midfield. Had he played three at the back that would have been possible. It is much harder to encourage it with two centre-backs, so Rio was expected to play the same way for England as he did for Manchester United. He was never encouraged to take risks and dribble out of the back four at Old Trafford.

Neither 3-5-2 nor 4-3-3 would have solved England's selection conundrum in midfield, though. Eriksson would still have had to make big calls on star players.

Think about England's best line-up between 2001 and 2006. Who would not start in a 4-3-3? His main goalscorer Owen? Would he have used Wayne Rooney as a left-sided striker? Rooney did not like that position when occasionally picked there for Manchester United. There would have been criticism no matter who was left out, or who was compromised.

Experimenting with 3-5-2 or 4-3-3 does not answer the question of who plays as defensive midfielder. Gerrard, Lampard and Scholes form a terrific trio on paper, but which of them would sit in front of the back four? And where does Beckham, England's captain and the nation's biggest superstar of the era, play in a 3-5-2? Right wing-back?

'In hindsight, I wish Sven had had a bit more strength in terms of telling people they're not playing because they don't suit a system,' said Gerrard. 'If it was me, Scholes and Lampard, just saying to one of us, "Well, no, we're playing 4-3-3 today and you're on the bench, and if he's not playing well, you're coming on," or vice versa. So maybe the big decision he needed [to make] was, is it Wayne Rooney or Michael Owen? And it had to be two of the three from me, Frank [Lampard] and Scholesy because normally you need that natural sitter in there, someone like Nicky Butt – or whoever he decided to play.'

England's post-tournament debrief always fixated on individuals. The arguments focused on whether Gerrard and Lampard should or could play together and who should play on the left wing. In South Africa in 2010 I remember Capello not selecting Joe Cole as a headline-grabbing story.

There was also the annual club versus country debate which some think undermined the squad, certainly those outside looking in.

'You know as well as I do the English people and all the journalists always said, "Oh, they've got to play Scholes, Lampard and Gerrard,"' said Hamann. 'I never saw a game where I saw all of them play well. You have to complement each other, and I always felt they never did. In terms of quality, I don't think you can say too much. England had five or six players of Manchester United's treble-winning side. You had Stevie and Michael. In terms of personnel, you were better than us. But in the national team you always have the divide, Liverpool and Manchester United.'

I am not sure club rivalry was as harmful to England as many suggest, and David Beckham agrees. 'I have heard some say we were never together as a team,' he said. 'There were groups of United lads, the Liverpool lads and the London lads, but there was never a situation where you would not pass to someone because they played for a rival.'

I have made no secret of the fact that I was more preoccupied with my Liverpool career than with international football. Even today, despite my presence in the squad or on the pitch in these matches, I do not look back and consider myself an 'England player' in the same way as Beckham, Gerrard, Owen, John Terry and Lampard. Even some of them accept that most overseas players see their national team in a different way.

'First and foremost, for their players the country is the be-all and end-all,' said Gerrard. 'It's like their priority type-thing, where I think in England, with all due respect, it's club football and England's the bonus type-thing. I think other nationalities actually love being away with each other. They bond better. I think they have a better atmosphere around them. This is just what I think from the outside and from speaking to international players. They actually adore going away, so they're relaxed. They enjoy it. They definitely handle the media attention better than we've done in the tournaments. I also think their most successful managers are tactically shit-hot. They don't just pick the best players. They pick the best team.'

As captain, Beckham was frustrated England could never replicate the excellence of their qualifying campaigns. 'We didn't handle tournaments as well as we should have,' he said. 'That's what was disappointing because as individuals we had an amazing team that performed week in, week out for our clubs at the highest level, so I always felt going into World Cups and Euros we had a great chance. When we got knocked out it took a long time for me to get over the disappointment.'

Sven's period in charge has aged well because of the failings of his successors. England did not qualify for Euro 2008 under McClaren, and Capello's World Cup campaign ended in symbolic embarrassment against Germany. I was on the bench that day too, one of four England players involved against the Germans in 2001 who was part of the squad against them in South Africa nine years on, Gerrard, Ashley Cole and Heskey the others. Klose was Germany's sole survivor.

Whatever disappointment I felt under Eriksson, it was greater under Capello.

In 2010 my agent, Struan Marshall, took a call from Capello's right-hand man Franco Baldini, asking if I would reverse my decision to retire from international football, made four years earlier. I was so in awe of the great AC Milan team for which Capello had played and then managed, I knew I would regret it if I declined. We had no meeting. I just told my agent that if I was picked, I would go. I knew there would be a backlash from some England supporters. My feeling was, if a manager as good as Capello – the manager who worked with my defensive hero Franco Baresi – rated me, I was good enough to do a job.

Unfortunately, I never felt the benefit of his immense knowledge and experience. The Italian's grasp of English was so poor, and his style of management so distant from the players, he was difficult to communicate with.

What bonds Eriksson and Capello is that after being appointed to import Continental methods, they went native in the England job, employing the traditional British tactics of direct football with a target man and a line of four across defence and midfield.

We felt a long way from Munich on that afternoon in Bloemfontein when Capello's ageing and rigid 4-4-2 was ripped apart by the flexibility of Joachim Löw's young team, the story of the era completed with Germany brutally exploiting those spaces between England's flat back four and midfield.

A combination of injuries, loss of favour and disillusionment meant the international careers of players like Owen, Scholes and Ferdinand were already over. 'I am gutted the way it ended,' Owen recalled of Capello's ruthlessness. 'It stopped very abruptly. A new manager came in and basically that was that.'

Between 2012 and 2016, England continued the theme of qualifying impressively and giving abject performances in the major tournaments, the loss to Iceland in Euro 2016 the most humiliating of them. Southgate reversed that trend by leading England to the World Cup semi-final in 2018, doing so by openly acknowledging past mistakes and aiming to create a team that was better in and out of possession.

'Maybe this is the second Golden Generation,' said Eriksson.

'Please never call us that again' was the collective scream of players, coaching staff, fans and journalists, many of whom think our generation lost more than golden.

Despite the negative connotations, consider this: between them, the fourteen England players who featured in the 5-1 win over Germany won 144 medals during the course of their professional careers. That includes fifty-one domestic titles and thirteen Champions League wins. When you add Rooney, Terry and Lampard, who came into the side over the next three years, the medal haul increases to 191.

The players who tore Germany apart in Munich *were* founder members of a golden generation. Just not wearing those three lions. We would all sacrifice one spectacular result in a qualifier in Germany for happier World Cup and European Championship experiences.

'I look back and think, "Wow, some amazing occasions,"' Owen told me. 'But I definitely look back and think "missed opportunity". Deep down I feel as if I was successful for England but that didn't translate into trophies. Who does win a trophy at international level? Do you only calculate success for England as winning a trophy? If not, then I do look back with England and think I had a successful England career. Then again, I would say we probably underachieved – which does leave a sour taste.'

That is the eternal disappointment of all of us who played a part in England history that night in Munich. None of us believed beating Germany 5-1 would be as good as it would get in an England shirt. It was supposed to be a beautiful first stop on the journey towards the peak of our England career, not the final destination.

5

Tuesday, 18 June 1996

1996 UEFA EUROPEAN CHAMPIONSHIP, GROUP A
Wembley Stadium

ENGLAND 4-1 HOLLAND

Shearer *23 (pen), 57*   Kluivert *78*
Sheringham *51, 62*

'By an absolute street, Terry was the best
England coach I worked with'

– Gary Neville

TERRY VENABLES IS RESPONSIBLE FOR my first international snub.

Euro 96 was approaching, the Lightning Seeds were promising to bring football home, and I was celebrating winning the FA Youth Cup when Liverpool's academy received a call from England staff. National coach Venables was thinking ahead and wanted a couple of those who had shone in the youth final to join his squad ahead of our first home tournament in thirty years. What an opportunity.

Since I was man of the match in Liverpool's victory against West Ham, I fancied my chances.

Frank Lampard and Rio Ferdinand represented East London. On Merseyside, the offer was extended to my friends David Thompson and Jamie Cassidy.

Gutted.

I had already represented my country and wanted more. Between 1992 and 1994 I was among the elite group of youngsters selected to attend the Football Association's School of Excellence at Lilleshall, the former boarding house for aspiring England footballers. I savoured every minute under the guidance of straight-talking Yorkshireman Keith Blunt, a former youth coach under Venables at Tottenham Hotspur.

My first coaching session with a senior England manager was as a fourteen-year-old under the late Graham Taylor. My abiding memory of his Lilleshall visit is of a particularly attentive teammate, Arsenal apprentice Jamie Howell, going above and beyond to get noticed.

'Hello, Mr Taylor. Would you like a seat, Mr Taylor? Can I open the door, Mr Taylor?'

Fate ensured there would be no reward for such professional boot-licking. A year later we were all assembled in the Lilleshall lounge awaiting a less favourable insight into the England manager's methods, giggling with the rest of the nation as the fly-on-the-wall documentary *The Impossible Job* recounted the final months of Taylor's reign. The phrase 'Do I Not Like That' entered footballing folklore when Holland's Ronald Koeman planted a free-kick past David Seaman to reduce our participation in the 1994 World Cup to a watching brief. The England team had literally turned itself into a laughing stock, while our conquerors seemed to be playing football from a different stratosphere.

'We always loved to play English teams,' Ronald de Boer, who played in that 1993 qualifier, told me. 'At that time? Honestly? We thought they had a lot of running but not a lot of ideas. They were physical, but we always thought if we keep the ball and use our brain we were always ahead of the opponent.'

This was a period when every layer of England football was indoctrinated by FA director of coaching Charles Hughes's 'POMO' philosophy — Positions of Maximum Opportunity. Hughes's study of elite football, summed up in his divisive coaching bible *The Winning Formula*, suggested that 85 per cent of goals are scored after five passes or fewer, and a quarter are a result of set-pieces, defensive rebounds and interceptions. Taylor was among the generation of coaches who believed and executed Hughes's methods.

At Lilleshall, we were guided along these principles, the idea being to pass directly towards a target man who would hold the ball and lay it off to advancing midfielders or glance it on to a strike partner to get into dangerous situations.

Hughes denies that his work is an argument in favour of 'long ball football', suggesting the negative association of that term created a simplistic and false impression. Rightly or wrongly, there is broad agreement that his vision was absorbed by those encouraging a direct style in England, and after the failure to reach USA 94, the criticism escalated. To many, the imperfections of Hughes's philosophy at the highest level had been exposed.

Beyond the euphoria of England's result against Holland, that is what makes Euro 96 so tactically significant. Three years after Taylor's downfall against the Dutch, the same opponents were swept aside in one of the most celebrated and untypical England performances, certainly at Wembley. The symmetry was poetic as co-commentator and future national coach Kevin Keegan observed that England 'were doing to the Dutch what they usually do to us'.

Was the transformation really so radical?

Keegan's enthusiasm may have got the better of him, but there are two prolonged passing sequences during the victory that support his claim. Neither led to a goal. They did not even produce a chance or a shot, one petering out with a wasted Gary Neville cross from the right wing, the other with an aimless punt upfield by Seaman. Pretty unremarkable, on the surface. Hughes's disciples might say it proves the point that possession means nothing without an end product.

Both sparked a stirring Wembley ovation.

The first was after 11 minutes. Seaman eased the ball to centre-back Gareth Southgate on the edge of the penalty area to start a twenty-four-pass move in which every outfield England player touched the ball. It was still 0-0. Eighty minutes later, England matched it, the talismanic Paul Gascoigne indulging in a couple of party pieces as the deflated Dutchmen were made to resemble training cones.

'The crowd are loving this,' said ITV's Brian Moore, so amazed it was as if he was watching man's first steps on the moon. 'After many years watching England, I cannot remember a better all-round England performance.'

Having completed his last give-and-go of the evening, Gazza turned to the stands and gave them a roar accompanied by a couple of clenched fists. England were 4-1 up, easing into the knockout stage to 'Three Lions', the anthem of that summer.

'We have shown England players can play football,' Alan Shearer said in a feisty post-match interview – a message to those who had been ridiculing the national team's lack of style and technique since he was part of Taylor's final bow in front of the documentary crew in Rotterdam.

Venables's side seemed to be mapping out a scenic future for the national team away from Hughes's concepts, embracing aspects of the progressive game the manager had absorbed while coaching Barcelona in the mid-eighties. Glenn Hoddle, who had been similarly influenced by his spell under Arsène Wenger at Monaco, replaced Venables at the end of the tournament. Hoddle endorsed the fashion shift. England evolved.

Out went 4-4-2 with strikers chasing long balls down the channels. In came 'Christmas Tree' formations, midfield diamonds, roaming number 10s, three centre-backs and full-backs given the innovative description 'wing-backs'.

Like the fans, those of us waiting to complete our apprenticeships sensed an exciting future, years of false promise seemingly on the threshold of belated remedy, the overseas influence growing in our chic, cosmopolitan Premier League.

And then it all came to an abrupt halt. The England bandwagon which the nation cherished for those few years of reform went into reverse after Hoddle lost his job in January 1999. Rather than become the model for future tournaments, Euro 96 and France 98 became stylistic anomalies until current manager Southgate, openly influenced by Venables and Hoddle, restored aspects of their methodology at the 2018 World Cup in Russia.

That is the regrettable contradiction in our national team's history which screams out when reviewing the victory over the Dutch in 1996. The England coaches of the last three decades who most passionately preached the merits of European culture were English, and those who believed our players should play a predominantly physical and direct brand of football were a pragmatic Swede and an uncompromising Italian.

I am not re-emphasizing this to condemn or point an accusing finger at Sven-Göran Eriksson and Fabio Capello. English-born coaches Keegan, Steve McClaren and Roy Hodgson fared no better. McClaren even recruited Venables as his assistant in 2006 in a nod to the enlightened approach ten years earlier. McClaren subsequently became the first English coach since Taylor to fail to qualify for a major tournament.

But it is simply impossible to place two of England's most iconic victories, in 1996 and 2001, alongside each other, or to consider my own international experiences between 1999 and 2010, without identifying profound differences.

The illogical timeline fascinates me. Venables and Hoddle executed in 1996 and 1998 what was lacking in championships until 2018. You will be hard pressed to find an England player who featured under Venables in 1996 or was part of the structure under Hoddle who did not believe the national team was heading in the right direction. Many of my generation compare England in the 1990s and 2000s and wish Venables or Hoddle had been able to stay longer in the job. Both left for non-footballing reasons, Venables walking away on a matter of principle because the FA refused to extend his contract until they could evaluate England's performance in Euro 96, and Hoddle when he was sacked after giving an interview to *The Times* newspaper explaining his contentious religious views.

In both instances, the players felt that English football sabotaged itself when we were getting it right. That impression has escalated since.

'As a coach I loved Hoddle, I absolutely loved him,' Michael Owen told me, believing the tactics and psychology of the England team were never better than when he was eighteen. 'He was years and years ahead of his time.'

England lost in the last sixteen to Argentina in France 98, but they came back stimulated by their performance as much as deflated by their penalty shoot-out defeat having gone toe-to-toe with one of the tournament favourites.

'He may not have been popular with everybody, but I think if you asked everybody who worked with him what they thought of Hoddle as England manager, they would say that he was amazing,' Owen added.

The FA's decisions impacted on the direction of my England career, too. Hoddle's friend, Peter Taylor, was my Under-21 coach from 1997 until I received my first senior call-up in 1999, guiding the junior team along similar footballing principles. I never enjoyed playing for my country more than when I worked under him. During Taylor's reign I became the most capped England Under-21 player, and our record was exceptional, winning fourteen of his twenty-three games in charge. He lost only one competitive match, but following an FA review after Hoddle's sacking, technical director Howard Wilkinson – another student of Charles Hughes's teachings – decided he would do the job himself. Taylor was in tears when he brought the Under-21 side together to announce his departure. Even then I was baffled by this unnecessary change made for political rather than sporting reasons.

We will never know how Venables or Hoddle would have led the 'Golden Generation' that followed. What can be guaranteed is England would have been more inventive and less formulaic.

In Eriksson and Capello, especially, I played under managers who refined what Europeans knew to be established England characteristics similar to those I was taught at Lilleshall: two blocks of four across defence and midfield, strict organization with players in fixed positions, moving the ball from one end of the pitch to the other quickly, limited flexibility.

As I wrote in my analysis of the 5-1 victory over Germany and Sven's reign generally, there are strengths and flaws in any system and a manager must decide what is plausible and sensible based on players available. Owen and Emile Heskey were a productive, sometimes devastating strike partnership for club and country and a different profile as a pairing to predecessors Shearer and Teddy Sheringham.

Heskey was an upgrade on a typical target man because he had such pace to go with his strength and height. His main quality was his ability to bully centre-backs and stretch the opposition, not drop into deep positions to link midfield or even defence with the forward line. Along-side Owen, it made the teams in which he played more suited to high-intensity football – making it as physically uncomfortable as possible for defenders rather than encouraging intricate passing between the midfielders and forwards.

As a young full-back at Liverpool, it was a blessing to be able to look up and see Heskey available for a chipped pass down the line which he would hold up or use to dash away from defenders. There is nothing wrong in playing football this way. When executed well, especially at club level, it is still highly effective.

The pity for us as a nation is this: I do not believe it is the brand of football the FA should have had in mind when they appointed overseas managers to the England job. The purpose of looking abroad had to be to hire an elite coach who would educate us to implement much of what France, Italy and Germany did so well, not to impose the Swedish or Italian interpretation of the English game, which was in essence a modernizing of methods used by most of our clubs in the 1970s and 1980s.

I have placed this chapter after England's 5-1 win over Germany for that reason. Although the victory over the Netherlands took place five years earlier, anyone without knowledge of the chronology will analyse how England played and believe it must be the wrong way round.

Euro 96 should have been the cut-off point between England's past of misguidedly believing we could apply the same energy and passion of a domestic league game in World Cups and European Championships, and the switch to a more sophisticated era when teams less preoccupied with keeping possession were unlikely to succeed.

When I studied the win over the Dutch, some of the distinctions were glaring, especially in the movement of the midfielders and how few high balls were played from back to front. From Seaman's first goal-kick, full-back Neville was standing high up the pitch while centre-backs Tony Adams and Southgate waited on the edge of their penalty area to receive the short pass from the keeper, exactly as we would see from the top sides in 2020.

When Adams looked up, he was not thinking of a long pass down the wing, or seeking a target man to withstand the challenge of a centre-half. Instead, England's wide midfielders, Steve McManaman and Darren Anderton, moved infield to take possession and reproduce choreographed patterns from the training pitch. The alternating of positions, with defenders occasionally striding forward, wide men often through the middle, full-backs flying down the sidelines, and a supporting striker covering every conceivable blade of grass, was tailor-made for international competition.

My Sky Sports colleague Neville worked under five England managers and ended his international playing career as an unused reserve under his sixth, Capello. When we discussed the most impressive international manager he played under, his response was unequivocal.

'By an absolute street Terry was the best England coach I worked with,' he said. 'He trusted players. Because he had been at Barcelona he had subtleties to his coaching I did not feel other English coaches had. On reflection, Glenn had that too. Glenn saw the game in '98 as most see it today. Everything had to be played from the back and nothing direct. They knew we had to control possession if we were ever going to win a tournament. Terry was more adaptable than Glenn. We could play three systems in a game under Venables and he trusted the players to change it themselves on the pitch. If Tony Adams felt it was not right, or he was uncomfortable, Terry would allow Tony to go to three at the back. We had the licence to see something.'

Venables's era is lauded by those he worked with because this fluidity fits our contemporary ideas of how football should be played – or at least how we should try to play – and it has been so depressingly rare in an England team since. Today, we consider this Holland game, and Euro 96 generally, as the perfect England performance. We did not win the tournament, but we competed with the best and made a nation proud because only misfortune and a penalty shoot-out against eventual winners Germany stopped us.

Ask any England fan to pick their highlight of that summer and it is likely to be Gascoigne's mesmerizing piece of skill and volley against Scotland, or the third goal against the Dutch. That had everything, Gazza weaving past Dutch defenders, exchanging passes with Anderton, then a one-two with McManaman before Sheringham dropped the shoulder, feigning to shoot and unbalancing centre-half Johan de Kock with his disguised tee-up for strike partner Shearer, who slammed the ball into the top corner. Flawless.

There are many incidents throughout the tournament and in the Holland game especially that illustrate clever tactical variations. To me, England's balance with and without the ball can be emphasized by focusing on the role of one player.

Teddy Sheringham was exceptional. He typifies how Venables's England team should be remembered, as a blend of the best of British football with a dash of flair more commonly associated with foreign imports.

'It is not often you watch games back and think "I really want to watch this because I played really well",' Teddy told me. 'Sometimes you can watch a game you thought you did well in. Then you watch it back and think, "Oh, did I?" When you are involved in a game you feel it differently. You know if you are losing your marker when dropping off, sense you are causing problems, feel your touch is good. It is possible to feel you are having a good game without actually having that much of the ball. When you watch it back on TV you might think you did not do much. It was not like that at all when I watched this game again. I was purring. It really was fantastic, especially the interchanging between the players. I loved every minute of it.'

In any list of the most tactically important England players of the last thirty years I would position Sheringham close to the top. He was a multi-tasking striker, making Venables's fluid formation work because he had the ability to play as a traditional English number 9 or the modern number 10.

'Teddy was the glue,' said Neville.

He could slot into any top Premier League line-up today, drifting between defensive and midfield lines. One minute he was occupying the space of a deep midfielder, in the next that of a supporting striker. Sheringham would have been equally at home in a 1980s line-up, playing in a 4-4-2 as a static target man winning headers against a bustling centre-back.

Over the ninety minutes, more than half the passes Sheringham received were in his own half. Just as importantly, he won eleven of his aerial duels with Dutch defenders high up the pitch.

That fusion enabled England to exhibit different faces – comfortable with the ball and unashamedly direct if and when necessary. They were a constant threat from corners and set-plays.

Sheringham's input in the twenty-four-pass combination demonstrates why he was indispensable. He was involved more than any England player, receiving and delivering six times, supervising what modern coaches refer to as the 'transitions' from one area of the pitch to the next. His first touch was in a defensive midfield position, deep in England's half, where he formed a triangle with anchorman Paul Ince and centre-back Southgate. He then replicated this shape moving through midfield and to the edge of the Holland penalty area after a series of short-range passes with left-back Stuart Pearce and midfielders McManaman and Anderton. The only outfield players he did not link up with during the sequence were his strike partner Shearer and centre-back Adams. Throughout the move Sheringham was always in space, shadowed by different Dutch markers who were unsure about who had the responsibility of tracking him.

Venables knew such a player was critical to international football, where the technically strong teams lived by the mantra 'control midfield and control the game', as he explained in his 2014 autobiography *Born to Manage*. 'What we had worked on since the moment we would face Holland was this: we would play a basic 4-3-3, with three attackers – Shearer in the middle, with Sheringham to the left and McManaman to the right. The middle three were Anderton on the left, Ince in the middle and Gazza on the right. By doing this, I believed the Dutch plan to stifle our attack would be in trouble, and I was sure they would then have to play an extra defender, which would reduce their attacking threat. Until they adjusted, the Dutch defence was left with a dilemma, as defences hate it if they do not have a numerical advantage. When they changed to play an extra man at the back, we were able to out-number them in midfield as Teddy could drop deeper to find space. It was almost as if Teddy were saying to the defender: "Well, then, are you coming?"'

Sheringham's inclusion changed England's profile, moving from Taylor to Venables. He was thirty by Euro 96 and had made only two England appearances prior to Venables's appointment. He featured in seventeen of Venables's twenty-three games in charge and a further eighteen under Hoddle.

'Terry gave me the licence to go wherever I wanted,' Sheringham explained. 'He loved the way the Dutch played because they were so interchangeable, with Dennis Bergkamp dropping off. Before Terry changed it, whenever we played against the top sides at Wembley they used to outnumber us in so many areas. Their defenders were passing it out around our two strikers, and before you knew it you would be turn-ing around and seeing they had six against four up front as well. I would be like, "How have they done that?" So I evolved my game from being a centre-forward, which I had always been as a youngster, to a number 10.

'I would see where we were in trouble and realize if I did not drop deeper we would be outnumbered. When we had the ball it was always about making an extra passing option so we could get out of defence and through midfield. That is how I saw the game, and Terry gave me the freedom to drop into the hole in midfield if I thought it was the right thing to do. What happened was their midfielder was watching me and did not know whether to follow me or stay back because someone had to watch Gazza and not allow him space to get on the ball and run at their defence. It caused them a problem. In that half a second, Gazza might be away, over my shoulder, and I could put him in space.'

As a centre-half, playing against a player such as Sheringham was a challenge. When I prepared for any match, knowing I was facing an orthodox number 9 or a target man was uncomplicated. Of course they can get the better of you with their height or speed around the penalty area, but generally you know which man to stick to and that your opponent will operate in one zone of the pitch. You occupy a particular space, intuitively knowing the opponent wants to get to in and around the penalty area as attacks develop. You can stick with your man, duel for ninety minutes and shake hands at the end hoping you have won your personal battle. When you next meet there are few surprises, centre-forwards and defenders familiar with the strengths and weaknesses of each other. When you have had good experiences against great strikers, you always fancy yourself to have a good game next time, and vice versa.

Sheringham was one of those who created tactical dilemmas because he was never in one spot, so the manager had to decide who was responsible for following him when he went roaming into his own half. A greater level of concentration is required from midfielders and defenders out of possession.

Over the last ten years the game has changed again at the highest level with even more mobility between deep strikers and advancing midfielders switching positions, blurring conventional definitions of attacking players.

But for at least thirty years, the greatest sides for club and country saw the second striker or number 10 behind the main goalscorer as vital. Think of some of the legendary teams in England and they had such a player, from Kenny Dalglish and Eric Cantona to Dennis Bergkamp and Wayne Rooney. The best were difficult to stop. To date, Sheringham has been utilized in that role more effectively than any England international player because, allied to the system which suited him, he possessed those other potent weapons – his heading ability and knack of scoring as much as he created.

'Everyone who played the number 10 role in English football during that time was similar and different,' he said. 'What I mean by that is you had Dennis Bergkamp, Gianfranco Zola, Paul Merson, who played the same position in the Premier League but in a different way. I always felt I needed a regular number of goals. Bergkamp scored fantastic goals, but – and I obviously mean this with total respect for a brilliant player – he did not score enough for me. Zola was the same. I just felt I was a striker so I was there to score as well as make goals. I knew I could score different types of goals – left foot, right foot and head, a poacher's goal or one outside the box. Obviously there is always something missing from a player otherwise we would all be the complete footballer. I enjoyed how I played, but whatever I was contributing I always felt in whatever team I played in I had to score.'

The Dutch know all about players like Sheringham. They had one of the greatest of all time, Bergkamp, in their Wembley line-up. When they reflect on the 4-1 defeat, not surprisingly they pinpoint Sheringham's performance.

De Boer, one of three Dutchmen to feature in the 1993 and 1996 meetings with England, noted Sheringham standing alongside him in midfield as much as troubling Holland's centre-backs. 'Yes, yes,' he said. 'I am a fan of this kind of player who brought depth to the game and also had the scoring ability, like Bergkamp, like Jari Litmanen at Ajax. We produced many players like that. That is what we always try to find in our way of football and Teddy did an incredible job in that tournament. He was physical, but he was good with his head and feet. He could play very deep in the pitch and also be a second striker. The number 9 could take advantage of his runs because the opponent has to spend a lot of time focusing on the number 10. A good number 9 and 10 combination can be deadly.'

Sheringham was involved in all of England's goals, scoring two.

In his memoir, Venables argued that the contribution of McManaman was more important against the Dutch. 'For all the influence Teddy had, with his intelligent movement, use of space and distribution, it was McManaman who was the key in this system,' he wrote. 'He played up and down that right side and tormented [Winston] Bogarde so the Dutchman had to stay back.'

I am loath to disagree with the manager who masterminded the win. The England pair brilliantly complemented each other, but that is because Sheringham was taking up so many canny positions to feed a wide midfielder. It is the opposite of what we were generally accustomed to in England at that time, where the wingers were in the side primarily to supply the striker.

Sheringham and McManaman's understanding led to the first two goals, a consequence of blistering breakaways. For the opener, after 22 minutes of play, there were nineteen seconds between Richard Witschge taking a Holland corner and Danny Blind fouling Ince for an England penalty. After Shearer and Anderton headed clear the set-piece, Ince collected the ball on the edge of his penalty area and picked out Sheringham, who sent McManaman scampering down the right wing. Ince's contribution is magnificent, dashing from one box to the other to be in position to receive McManaman's clever pass, trick Blind into a clumsy challenge and win the spot-kick, emphatically dispatched by Shearer.

'Incey was meant to sit deeper but he would always get forward too,' said Sheringham. 'There was so much interchanging in that game.'

Ince gave a complete box-to-box midfielder performance in this match, his only blemish a yellow card which ruled him out of the quarter-final against Spain.

England's second followed the same pattern, Sheringham freeing McManaman who made tracks from his own half, leading to the cross which earned a corner off Michael Reiziger's sliced clearance. In the first half Witschge stood on the near post during corners, blocking an early Shearer volley. When he was subbed at half-time so the Dutch could add another defender, no one took over his job. Sheringham's header would have been cleared had Witschge still been on duty.

If this was a self-inflicted Dutch wound, the contrast between England's third and fourth further demonstrated how adept Venables's side were at mixing it up.

After the sensational third, England's fourth came about with route one football after Seaman kicked long. Sheringham won a headed challenge to flick on towards Shearer on the edge of the penalty area, and he found the advancing Anderton. His shot was parried by Edwin van der Sar. Sheringham pounced on the rebound.

Wembley, and the country generally, was in a state of blissful disbelief. England had not beaten the Dutch since a friendly in 1982. It was England's first victory against a tournament favourite in a championship since a group win over France at the 1982 World Cup. Since then, England's wins in major tournaments had come against Poland, Paraguay, Egypt, Belgium and Cameroon.

'We took the Dutch apart,' said Venables.

Playing devil's advocate, I am not sure that is entirely correct. Anyone researching the background to this game and reassessing the balance of play might argue that certain features have been exaggerated.

It cannot be ignored that while England had improved beyond recognition since the nations' previous meeting in 1993, the Dutch were not as strong. I was surprised during my analysis by how weakened they were.

Ajax won the Champions League final in 1995 with an amazing side packed with current and future legends – Van der Sar, Blind, Frank Rijkaard, Marc Overmars, Edgar Davids, Clarence Seedorf and the de Boer twins, Ronald and Frank. Six of Ajax's line-up were in the Holland side at Wembley, but there were setbacks in their preparation, the absence due to injury of centre-back Frank de Boer and winger Overmars especially damaging. With respect to Peter Hoekstra, Witschge and de Kock, theirs are not the illustrious names we associate with the most dangerous, free-flowing Dutch teams, or the side that made the World Cup semi-final two years later.

In their opening Euro 96 games, Holland drew 0-0 with Scotland and struggled past Switzerland. Their squad was divided, one photograph showing how the white and black players ate at different tables, implying racial tensions, which were later denied.

The split was more generational and financial.

Davids accused manager Guus Hiddink of being 'too deep in the ass' of captain Blind. By the time of the England game, Davids was exiled, returning to Amsterdam.

'There was some trouble in the group which we took into the tournament,' explained Ronald de Boer. 'Ajax were dominant between 1995 and 1996 and Guus Hiddink made a mistake thinking he could just go along with the success of Ajax, make sure everyone was happy and everything will go smoothly. But Ajax is not the Dutch team and the Dutch team is not Ajax. He underestimated that. He had to be much more like he was in 1998 which was basically the same squad. In 1996 we needed more guidance. You still have to have rules and show players the way forward. He let the rules be set by the players in that tournament and that is where he went wrong. We also had a contractual issue with some players and there were irritations with some guys feeling they should be on the senior contract rather than the contract for younger players; they took that into the tournament. So it was not a united group. It does not matter if you are Barcelona, if you lose 5 per cent you can lose to any team in La Liga. The quality will win you most of the games, but if you are not focused, forget about it. Our focus was not there as a team and that makes you average. What we did in 1998 was totally different. We had a group that was fighting for each other. In 1996 we started with a group that was divided.'

Football author and journalist Michael Cox has studied the tactical development of the game across Europe and believes England faced Hiddink's side at the right time. 'It was not a vintage Dutch team,' he said. 'They had a lot of problems that year. After Ajax won the Champions League in 1995 they played in the Intercontinental Cup in Japan and had a lot of travel issues, where the plane had to turn back and it took longer to get home. They still made the 1996 Champions League final and won the Dutch title, but their manager Louis van Gaal said the players were left completely exhausted by the season.

'They were one of the favourites for Euro 96, but although we think of the Dutch as always having that Johan Cruyff philosophy of Total Football, for a while they actually went away from that and it was not as classically Dutch as people might think. From the late 1970s until the international side's re-emergence when winning Euro 88, they were as likely to play 4-4-2. Although we think of Bergkamp as one of the great number 10s, for a while in Holland he was thought of as a number 9. That really only changed when he came to England.

'The Dutch were not entirely sure Hiddink represented that classic style of play in '96 and saw him as a soft touch who tried to placate the big names. By the next World Cup in 1998 they had moved more towards the Dutch style we think of today.'

Cox's observation about Bergkamp is identifiable in this game. Until he created the consolation for substitute Patrick Kluivert – the goal that sent the Dutch through on goal difference at Scotland's expense – Bergkamp played as a lone striker, not as the 10. He had several early chances, causing problems for Southgate and Adams after – wait for it – long balls over the top of England's defence for the striker to chase on to. The football-romantic Dutch were not immune to going direct when necessary. The idea made sense because Adams and Southgate were always looking to push high up the pitch, leaving space behind. My memories of playing against Bergkamp are of how deceptively quick he was, able to spin you and speed away.

Seaman made a crucial save one-on-one with Bergkamp in the 38th minute after a Southgate error, and Seedorf was excellent in central midfield. 'Seedorf was substituted twenty-six minutes into the previous game against Switzerland because he was on a yellow card and struggling in a deep, defensive position,' said Cox. 'It was a big decision to play him in the same role against England. I suspect Venables wanted to play off that.'

The Dutch were well beaten by the end, but it was not as comprehensive as the score suggests. Adams was outstanding in England's defence, and needed to be, especially in the first half. The game was even until England's twelve-minute, three-goal blitz early in the second half after Hiddink's decision to replace midfielder Witschge with centre-back de Kock backfired horribly.

Twenty-four years on, the Dutch do not reflect on the loss and believe they were beaten at their own game. De Boer says the difference was England's combination of skills. 'The England team in 1993 was still a little bit like the typical English style, more physical, getting the ball forward and leaving space in dangerous areas. In 1996, they could do both sides. That is the way I would say it. They could do the way of getting the ball forward quickly, and they also had players who could be more comfortable on the ball and play football more as we see today.'

To me, de Boer has it exactly right. What's more, that is all the more reason to celebrate Venables's approach.

As fans and pundits we often make the mistake of seeing football in simplistic terms, picking out those moves we like such as England's third goal against the Dutch or the passing sequences I selected at the start of this chapter and suggesting this was typical of the entire ninety minutes. That is dangerous. These moments shine for a reason. That is why an England team keeping the ball for twenty-four passes in 1996 earned such applause, while for other nations it would have been routine.

Once he was in place as the Under-21 coach, Howard Wilkinson explained to me what he considered to be the fundamental difference between playing for club and country. 'People think you can't score a shit goal at international level,' he said. 'Because it's the top level of the game, they say everything has to be top quality. It is nonsense.'

Wilkinson is correct.

Rewatch our most encouraging performances in international tournaments and you will not see a highlights reel of spectacular goals. England reached the World Cup semi-final in 1990 thanks to two Gary Lineker penalties against Cameroon. In the 2018 World Cup, only three of England's twelve goals came from open play, the rest from free-kicks and penalties. And on the night Venables said his side 'took apart' Holland, three of the goals came from a penalty, a corner and a long ball from the goalkeeper with the home attackers pouncing on the second ball. Hardly 'total football'. The build-up to three of the goals fits Hughes's 'five passes or less' POMO theory.

I believe the Wembley crowd reacted as it did when England completed those extended passing sequences because there is a greater demand for the purest form of the game in the national side, the expectations set by our images of Brazil with Pelé and Zico, the Dutch in the late seventies, the great France side of Zinedine Zidane in 1998, or in more recent years the Spanish team that won the World Cup of 2010 and the Euros in 2008 and 2012.

Unlike at club level, where inconsistency is a natural hazard – even the greatest teams will occasionally throw in a dud performance – there is no tolerance of mediocrity in the international arena. Even when you win, if you do so playing poorly there is severe criticism.

There is not much logic to that. Club football is generally a better spectacle than international football, especially at the highest level, because managers have a broader choice of players to work with and, more importantly, much longer to work with them.

I have often said I find a lot of international football boring and predictable, especially in Europe. The seedings for qualifying stages favour the strongest nations to ensure that few, if any, fail to reach the major tournament. That leads to uncompetitive qualifying fixtures where nine times out of ten you already know who is going to win before kick-off. Only during World Cups and European Championships is there an element of uncertainty to quicken the pulse. Every two years we get a chance to assess fairly how good a nation is. It only needs one shocker and a coach has to wait another two to put it right, or the public reaction might be so brutal that opportunity never comes around again.

That is soul-destroying as a player and a career threat for a manager. Whenever you lose a game, or do not perform to your highest standards, you are desperate for the next fixture so you can make amends.

As Eriksson, Capello and Hodgson know to their cost, you can have an impeccable qualifying record, but when you fail to impress when the stakes are at their highest it is the flaws exposed in your final knockout-round defeat that become your legacy. Capello's England reign will be forever tarnished by the misery of exit to Germany in the 2010 World

Cup. Hodgson can never escape the dismal performance against Iceland in Euro 2016.

Their general win rate compares well to Venables's. He only managed England in five competitive games, all in Euro 96, winning two and drawing three, the final two knockout fixtures decided by penalties. But there was a general, justified sense across the country that we were aspiring to something greater than before.

'The difference with Glenn and Terry is this: they could do what Sven and the others could not,' said Neville. 'Glenn and Terry could tell you how to get from one penalty box to the other with control of the ball, transitioning from defence to midfield to attack without lumping it up the field. The modern managers – Jürgen Klopp, Pep Guardiola, Mauricio Pochettino – can all coach their players to do that. I am the first to admit, when I was a coach in Valencia I could not do it.'

Neville says the players felt educated by Venables.

'I was challenged under Terry. Glenn also challenged us, and the big disappointment for me after that is it was so basic it was untrue. I would ask Terry questions about his method. Why he wanted me standing where I was. Why he wanted Anderton to come inside. He explained to me we could never be outnumbered in midfield. That meant we could play 4-4-2 in possession, but out of it we had to be 4-3-3 if they had three in central midfield. That was his main stipulation. So we could flip in-game.'

In the Scotland game, which immediately preceded the Dutch victory, England won playing three centre-halves. The same line-up played in a flexible back four against Holland. 'We had friendly games in the build-up to the tournament and worked on different ways to play, and systems,' Neville told me of the Euro 96 preparations. 'We were working on the Holland system four or five games before we played them.'

Although it is true England's goals were not all works of art, that does not undermine the reality: when we had the chance to show we could exert control with our passing and movement, the display was worth the acclaim received at the time and in the years since.

What the Venables era showed is the importance of players being comfortable switching between different ideas and formations, having the confidence and understanding to solve tactical problems for themselves. And do you know what? There is no harm in the occasional aerial bombardment too, if that is where we see a weakness. Just make that part of the ammunition, not the main weapon.

England's problem is in the struggle to pinpoint our 'identity', bridging the philosophical divide between those managers associated with Charles Hughes and deemed 'route one', and those considered 'possession-based'. As de Boer's observations suggest, England can be at their most effective when assuming elements of both.

There is now broad acceptance that a rigid 4-4-2 is inadequate for an aspirational international side. At the same time England cannot, and never should, try to be *exactly* like Spain, or Holland, whose players are indoctrinated from the age of ten to play slowly and methodically from back to front in the knowledge that any diagonal long ball will provoke howls of derision from supporters.

France did not win the last World Cup playing that way. They were a defensive, counter-attacking team in 2018, their coach Didier Deschamps keeping it simple and realizing that if his side was well organized at the back he could utilize the power and pace of his world-class game-changers such as Kylian Mbappé.

In the 2016 European Championship and the 2018 World Cup there was some evidence of nations needing less dominance of the ball to win.

The overall point remains that whatever formation a manager favours can only work with players of flexibility and the technique to produce incisive passing combinations through defence, midfield and attack.

There is no question that many of our coaches see the English game exactly as Eriksson and Capello did, with our greatest assets being those apparent in our domestic football – intensity, athleticism, power and pace, quickly moving the ball forward back to front with 30-yard passes from full-backs into a target man. Venables belongs to a tradition of British managers, now more common, who recognize that the energy levels of a Premier League game cannot be sustained over ninety-minute performances (let alone 120) at a major international tournament.

That instructive approach is a consequence of overseas experience. De Boer says that once you spend time at Barcelona, the influence never leaves you. 'You see it, experience and feel it,' he explained. 'Until you get into the middle of it, you never know it. Once you see it and understand it, you think, "This is the way I want to play football and how it should be played." That is how it is for so many coaches who have been to Barcelona. When you get involved with that kind of philosophy you take it with you. Terry Venables understood that.'

Amid the regret, there is also some anger that the opportunity was there to maintain the trajectory – especially given the calibre of players which followed that Euro 96 side – and instead we put our faith in those who, emboldened by sensational qualifying results, failed to adapt.

'Sven was a lovely man, a good coach, and he treated you well, but he did not bring the foreign touch to us,' said Sheringham. 'He brought that traditional "English" mentality without being English. He was rigid. Capello was exactly the same. We wanted Italian flair and he made us even more rigid and disciplined. I did not play under him, but outside looking in, it looked too much for the players. We looked for overseas flair and those two did not bring it.'

Whenever Neville and I discuss this topic, the sense of frustration grows.

'I see wasted years beyond Venables and Hoddle,' he said. 'Players want more now. They want better information and to be shown how to unlock the doors. Look, you played in the Sven team and in a side where for a lot of the game you think you are chasing fucking shadows. The opposition would have players in between the lines and we had no idea where they were. You imagine if we had used Paul Scholes, David Beckham, Steven Gerrard, Frank Lampard, Wayne Rooney and Owen like that. It would not have taken much to put Rooney a bit to the left, Michael up front, Becks to the right and Stevie, Lamps and Scholesy in a 4-3-3. That is what we lost with Sven's rigidity. Terry would never have had us in a rigid system with Scholes on the left in a 4-4-2. He might have told him he had to be on the left to defend. But on the ball, he would have said go into the centre.

'Seriously, when you mention Scholes, Lampard and Gerrard, you wouldn't play four-four-fuckin'-two, would you?'

Neville was assistant manager to Hodgson in 2012, 2014 and 2016, when England faced the same criticism for being technically deficient. Over the course of three major championships, Neville said there were attempts to shift the pattern of play, but there were different challenges to overcome during a transitional era for the national team.

'In the first two years, I'll be honest with you, it was not enjoyable in the England set-up. I could not see the future that much. We had a lot of players coming to the end of their international careers – Glen Johnson, Joleon Lescott, John Terry, Ashley Cole, Scott Parker and James Milner. Wayne Rooney and Steven Gerrard had evolved their game by then. By 2014, Gerrard had gone from being a marauding box-to-box midfielder to someone who sat in front of the back four. Wayne was also a different type of player at that stage of his career.

'Everyone gets to that point where they can't quite do the same things as when they were younger, like when Ryan Giggs changed from being a flying winger to a midfielder. At his peak around 2004, Rooney was unbelievable, someone who I would have in my all-time Manchester United XI. He could do everything, able to drop deep or run in behind a defence because he was quick. He could score, head, go to war for the team because he was a fighter. He could do everything Teddy did in 1996 and more because Wayne had the dribbling ability too. You could give him the ball on the half-turn and he would go past his man. By 2014, Wayne was moved around more and played a few games in midfield. So I enjoyed the job much more in the last two years because the young ones emerged before Brazil in 2014 – John Stones, Ross Barkley and Raheem [Sterling]. And then you saw a younger side emerging heading into 2016.

'Towards that tournament, we had two distinct systems, a diamond and a 4-3-3, and the players were comfortable switching. We had [Marcus] Rashford and Sterling and obviously Harry Kane, although we did not have a holding midfielder. We used Jack Wilshere there a few times.'

England's possession stats were not a problem in the 2016 Euros. In their last four games, including defeat to Iceland, they had 52 per cent, 70 per cent, 61 per cent and 68 per cent of the ball, but won only once. The main issue was the lack of creativity and productivity in possession, as well as an alarming sense of panic when the pressure was on in that final, horrendous loss.

'There is no defence for that result,' said Neville. 'It was a mess. There is no excuse. We have to take the criticism. It came out of nowhere and it killed us. We were absolutely gutted. We had never seen our team perform like that before. We had never lost a qualifier. Iceland did a job on us, there is no doubt about that, but we were used to playing teams with that stifling approach, especially in the qualifiers. It was no different to playing a side like Burnley in the Premier League. We just did not deal with the occasion. There was at least development in the make-up of the squad, with Dele Alli also joining that group. You could see there were talented players emerging, but after our third tournament, if you get a result like Iceland there is no hiding place.'

I realize my two chapters on England read like laments rather than celebrations of our greatest games. That was not the tone I anticipated when reassessing the victory over Germany and this emphatic win over the Dutch, but it is dictated by those who have contributed. These were great games in generally unsatisfying eras.

I suspect the debate as to why that proved the case will dominate these chapters of English history for ever, or certainly until what has now become 'six decades of hurt' end. Southgate has revived hope as we look ahead to the European Championship in 2021 and the 2022 World Cup, the reputation of our young players never higher.

'It has changed so much from the time we saw England's qualities as mainly physical,' said de Boer. 'I could give you a list of twenty-five exceptional players in the England squad – young players and experienced players who can play a European style and fit into the Real Madrid, Barcelona or Ajax way of playing.'

It is maddening that it has taken us so long to start getting it right.

Neville also believes the attitude of the public and media surrounding the England team is changing for the better. 'Go through all the England managers you have mentioned over the last thirty years,' he said. 'Terry, Glenn, Kevin, Steve McClaren, Sven, Fabio Capello, Roy. They are all good coaches, and yet they all come out of the job tainted by it. Roy is one of the few who has managed to quickly re-establish his reputation, doing so well at Crystal Palace.

'Through the eighties into the 2000s there was a culture in the media of showing no respect for any England manager or player who failed at a major tournament. I can give you a long list of managers and players who suffered assaults on their personalities. It was personal. They were mocked, not analysed for football performance. I do think that has changed recently. There is a more mature outlook on football underperformance in the conversations around England, with more tactical and technical understanding.'

So where should we place Germany v. England and England v. Holland in the pantheon of our great international performances? Both momentarily made us believe in the national side again, our players discrediting arguments about technical inferiority. And yet they are so different that re-analysing them is rather like comparing the strategy of two separate nations.

Ultimately, the emotions of the players are similar in that Venables and Eriksson took a different path to the same destination – defeat by penalty-kick.

'I look back at Euro 96 with pride,' said Sheringham. 'We played in the right manner and took the game to top European teams to hold our own. But there is a little bit of "if only". We could have been legends. We were so close. We don't know if we would have won the final against the Czech Republic, but I like to think we would have. Instead, we were nearly but not quite. Football is not about nearly. Football is all about winning things.'

Sheringham's time would come. His unique skill set was identified by Sir Alex Ferguson as he sought a replacement for Eric Cantona in the summer of 1997, although Sheringham initially thought he was heading elsewhere. 'I went on holiday, and when I came back I had a message that Tottenham had agreed a fee with an English club. At first I thought it was Newcastle because they had been in for me. Then I was told "it's even better than that". So I thought it must be Liverpool. Then I was told "even better than that". I was like, "It can't be Man United?"'

As with all of us preparing to build on English football's feel-good factor after Euro 96, victory in Europe would follow for club rather than country.

6

Saturday, 20 May 1989

1989 FA CUP FINAL
Wembley Stadium

LIVERPOOL 3 – 2 EVERTON

Aldridge *4*   McCall *90, 102*
Rush *95, 104*

'It was the only time I ever felt sorry for Everton'
– John Barnes

I REMEMBER THE SILENCE.

My dad was driving away from Villa Park and I was staring out the window counting the miles back to Merseyside.

Nobody spoke. Nobody wanted to. Such journeys were usually filled with enthusiastic match reports and heated discussions about which players were good enough or unfit for the Everton shirt. An hour earlier I'd imagined the jubilant scene to which we had become accustomed, having rejoiced in the club reaching its fourth FA Cup final in six years. Aged eleven, I was now a semi-final veteran, this being my third trip to the same fixture at the same neutral venue to see the same triumphant outcome.

The celebrations after victories over Luton Town in 1985 and Sheffield Wednesday in 1986 are the most joyful I remember as a boyhood blue, and when Pat Nevin tapped in the winner from a yard against Norwich City in 1989, I briefly experienced the same emotions. Another Wembley final beckoned, and Everton had a chance to avoid the unbearable, unthinkable prospect of suffering a second full season without a trophy.

While walking to the car, there was an unusual, uncomfortable mood change. Rather than overhearing discussions about the win, there were an increasing number of rumours about why there was no result from the other semi-final between Liverpool and Nottingham Forest. 'There has been some crowd trouble' was the most repeated explanation, at that stage failing to grasp the gravity or cause of what had happened 90 miles away in Sheffield.

A suggestion of a problem had come at half-time because there was no latest score announced over the Villa Park tannoy. All we knew was the other semi-final had been abandoned.

I was so focused on Everton I did not give events elsewhere a thought in the second half. You can see that in the fans' celebrations at full time, many of them rushing on to the pitch. In a world before mobile phones there was no way of knowing what was going on in other matches unless you took a radio into the stadium.

Only when trying to discover who Everton were playing in the final did we learn how serious the situation was.

We got into the car and turned on the radio.

Seventy-four Liverpool supporters were dead, the broadcaster said.

That figure would rise to ninety-six.

The world of everyone in my city would never be the same again.

Until 15 April 1989, Hillsborough was just some away ground in Yorkshire we visited once a season. Saying and writing the name would mean something tragically different from that day on.

I recall the feelings of shock, bewilderment and helplessness as the hush between us on the drive home was broken by the increasingly grim reports on BBC bulletins. These rapidly transformed into a deeper, more personal anxiety as my dad worried about which family and friends were at Hillsborough.

My cousin, Jamie Keggin, was in Sheffield. We needed to get home so my dad could make the phone calls to ensure everyone was OK, and head to the Chaucer pub in Bootle where the Liverpool and Everton fans' plans to meet to exchange views about the day's events would take on a graver meaning. Now everyone was praying that relatives and mates had made it back alive. The horror of thinking and writing that is no less terrifying and appalling three decades on.

My cousin Jamie was safe, thank God. The numbness of that car journey returns whenever I think about how many families were not so lucky.

Hillsborough scarred all of us to varying degrees, the grief shamefully extended for the bereaved, who spent years fighting the malicious reports in the aftermath. The families would campaign for justice for twenty-seven years until a second inquest delivered the verdict that innocent supporters were unlawfully killed. The legacy of the disaster changed Liverpool as a club and Merseyside as a region, and it had a far-reaching impact on how English football was governed. The immediate, most visible consequence was a community united in sorrow and solidarity.

Liverpool went on to beat Nottingham Forest in the rescheduled semi-final, thus ensuring a Wembley final like no other, one of unmatchable poignancy. When 'Merseyside' was briefly chanted by both sets of fans, drowning out the opening bars of 'God Save the Queen' as the teams lined up in front of the Royal Box in the nation's capital city, it was done so with pride and defiance.

'That "Merseyside" chant was all I could hear when I went out before the game,' said Ian Rush, who would upgrade his legendary status with two goals in the final. 'When we got inside Wembley all I saw was red and blue. Maybe it was like that in 1986, too, but I was concentrating on the game so much I did not notice then. It was different for me in 1989 because I was on the subs bench, so I was taking it all in. I was looking around and thinking, "If I score, where do I run? Which end is ours?" I suppose that tells you that somewhere in my mind, I must have known I was going to score.'

The camaraderie inside Wembley was neither surprising nor rare. The 'Merseyside' chant debuted at the 1984 League Cup final between the clubs, and the meeting in 1989 was the fifth in the stadium in as many years, making it an annual pilgrimage south.

Those bonds were never stronger. When Gerry Marsden sang the Kop anthem 'You'll Never Walk Alone' before kick-off, it was striking how many blue scarves were held aloft as much as red. The emotions were raw and real.

That shared sense of a community preceded Hillsborough, but the tragedy reinforced it. The majority of Everton and Liverpool fans are conscious there is more that binds than separates us.

What those from outside Merseyside often fail to understand is that Liverpool is the smallest of big cities. We often think of it more like a large village. Football allegiances are not geographical, nor religious. Deep into the 1960s, fathers and sons loved football so much they headed to Goodison one week and Anfield the next, before deciding whether they offered permanent loyalty to the midfield Holy Trinity of Howard Kendall, Alan Ball and Colin Harvey, or were lured to the red revolution of Bill Shankly. In those days fathers might choose blue, their sons red, and vice versa.

By the 1980s, the clubs were so successful in their own right, their history so evolved, each had a proud, fiercely protected identity. Families were divided and allegiance passed through the ages. It had to be one club or the other. That was how it was for me. My dad was a blue and there was no other colour for his lads.

I grew up resenting Liverpool for no better reason than that they were our nearest competitive rivals and if we wanted to win a trophy we had to beat them, or finish above them. I did not hate Liverpool. I simply hated losing to them. That is an important distinction, and one I fear too many younger supporters fail to recognize. Everton and Liverpool fans took the piss out of each other. We swore blind our past and current players were better than theirs. But hate? Never.

It was like a family feud. I would never go so far as to say Liverpool v. Everton was the friendly derby that some in the media portrayed it in the 1980s. There was too much intensity to the game, the stakes were too high for supporters and players – it could never credibly come under the category of 'friendly'.

There was always respect, though. Even if it might take weeks or months to get over derby defeats, in the mid-eighties you knew you might win the next, or finish the season with the league title or FA Cup to ensure you had the last word over the summer. Football was all we ever talked about. The next game was all we seemed to live for.

For my generation, the media voice of Merseyside football in those years will always be Clive Tyldesley. Before he became known nationally as a TV commentator, Clive worked for Radio City in Liverpool, rotating second-half commentaries (all that was permitted for league football in the 1980s) between Liverpool's and Everton's trophy-winning campaigns. Clive's radio commentaries were my window into the world of sporting heroes, the audiotape to a glorious decade on the pitch, while off it the city's economic and political troubles escalated.

'I lived on Merseyside from 1977 to 1992,' Clive told me. 'The context that is important is Margaret Thatcher came to power in 1979. Then you had the Toxteth riots two years later, shortly followed by the Militant Labour City Council most associated with Derek Hatton. You had Alan Bleasdale's *Boys from the Blackstuff* perfectly chronicling how the people were feeling and were represented. At the same time, you had the start of this period when Everton and Liverpool were arguably the best two teams in Europe, let alone in the country. There was an "us against the world" kind of mentality growing within the region. The 1984 League Cup final is a little lost now but that was really the start of that five-year rivalry.'

Between 1984 and 1989, Liverpool and Everton won eleven major trophies between them. To me, the FA Cup was the biggest knockout tournament, even more meaningful than the European Cup Winners' Cup, which Everton had recently won. In the years Everton did not make it to Wembley, I would spend all day watching the hours of cup final build-up; all those interviews with celebrity fans and all that behind-the-scenes access. Watching a team bus leave a London hotel and make its way with a police escort towards Wembley Way felt like thrilling, breaking news.

Everton's 2-0 win over Watford in 1984 is my first memory as a boyhood supporter. Losing to Liverpool in 1986 was my worst. 'Hand on heart, the 1986 FA Cup final is the biggest game I have ever covered,' Tyldesley said. 'We honestly felt that the FA Cup final was a bigger deal than the European Cup final at the time. It had a higher profile than the European Cup, and 1986 was the derby to end all derbies as a week earlier both clubs were dreaming of the league and FA Cup double. It just felt like there would never be another game like it.'

Within an hour of reaching another final, everyone connected to Everton knew 1989 was not going to be like that. The satisfaction of getting to Wembley was diminished, and there was no chance to talk excitedly about winning, or openly seek revenge for the defeats in 1984 and 1986. Not given the revised priorities and heightened sensitivities.

'Do you know what I most remember about that journey home from the semi-final?' Everton's captain, Kevin Ratcliffe, confided. 'Things were getting filtered back about the fatalities getting higher and higher. Then as we got closer to Liverpool, coming down the M62, there were coaches coming back from Hillsborough arriving back at the same time. They were pulled over and you could see they were not full. It was eerie and scary. You're on a high. You have just won an FA Cup semi-final. And the next minute, you are hearing people are actually dead.'

For a while, no one was sure if the season would or should continue. A friendly with Celtic in Glasgow helped Liverpool back on to the pitch on 30 April, a mere fifteen days after Hillsborough.

Liverpool's first league game back was again, appropriately, against Everton at Goodison Park, on 3 May, a sombre occasion that felt more ceremonial than competitive. *Daily Mirror* journalist Brian Reade, whose campaigning coverage of Hillsborough and its aftermath was widely commended, looks back with incredulity that the players were asked to return so soon. 'At the time, as a Liverpool fan, I wanted football to come back as quickly as it could,' he said. 'I was at Hillsborough and I was at the Old Trafford semi-final replay, and like everyone else we were all affected by it. But the brain kicks in and the thought of it not coming back just did not occur. Now I look back and think they should not have played the FA Cup. Even though we won, I regretted it. They should just have left it and dedicated the competition to the ninety-six victims. The pain was still so raw and I do not know how the families watched it.

'Fortunately, as a club Liverpool were great. The players and manager attending the funerals in that week were more like social workers. Then you go from that to telling them, "OK, put your boots back on now." You look back and have to say that was too much.'

Having heard the players' heart-wrenching accounts, I agree. It is hard to believe the Liverpool squad returned and performed as well as they did.

John Aldridge was effectively playing in a post-traumatic trance in those weeks, Liverpool's players continually leaving training sessions to attend funerals, sometimes more than one in a day. 'Replaying the semi-final was the worst,' he recalled. 'We were going to so many funerals, and there was one all of us remember when we were sitting in the church, and saw a coffin going by. The next thing there is another. A father and son being buried. My stomach was churning. The whole thing was like the worst nightmare. Then you have to think about playing the semi-final. We were all thinking, "What if we get beat here? We just can't. The fans need this." It was all getting on top of me but you had to motivate yourself. I sorted my head and got two in the semi-final, which meant the world to me. We just wanted to get over the line.'

The strain impacted the Everton players, too. 'We had been to Anfield to lay a wreath to show our respects and we were applauded by Liverpool fans,' recalls Ratcliffe. 'It was a little bit unheard of, you know? It's something you never forget.'

The 0-0 draw at Goodison was the signal for renewing rivalries. Liverpool's 3-1 semi-final win over Forest followed four days later, and they were in the midst of a title run-in that would conclude six days after the final, against Arsenal. Such was the backlog of fixtures, had the final ended in a draw after extra-time the replay would have been on 8 June.

Without the context of Hillsborough the 1989 FA Cup final could be studied solely as a classic all-Merseyside derby in which fortunes ebbed and flowed. But even now, I am hesitant before shifting the tone of this chapter from one of solemn respectfulness to the trivial matter of the tactics that decided the game. There is as much awkwardness in that today as there was then, when nobody knew what the right thing to do or say was. How could they?

People are always quick to say in times of tragedy that football does not matter. Equally, the game is the heart and soul of a community like

Liverpool so I wrestle with my feelings whenever I hear that. Football may not be the most important thing in our lives, but it is a close second.

As a child, I headed to Wembley as desperate as ever for an Everton win while appreciative of the fact that we felt like we were there in a supporting role on and off the pitch.

'It was the only time I ever felt sorry for Everton,' John Barnes told me. 'Normally, the neutral wanted the underdog to win. After Hillsborough, everyone wanted Liverpool to win, apart from Evertonians.'

Rush's sense of inevitability as he pondered which end to run to if or when he scored was not exclusive. I was so expectant of defeat I could not bear to watch kick-off. My seat was directly in line with the edge of the penalty area where Aldridge scored the first goal after 4 minutes. I never saw it. I was a nervous wreck in the Wembley toilets.

Once I heard the roar from Liverpool fans I accepted our fate. Returning to the action thirty-one years on, I found myself dissecting a game I had watched live in the stadium in hope more than expectation.

My suspicions in 1989 were confirmed in 2020. Anticipation of a Liverpool win was not entirely based on destiny.

Over the previous two seasons, Everton manager Colin Harvey had been unable to match the levels reached by predecessor Howard Kendall, and Liverpool were by now the superior side. Although the ninety minutes did not have the same goalscoring excitement as extra-time, there are plenty of illustrations why Kenny Dalglish's team has for so long been considered the best in Anfield history, and certainly the one everyone feared in the late eighties.

Everton's excellence in previous years was based around their combination of feisty football with the skills of a group of players who peaked at the same time. There was a directness to their style typical of the decade, with runners feeding off the target man, Graeme Sharp. There was more to them than that at their best, of course, but overall I would say the club enjoyed success because between 1984 and 1987 they brilliantly executed what other sides tried to do.

Liverpool, by comparison, were not a typical eighties team. The clearest demonstration I can find to justify that is an unusual incident in the 32nd minute of the first half, which in other matches of this period would barely be worth referencing. Liverpool's centre-back Alan Hansen collected the ball in a defensive position near the left corner flag, controlled it, briefly looked up and kicked as long and high upfield as he was able. In doing so, he gave Everton the ball, albeit in the centre circle, far away from danger.

Why is this so significant? Because it was the only time in 120 minutes that Hansen cleared long from Liverpool's half. He only did it because Everton striker Tony Cottee closed off the option to pass back to goalkeeper Bruce Grobbelaar, and Sharp was close enough to intercept if Hansen tried a risky pass down the line to left-back Steve Staunton, or inside to one of his deep midfielders.

I hesitate to call it a pass. It is more of a clearance than an attempt to find a teammate, but for the sake of argument we will call it a 'long ball' as it was intended for Aldridge. That means it was the first of only two occasions in the FA Cup final when a Hansen pass failed to reach its intended target.

Think about that.

Twice in 120 minutes, and one of those was barely a pass at all.

The second was in the 50th minute when, deep in Everton's half, Hansen attempted an over-ambitious ball to Aldridge on the edge of the opposition penalty area, which was intercepted.

Unlike most central defenders in the 1980s, and a couple of thousand who have played the game at the highest level since, every decision Hansen made was about ensuring that Liverpool kept possession.

He was years ahead of his time. His starting position at the edge of the penalty area was exactly where you might see Virgil van Dijk or Aymeric Laporte receive it from the Liverpool or Manchester City keepers in 2020.

Often it looked simple as Hansen took a pass from Grobbelaar, made a stride forward, assessed if midfielders were in space, and then either picked one out, redirected to full-back Steve Nicol, or retreated to Grobbelaar, Liverpool never shy to exploit the old rule about keepers picking up backpasses. This was a deliberate time-wasting ploy, especially when Liverpool were ahead both in the ninety minutes and in the second period of extra-time. The change in the laws had a massive impact on teams' ability to slow the tempo and kill the game like this.

Nicol also had the skill to instantly risk-assess and pick out a teammate every time, helped by midfielders' confidence and ability to collect the ball in deep positions. Nicol's pass success ratio at both ends was amazing, instrumental in the first two Liverpool goals. The experience and understanding of Nicol and Hansen stood in vivid contrast to every other defender on the pitch, including those in their own team.

You can see the duo's positive influence on the less confident, inexperienced Staunton and Gary Ablett, both of whom performed well on the day but when pressured by Everton strikers were more prone to the occasional long ball forward rather than midfield pass along the floor. Hansen and Nicol were blessed with a calmness which defied the stress of a cup final. They were world-class players, and Hansen's performance is astounding given it was only his sixth game of the season because of a knee injury sustained the previous July. Incredibly, his first appearance of the season was at Hillsborough. Liverpool's captain was so short of matches he did not even wear the skipper's armband, generously allowing vice-captain Ronnie Whelan to keep it and later lift the trophy. You would never believe Hansen lacked match fitness. It was a masterclass which any modern defender can study.

During the 1980s, whether it was the goalkeeper, centre-backs, full-backs or deep midfielders kicking long to a target man, the ball was generally treated carelessly. Even Liverpool were not averse to going direct when it suited, Grobbelaar's goal-kicks occasionally sent towards Aldridge, whose aerial prowess added another dimension to Dalglish's side during the striker's two years at the club. Generally, though, Grobbelaar tended to throw to his defenders rather than kick long.

Hansen typified how Liverpool controlled the tempo of games. He was not alone. The central midfielders, Steve McMahon and Whelan, were in tandem with every move. Even in a 4-4-2, there was barely a space between them, persistently exchanging passes in midfield as though they were playing a five-a-side at Melwood.

A few years earlier Everton had the tenacity of Peter Reid and Paul Bracewell to deny Liverpool space. Reid's presence was sorely missed when he was sold to QPR in 1989, and Bracewell had suffered numerous injuries by then. Everton played Trevor Steven in the middle to try to keep possession and, when given the chance, he played well. His problem was he could not get on the ball enough. That is partially because Everton did not have defenders like Nicol and Hansen confident or technically proficient enough to link defence and attack, so although Southall sometimes chose to throw the ball, he mostly kicked long. Despite Steven's obvious class and some enterprising runs by Nevin, from an Everton perspective the midfield was a depressing mismatch, and it was sad to see one of my boyhood heroes, Bracewell, correctly replaced by Stuart McCall before an hour was complete.

While Everton's ball-players Nevin, Steven and Kevin Sheedy hunted for passing options, Liverpool's always looked obvious. Barnes and Ray Houghton regularly supported McMahon and Whelan from the wings, finding space and taking possession from defenders when facing their own goal. Peter Beardsley dropped so deep the formation was more 4-5-1 than 4-4-2. That meant Liverpool could outnumber Everton in midfield which gave McMahon, especially, the confidence to know that if he did break upfield he would be protected.

This is never more apparent than when Aldridge scores, McMahon resembling a strike partner rather than central midfielder, the furthest forward in support of the goalscorer.

Elsewhere in this book you can read my description of a goal by Emile Heskey for England against Germany, the fifth in the later stages of that famous 5-1 win. It comes during a period when England are relaxed, exchanging passes in their own half before quickening the pace when an advancing midfielder, Paul Scholes, plays a perfectly weighted pass for Heskey. It is an action replay of the opening goal of the 1989 FA Cup final.

The difference? Liverpool did it four minutes into their biggest game of the season, not when playing keep-ball with the game won. Such football was programmed into Liverpool, whatever the situation. Their supporting striker, Beardsley, was in his own half when he played a 6-yard ball to Nicol, who spotted the run of McMahon and instantly made an immaculate 40-yard pass. Everton's high backline was exposed, and McMahon's touch enabled Aldridge to shoot with his right foot without breaking his stride, the first time he ever scored against South- all. Brilliant goal.

Nicol's pass reminded me of one of Liverpool coach Ronnie Moran's instructions before every game. 'Turn them,' he would say, basically ordering us to make their defenders face their own goal.

Two years earlier, I doubt Liverpool would have scored from this move. Ratcliffe had returned from a knee injury earlier in the season and could not keep up with the midfield runner. Before that injury his speed would have seen off the danger before McMahon had had time to make the assist.

Every time Aldridge scored for Liverpool after Hillsborough it would carry extra meaning. Given the added dimension of his experience at Wembley a year earlier, missing a penalty in the 1-0 FA Cup final defeat to Wimbledon, no goal meant more than this. 'The Wimbledon penalty was my last touch of the cup final in 1988,' he said. 'Kenny subbed me straight after it. I was devastated. Kenny tried to help me, telling me it was my goals in the semi-finals that got us to Wembley. It did not mat- ter. I remember being at Wembley, a grown man, locked in the toilets crying. I let all my emotions go. I was inconsolable. I felt I let everyone down.

'What helped me get over it was playing for Ireland in the European Championship that summer, especially beating England.

'As it happened, the goal against Everton in 1989 was my first touch and it was near enough the same place in the penalty area. Weird.'

Having only taken my seat at Wembley after Aldridge's goal, I missed the signs of promise for Everton before it, and forgot that the initial response to going behind was also encouraging.

Nevin and Steven were Everton's best players on the day, and Sharp was always dangerous, winning free-kicks from Hansen and Ablett because of his ability to jump early and hang in the air. There were a few attractive passing patterns in midfield, although none of the cutting edge of three years earlier when Gary Lineker's pace was a constant threat.

For all their ambition to play an attractive style, Everton could not land a glove on a Liverpool team so comfortable on the ball in the ninety-degree heat.

Beardsley should have doubled the lead early in the second half, and Southall saved from Barnes as Liverpool looked to be heading for what would have been remembered as an orthodox 1-0 win.

I was watching from the Wembley stands disheartened at how little Everton were offering. There was some anger, too. A well-known Everton fan, Ernie Herd, ran on to the pitch to reproach Steven, who was playing his last game for Everton before being transferred to Rangers. There was growing disillusionment in the fan base about the club's direction and the failure to build on the 1987 title win. Everton's first attempt on target was an 80th-minute header from Sharp, and had the game ended in a whimper there would have been further recrimination after a poor season.

As a last resort, centre-back Dave Watson was used as an emergency striker shortly after that chance. Nothing summed up Everton's decline and limited options more than the number of times I saw this 'plan B' put into action in subsequent years.

That was the only time Liverpool's defence started to suffer, particularly on the right wing when Steven or Nevin took on Staunton. Unlike Everton, the starting position of Liverpool's back four was deep, making them vulnerable if they lost the first header and did not pick up the second ball.

That is how Everton equalized through substitute McCall in the 90th minute.

Southall's goal-kick was headed on by Watson, Cottee got on to it and laid it off to Sharp who passed to Nevin. Nevin's ball to Watson, now an overlapping right-winger, was a gem in an otherwise untidy move. Watson pinged in the cross which Grobbelaar failed to deal with, allowing McCall to pounce for an equalizer so scruffy, the Liverpool players appeared to be appealing for it to be disallowed on the grounds of taste.

'This was typical of the derbies around this time and it happened in the 4-4 a few years later,' Barnes summed up. 'We scored great goals and they scored spawny ones. We played great football and they battled. We scored great goals and then all of a sudden they would equalize.'

There was minimal injury-time played by referee Joe Worrall. Had there been another three or four minutes, Everton might have nicked it. Their fans had all the belief and Liverpool's were silent as the teams gathered at full time. Harvey's side started extra-time with greater momentum.

Liverpool's coaching staff, so close to Everton's on the touchline they look like they are sitting on the same bench, were fraught with anxiety and then despair. Liverpool reserve manager Phil Thompson was saying prayers for the last ten minutes, and Aldridge looked disconsolate, his head bowed and in his hands in his seat while Dalglish tried to re-energize the side. You could first see Aldridge's dismay when he was taken off with seventeen minutes remaining, Dalglish trying to console him.

Had the result stayed 1-0, the story would have been one of redemption for Aldridge, with the added poignancy of a born-and-bred Scouser dedicating a cup final winner to the Hillsborough victims. 'When Everton equalized I booted the water bottle all over the place,' said Aldridge. 'Fuckin' 'ell, I was gutted. Devastated. I thought I had scored the winning goal for the families and then it was snatched away. Then you are just desperate to make sure you win and it doesn't matter who grabs the headlines. It was just about winning.'

Those few minutes either side of full time reminded me of Cardiff in 2001, when I was in the Liverpool team played off the park in the FA Cup final by Arsenal. Arsène Wenger's team looked in no danger, then suddenly Michael Owen equalized with a few minutes left and we got the winner before Arsenal could regroup and reassess.

Everton did not have long enough to take advantage in the same way.

Three substitutions changed the course of the cup final. The first are obvious because McCall and Rush scored two apiece. The third is overlooked. Barry Venison replaced Staunton for the start of extra-time, which meant Nicol moved across to become a right-footed left-back, a critical tactical change because of his natural instinct to combine with Barnes in attacking positions.

One of the decisive duels during the ninety minutes was between Everton's right-back Neil McDonald and Liverpool's attacking talisman Barnes. McDonald's plan was to nullify the winger by pressuring him to cut inside on his less favoured right foot, blocking him from dribbling to the byline and whipping in crosses for Aldridge.

This move was a focal point of Liverpool's success from Aldridge's and Barnes's competitive debut together at Arsenal two years earlier. Barnes's cross and Aldridge's header after 9 minutes at Highbury was the first goal of the 1987/88 season, triggering a prolific relationship.

'Aldo liked you to go down the line and cross the ball for a header,' Barnes explained. 'If you look at the goals I made for him, I would get past the full-back and cross it back into the box where he would be there to head into the net. The pass or cross was straight across because that is how Aldo liked it and he was always able to find space to get away the header.'

Everton still nearly suffered for causing Barnes to cross from a deeper position after 17 minutes, when a replica move to that which fed Rush for the winner was headed wide by an unmarked Aldridge.

Generally, McDonald's idea worked during normal time. Barnes often checked many of his runs, certainly until the later stages when there were more spaces, because Nevin was assisting his right-back to prevent Liverpool's winger taking him on around the outside. 'He either got tight to force me inside, or he stood off me to force me on to my right so I could not go outside him. His angle was always forcing me inside,' Barnes recalled.

On the one occasion Barnes succeeded in getting to the byline in the first half, it was courtesy of a give-and-go with Whelan, Aldridge just unable to get on the end of a cross swept into the 6-yard box.

Barnes also tested Southall in the 70th minute when he was able to get away from McDonald.

Each time this happened Staunton was hanging back, cautious about offering an option as an overlap. When the full-back did receive a pass, he played it back inside to a midfielder with his favoured left foot.

Nicol's switch to left-back changed the impetus and Liverpool reaped the reward within five minutes. When Barnes advanced down the left, the Scottish full-back was supporting him.

There seemed no danger when Nicol received the ball near the touch-line, side on to the penalty area. Right-winger Nevin, socks around his ankles and visibly tired, was unable to get close. Because Nicol is right-footed he was able to make a 'dinked' pass, as if digging the ball out of the grass with his boot, towards Rush who was prowling in the penalty area. Nicol would not have had the power to do that if he was left-footed. Everton were taken by surprise. Rush's body language indicates he anticipated the delivery, while Ratcliffe's behind him does the opposite. The difference in reaction time is decisive, the extra yard Rush steals enabling him to receive the ball. The rest is typical Rush: back to goal, able to finish with either foot, he turned and found the top corner. Everton switched off because they either forgot or did not notice right-footed Nicol was now on the left. Ratcliffe's furious reaction tells the Everton story.

This was a historic goal for Rush, the scourge of Everton. It was his twentieth in a Merseyside derby, taking him beyond a record set by Dixie Dean in the 1930s.

Liverpool would need his twenty-first because their shortcomings against long high-balls were exposed again seven minutes later. This time it was Ratcliffe's long, high free-kick near the centre circle which was met by Hansen and dropped to McCall for a first-time volley from 20 yards. For the record, it was the third and final time the ball left Hansen and fell to an Everton player, on this occasion because he won a headed, defensive challenge.

McCall's strike is superb, even if Grobbelaar seems slower than you might expect to react. The credit goes to the midfielder who took to the field with plenty to prove. This might have been his day had his side been able to compose themselves after equalizing.

Everton were level for eleven of the 120 minutes of the 1989 FA Cup final, conceding within four minutes of the start, five minutes into extra-time after their last-gasp equalizer, and two minutes after McCall's volley – Liverpool's third and winning goal.

This would be Rush's cup final. Again.

There was no more fearsome sight for an Everton fan than Ian Rush. 'You couldn't give him a sniff,' said Ratcliffe, Rush's roommate on international duty for Wales. 'If you gave him a chance he took it. It is the timing of the runs. People forget how quick he was. If he played on my shoulder, he'd be looking at the opposite centre-forward so he stayed onside. When he went past you, he got himself a 3- or 4-yard start. And he always used to make that arcing run so he'd never really get caught offside. He would catch every team out. On top of all that, he was just a fantastic finisher.'

Evertonians had hoped they'd seen the last of Rush when he moved to Juventus in 1987. He scored two in the 1986 FA Cup final and ended his career with twenty-five derby goals, four of which were in all-Merseyside Wembley finals and another four in one game at Goodison Park in 1983, still immortalized in a Kop chant.

'I would have had eighty if it wasn't for Neville Southall,' he said. 'I was an Evertonian growing up and [Everton manager] Gordon Lee came to watch me when I was playing for Chester. I never forgot what he said in the newspapers after, that I was not good enough to play for Everton. I was gutted. Three months later, when I signed for Liverpool,

I thought, "I am going to make them pay for that." I loved playing against them. They played a high line so in the first few years Kenny Dalglish and Graeme Souness just put the ball into space, and although Rats [Kevin Ratcliffe] was quick I was on to it before he could get going. They kept playing the high line against me.'

That Rush started on the bench at Wembley is a reflection of how well Aldridge responded to the challenge of the threat to his position. Rush also had difficulties after his return from Italy. He almost didn't feature at all at Wembley because his first season back was interrupted by illness and injury. He had chickenpox and shingles shortly after he re-signed in 1988, and was dealing with a chronic groin issue in the final weeks of the season. The same injury forced him off against Arsenal in the title decider a week after Wembley.

There was a chance the problem could have kept Rush out of the cup final squad. He'd briefly thought of ending his season prematurely, going to Lilleshall and preparing for the 1989/90 campaign. 'Kenny said no because Everton would shit themselves when they saw me on the bench,' he said. 'I was still easing back to full fitness throughout that season, and with the front three we had of Aldo, Barnes and Beardsley, Kenny was able to look after me.'

When he was ushered on for the final seventeen minutes by youthful fourth official Jeff Winter (later one of the most identifiable Premier League referees), Rush was unsure how much of an impact he could make. 'Because of the heat, I think everyone came down to my fitness level in extra-time. That brought me into the game.'

Once Rush was on, Liverpool's passing options and style slightly changed. Although his pace increased the counter-attacking threat, his teammates gave the ball away with greater frequency trying to find him with balls over the top. There had been a more considered build-up before that with Aldridge on.

Although Aldridge and Rush were both essentially goalscoring number 9s, there were clear differences to their games. 'The idea we could not play together was a fallacy,' said Aldridge. 'Until the last game of the

1989 season we never lost when we played together, and even that night [against Arsenal] Rushie went off injured before half-time. Until then, every time we played he created goals for me and I created goals for him. I think at one stage I had scored thirty in forty games that season. The team had changed a bit when he came back and was playing to my strengths after signing John Barnes and Ray Houghton – lots of balls into the box from wide areas. Rushie played more through the middle.'

As the chief provider, Barnes intuitively adapted to both strikers. 'Rushie wanted you to play the ball in front of him to run on to so you tended to look for more diagonal balls and earlier crosses from deeper positions ahead of him,' he explained.

Fatefully for McDonald, what had worked before would be his undoing. After 104 minutes, McDonald was fatigued. He and Nevin were not as close to Barnes as they had been all afternoon, but were still holding a position to push Barnes into releasing early rather than run towards the corner flag. The problem was no longer just what was in front of them, but the different profile of the striker behind.

'With the last cross, had I held on to the ball for another two seconds, I would have been forced to the right, or made to go diagonally towards the corner flag,' Barnes said. 'Because I put it in early, McDonald was unable to take the two steps towards me he needed to stop me putting the cross in. When I saw the space and they were holding their high line, subconsciously I saw the opportunity. It is not something you really think about until that moment comes, and then you see it and react. If Aldo was still on, I do not think I would have played that cross. It is a different understanding of each striker's strength. Because I can see Rushie making the lean forward, I decide to cross it early.'

The quality of Barnes's delivery was stunning and Rush's glancing header won Liverpool the FA Cup, the striker again evading the Everton centre-backs who looked at each other and wondered how he had made another run unmarked towards the 6-yard box.

With Liverpool's fans singing 'attack, attack, attack', seemingly worried that one more Everton long ball would secure a replay, only

Southall's saves from Barnes, Beardsley and Houghton in the second period of extra-time prevented a more one-sided score.

The final whistle was the signal for around two thousand young fans to rush on to the pitch – a depressing scene given the circumstances. It happened during the game too, initially when McCall equalized and after subsequent goals, and was remarked upon by the BBC's John Motson as being in jubilation but unacceptable for all that.

So soon after the fences were removed after Hillsborough, it is hard to conceive why those supporters did that.

'I remember being really angry about it and thinking, "What are you doing?"' said Brian Reade, who was at the game as a Liverpool fan rather than a journalist. 'Because we all know one of the reasons Hillsborough happened was because of the pens, and supporters being fenced in. The last thing we needed was people watching that and thinking, that is why we need to have fences. Even though it was a reaction to the goals or the final whistle, and it was mainly kids on the pitch, it jarred with me. How could people be so stupid and disrespectful?'

Although Liverpool collected the cup in traditional fashion, McMahon proudly doing so in an Everton hat, the pitch invasion meant they were denied the usual team photos with the cup on the pitch, and a lap of honour. That was an inappropriate conclusion to an otherwise sensitive, compassionate and ultimately thrilling final.

In the three decades since, Liverpool players and supporters have always had a complex, uneasy relationship with that day. 'To say I "enjoyed" winning it is the wrong word, but there was a satisfaction from achieving it like no other game,' is how Barnes articulated that to me. 'It was not just that we wanted to win. This was the one I really felt we had to win.'

For Everton, the 1989 final was one game too many for the core of a once brilliant but ageing team. The irreversible decline following Kendall's departure after the 1987 title had caught up with the club. Unlike Liverpool, Everton were unaccustomed to seamlessly building on success and preserving high standards by refreshing a winning team. The period between 1984 and 1987 was not the start of a dynasty in the same way as Anfield in the 1960s and through the seventies into the eighties. Everton dropped from first to eighth within two years and would have to wait until 1995 to win another trophy. That would have seemed inconceivable to me, even when leaving Wembley after another FA Cup final disappointment.

But I already knew the players I was watching were no longer good enough, and that performance underlined it. My annual final trips were over, and although I headed to Wembley for Everton's FA Cup win against Manchester United six years later, I could not get a ticket so was sitting in a London pub watching Paul Rideout head the winner.

The mid-eighties heroes had gone into the final in 1986 as Liverpool's equals, or with cause to believe they were even better. The gulf was massive three years on.

What is surprising about that is there were only four changes to the Everton starting line-up between the 1989 FA Cup final and the 1985 European Cup Winners' Cup semi-final against Bayern Munich, widely considered the best performance of any Goodison side. With respect to Derek Mountfield, Dave Watson was a better centre-back. The three other changes were McDonald, who replaced Gary Stevens at right-back after the England defender joined Rangers; Cottee, instead of Andy Gray; and winger Nevin, whose inclusion was the reason Steven played centre midfield at Wembley. You would not believe three out of the four Everton midfielders in 1989 were the same as those who outran and outtackled Søren Lerby and Lothar Matthäus four years earlier. The sizeable void was left by Reid. Losing one player with that profile across the midfield four reshaped the team's identity.

Reid's direct replacement was supposed to be McCall, another expensive signing from Bradford City. Gray moved on after Lineker's arrival in 1985, but when the England striker joined Barcelona after a year the difference in his replacement was vast, first Wayne Clarke and then Cottee unable to add the pace and consistent goals. When Gray and Reid, especially, left Everton, something greater than footballing ability went with them – call it heart, or fearlessness. It was a willingness to get into the face of an opponent and make sure that if they were going to win, they were going to have to earn it.

There was more to it than just a couple of players, of course. Injuries visibly impacted on Ratcliffe and Bracewell, so the spine of a great side was weakened. The club failed to address that.

'You have a shelf life, and that team was on its way out,' said Sharp. 'The transitional period was not a good one. We did not do it well and that was the start of the break-up of the team. We were getting older. The additions were not of the quality we had before. It was changing, and not for the better; Cottee, McCall and Peter Beagrie were compared to those they replaced. We thought it would take us to the next level. It was not to be, and we have been in the doldrums ever since.'

While Everton were unable to replace their stars, Liverpool identified the right moment to change theirs. McMahon, for example, was an unused sub at Wembley in 1986 but the dominant central midfielder in England for the next three seasons. Liverpool's starting line-up in 1989 contained seven changes to the double-winning FA Cup team that beat Everton 3-1 in 1986. The critical difference between the Merseyside clubs at the end of that decade was experience and sound judgement in the transfer market. That is the biggest reason why Everton faded and Liverpool remained at the top slightly longer, until 1990.

Liverpool's downturn was still closer than anyone at the time anticipated. There was no obvious sign of its approach in 1988/89 as Dalglish's side turned their attention to another league and cup double. This was the second of three years when they could, probably should, have achieved it. They lost the FA Cup final to Wimbledon in 1988, would lose the title with effectively the last kick of the 1989 season thanks to Michael Thomas, and lost to Crystal Palace in the FA Cup semi-final in 1990.

The hints of what was coming over the next eighteen months were at best mild. The way Everton benefited from a more direct approach to equalize before the final whistle caught the attention of rival managers.

Liverpool lost 4-3 to Palace in the next year's semi because they struggled with the same direct high balls towards the penalty area, and there are reminders of Wembley in the 4-4 draw in the FA Cup tie at Goodison Park in February 1991, which proved to be Dalglish's last game in charge. That was a night when, despite some wonderful football, Liverpool could not hold on to their lead because of a weak backline. Hansen had played his final game for Liverpool by then, retiring shortly after his friend's resignation. Rewatching the 1989 final reminded me that Hansen's departure should be regarded as a shape-shifting moment for Liverpool as much as Dalglish's.

Following Dalglish's title win in 1990, Liverpool's decline echoed their neighbours', unable to cope with the loss of their spiritual leader in the same way Everton failed to deal with Kendall's managerial move to Spain. Expensive new signings in the early nineties were not up to replacing those who had gone.

After the dominance of the mid-eighties, between 1991 and 2000 the Merseyside clubs won three trophies between them, one FA Cup each (in 1992 and 1995) and Liverpool's League Cup under Roy Evans (in 1995).

What gave Liverpool more hope was the quality of their youth talent, first Robbie Fowler and Steve McManaman in the early and mid-nineties, and then Michael Owen, Steven Gerrard and myself later in the decade. Gérard Houllier and Rafa Benítez helped put Liverpool back on the European map in the new millennium. It still needed two boardroom takeovers, most significantly by Fenway Sports Group in 2010, and Jürgen Klopp's appointment in 2015 to set the club back on course to being English champions in 2020.

My sadness as a player is I never experienced the same unity or sense of competitiveness between Liverpool and Everton at the top of English football that I witnessed and felt part of as a fan in the 1980s. I played against Everton in the FA Cup semi-final on 14 April 2012, the weekend of the twenty-third anniversary of Hillsborough. As in 1989, there was an impeccably observed minute's silence of remembrance, but there were no chants of 'Merseyside', nor mix of red and blue banners and scarves side by side scattered around Wembley.

The fixture had changed, Liverpool and Everton supporters struggling to come to terms with their new standing trying to catch those at the top rather than preserving an esteemed status. What was once a proudly parochial rivalry, focused only on events on the pitch, evolved into something less attractive.

'It is not the same,' says Sharp. 'When two teams from the city are successful, everyone is happy. When that is not the case, there is more friction. It was a common occurrence to get to Wembley then, even with the Charity Shield. I don't think it is necessarily an issue just on Merseyside. Football has generally changed, and the rise of social media may have something to do with it.'

The online world is certainly a factor. The majority of fans retain levels of respect, but the internet has given a louder voice to those who were once on the fringes, and as a result there is more negative influence contaminating the rivalry.

'I went to the Goodison derby in 2018/19 and it had a real edge to it – it just felt different,' said Clive Tyldesley, who was genuinely emotional when reminiscing, and spoke with a heavy heart when identifying how it has changed. 'In the eighties it not only divided streets, it divided households. But what was most important is everybody got on.'

The 1989 final captured a moment in time when it was Merseyside versus the world, whether in football, politics or, as was so painfully the case, in grief. It was a fixture which ended an era of triumph and tragedy for Liverpool and Everton.

I may be prepared to compromise the title of this book and admit it was not the greatest game between the clubs. What I will say is this: it was, and always will be, the game of which all involved should be most proud.

7

Wednesday, 26 May 1999

1999 UEFA CHAMPIONS LEAGUE FINAL
Nou Camp, Barcelona

MANCHESTER 2 – 1 BAYERN UNITED MUNICH

Sheringham *90+1* Basler *6*
Solskjaer *90+3*

'I always felt that we were going to win the game'

– David Beckham

THE 1999 CHAMPIONS LEAGUE FINAL ended with a travesty of justice. David Beckham was not named man of the match, overlooked for Bayern Munich's Mario Basler.

I would hazard a guess Basler was nominated because in the mayhem of the 101 seconds between Teddy Sheringham's equalizer and Ole Gunnar Solskjaer's injury-time winner, the dignitaries heading pitchside missed Manchester United's goals and had no time to change their mind. A final's most influential player tends to be a member of the victory parade, and as the trophy engraver got to work, Basler was prematurely declared the match-winner.

UEFA made a regrettable error.

Basler was not the game's best player.

Bayern were not the superior team.

Beckham was markedly better than anyone else on the pitch.

Manchester United were worthy champions.

All of that may sound contentious to those who have never rewatched or studied what Sir Alex Ferguson described as 'the greatest night of my life'. It certainly contradicts UEFA's approved story of the evening, which was recently recounted to European football's governing body by Bayern's ex-skipper Lothar Matthäus. 'It's very rare for a team to lose a Champions League final so undeservedly,' Matthäus said. 'We dominated the game for ninety minutes. It was one-way traffic. Manchester United didn't have many chances. We really controlled the match. There was nothing to suggest United would score.'*

Few have challenged these sentiments. Even some of United's heroes accept the established version of events. Sheringham describes the triumph as the ultimate 'smash and grab', Bayern unfortunate to strike the woodwork twice in the closing stages before the Champions League trophy was plucked from their grasp courtesy of a couple of well-directed Beckham corners. My former Liverpool teammate Markus Babbel played for Bayern that night and is adamant Matthäus called it right. 'We were the better team,' he insisted. 'We had so many good chances and hit the bar and the post.'

I felt no compulsion to query the idea that United only turned up for the last three minutes in the Nou Camp. Only after sitting through all ninety-three minutes for this chapter did I realize so many inaccurate claims about the 1999 final have gone unchecked.

With all due respect to Markus, Matthäus and everyone else who considers United's Champions League win of 1999 'undeserved', I completely disagree.

For a start, Bayern had only themselves to blame for what happened. Basler put them ahead after 6 minutes and they played the next eighty-four like they were the final ten, trying to grind out a 1-0 win rather than proactively pursue a second. Bayern's spectacular goal attempts came during a hectic finale because United took risks chasing an equalizer, making themselves vulnerable to counter-attacks.

It may have taken United too long to score, but when Sheringham did so it was not against the run of play, nor was it unwarranted. Bayern's defending in the last ten minutes was insecure and jittery. Their response to conceding in the 91st minute was calamitous, meekly surrendering possession to enable United to build another attack. The Germans

---

* https://www.uefa.com/uefachampionsleague/news/025e-0f8bbd7e5380-eb00803acfbb-1000--classics-bayern-1-2-united-1999/

invited heartache to the door just as their party was about to get going. The drama of the last act that night in Barcelona created a fiction that United stole the European Cup, but Matthäus's assertion that the game was 'one-way traffic' is absurd.

Tactically, Bayern were close to seeing it out and would have been rightly commended had they done so. Do not make the mistake of believing this means they were technically better and 'controlled the game'. United fans would have spent the last twenty-one years squirming at a missed opportunity had their side not done what they did. Sheringham and Solskjaer ensured there would be no regrets on the flight home to Manchester.

'Bloody 'ell, Carra, you must have thought we did all right to say that,' Sheringham chuckled as I delivered my re-evaluation. 'I don't know anyone who has ever said it before, not even Manchester United fans.'

Actually, Ferguson has always believed it. He first said it in the immediate aftermath of victory. 'We didn't deserve to lose,' he argued in his post-match press conference. 'We were the better team for most of the match.'

I found another enthusiastic ally to my United cause during the interviews for this chapter. 'I always felt that we were going to win the game,' Beckham agreed. 'Even though they had opportunities when they could have finished it off, we were a team which never gave up. Whether we were losing one or two-nil with five minutes to go, we always believed. The gaffer had so much trust in us as a team and individuals, he had faith we would do the right thing. He would often choose not to say much, but at half-time in the final I can remember him saying, "You are still in this game. Just play your football." The enormity of the final meant we did not create the chances we wanted or play as well as we could, but right until the end we always had a chance, and for whatever reason I always thought we would do it.'

I am happy to assist Sir Alex and Becks in setting the record straight and explain why they are right.

Cards on the table, I was as shocked as United legends and fans. As a former Liverpool player, this was not the first fixture I rushed to research and rewatch. Yet it was one of the most absorbing. Not because it was the highest quality, but because my preconceptions were stripped bare.

'It is one of those games, just like Istanbul for you, where everyone remembers where they were when it happened,' Sheringham said. 'Except maybe Liverpool fans.'

I think they vividly recall, too. I do.

I was on a post season holiday in Las Vegas on 26 May that year, sitting alongside friends from Liverpool believing we were about to celebrate United's failure to achieve a unique treble of the Premier League, FA Cup and Champions League. My reaction upon the final whistle in Barcelona echoed many from those not affiliated to United: 'Jammy bastards.'

Now I see it differently, recognizing those ten days for what they were – among the most extraordinary in the history of any football club. Until then, no side from the major leagues of England, Spain, Italy, Germany or France had completed that particular treble. Only Celtic, Ajax and PSV Eindhoven had managed it.

United had to beat Tottenham Hotspur to seal the Premier League title on 16 May, and they won 2-1 to finish a point above Arsenal. They eased to the FA Cup with a 2 0 win over Newcastle on 22 May before heading to Spain for the ultimate prize in club football – the trophy that had eluded the club since Sir Matt Busby made United England's first European champions in 1968.

'By the time we got to Barcelona we were excited more than anything else,' Gary Neville told me. 'I felt more pressure and nerves before the Spurs game. Partly because we had lost the Premier League to Arsenal a year before, and also because I was playing against David Ginola.

'Sir Alex thought if we won the first trophy, we would be OK. The FA Cup final was a procession, so when we flew to Spain I was thinking, "We are on the brink of something really special here. This is as good as it gets." You know as a player you are never going to be in that position again. We had waited six years for a chance to win the Champions League. We realized it was the biggest football moment of our lives.'

Shrugging off club rivalries and affording credit where due was impossible for me in those days. Privately, I recognized that United represented everything every fan wanted in their side, and everything I wanted Liverpool to become during my Anfield career. Ferguson's brand of football created an Old Trafford dynasty. Over the preceding nine years he had won five league titles, four FA Cups, one League Cup, one European Cup Winners' Cup and one UEFA Super Cup. He secured the domestic Premier League and FA Cup double in 1994 and 1996.

Whatever my arguments elsewhere in this book about who was really responsible for knocking Liverpool 'off their perch', United stood soundly on it now.

They had one of the best goalkeepers in the world in Peter Schmeichel, one of the best centre-halves in Jaap Stam, and a midfield some argue is the greatest in Premier League history. There has certainly been no central four more balanced than Beckham, Paul Scholes, Roy Keane and Ryan Giggs. Keane's and Scholes's suspension for the final due to bookings earlier in the competition tore into the heart of the team. 'I don't think any midfield can ever be better than that – not ever,' said Neville. 'Losing Scholes and Keane for the final was a massive problem.'

United also had four of the most potent strikers of their generation, Andy Cole and Dwight Yorke the preferred partnership, backed up by Solskjaer and Sheringham, who would have been starters for most clubs.

Europe, or to be more specific the Champions League, was the only territory left for Ferguson to conquer. He needed the European Cup to elevate him to Busby's pedestal. The fact the 1999 final was played on what would have been Busby's ninetieth birthday made it seem that the stars were aligned.

United had signalled English clubs' return after the five-year UEFA suspension with the European Cup Winners' Cup in 1991, but that was a couple of years before Ferguson built his first title-winning side. The legendary line-up with Eric Cantona, Mark Hughes, Steve Bruce and

Gary Pallister never had the chance to shine on the Continent because of UEFA restrictions on foreign players in the first half of the 1990s, knocked out by Galatasaray in the second round on their return to the competition in 1993/94.

When the Champions League was rebranded and group stages introduced, United struggled to adapt to the more technical and tactical brand of football generally required to become European champions. In 1994/95 they failed to reach the knockout phase, and although they showed more promise in 1996/97 and 1997/98, losing the semi-final to Borussia Dortmund and the quarter-final to Monaco respectively, it was a mediocre return for a top-class team.

By the start of the 1998/99 campaign, Ferguson knew something in his tactical approach had to change. History was repeating itself for England's finest.

In the 1970s, Liverpool overcame previous disappointments in Europe's elite event by introducing a slower, more patient passing style through defence and midfield, greatly influenced by the Ajax side of Johan Cruyff which dominated the European Cup at the start of that decade. That brought Liverpool eventual European Cup success in 1977, which continued until the UEFA ban following the Heysel Stadium disaster in 1985. Until 1999, Liverpool were still the last English team to win the European Cup (in 1984) and the last English side to reach the final (in 1985).

Rather than replicate how Liverpool dominated Europe, Ferguson took the reverse journey. He abandoned the Continental style of playing methodically from the back and instead instructed his players to get the ball forward as quickly and directly as they did in domestic games.

'Sir Alex's bad experiences in Europe were always when the team was lulled into playing it square at the back and into midfield,' explained Neville. 'One stray pass and then the opposition were away, we were 1-0 down, and at that level the game might be already done. Between 1993 and 1998 we lost a lot of counter-attack goals. We were a bit naive, so in 1999 Sir Alex changed it. He said he wanted more directness in Europe.

He said he did not want to see any playing it around or short passes in the defensive third, and he stuck with that. He absolutely hated the possibility of being counter-attacked in Europe so the big difference in 1999 was making sure that stopped.'

United's retro approach was my first surprise when reviewing the final.

In my analysis of the Everton v. Bayern Munich European Cup Winners' Cup semi-final of 1985, I wrote about the game's directness, Neville Southall repeatedly kicking far and high to test the German centre-backs. Fourteen years on, Schmeichel used an identical tactic against Bayern. Over ninety minutes, Schmeichel kicked the ball long out of his hands twenty-three times, mostly towards Yorke, and later to substitute Sheringham.

This is alien to modern football, certainly at elite level, and underlines where and when the advances have been made. The speed of evolution was evidently more dramatic in the 2000s than at the end of the last century.

Whenever I played United, they were a nightmare because of the quickness of their passing and movement back to front, gliding through midfield and manoeuvring the ball into wide areas.

Neville enlightened me on Ferguson's philosophy. 'Generally, Sir Alex was always about getting it into the strikers early,' he said. 'If I had a throw-in in the first twenty minutes of a match at Old Trafford, or anywhere else for that matter, and I threw it backwards, Sir Alex went mad at me. "Throw it to strikers and midfielders!" he would shout. We played directly from the back. I would get it at right-back and immediately look for strikers. When Becks had the ball, he would always immediately look for the strikers. Once we got ourselves ahead we would take more control with Scholes and Keane, but we never went for the possession style until the game was won. Until then, the instruction was "play it to the strikers, get it wide and then look for the combinations and crosses".'

This method served Ferguson for twenty-seven years. He was a classic 4-4-2 man, with two orthodox wingers, a dedicated goalscorer and a striker able to drop deep and link the play with midfielders, whether it was Cantona, Sheringham, Yorke or, in the later years of his tenure, Wayne Rooney.

United always seemed to have at least two players who could guarantee twenty goals a season, with a few more contributing anywhere between ten and twenty. In 1998/99, Cole and Yorke scored fifty-three as a strike pair. Solskjaer struck eighteen, which is amazing given he was a substitute. Three of the four first-choice midfielders – Giggs, Beckham and Scholes – contributed another thirty between them. That is six players with a combined 101 goals. Such a fearsome goal return, allied to a reliable defence, is a title-winning template. The signings of Yorke and Stam in the summer of 1998 took United to the next level.

In the group stages United drew 3-3 at home and away against Barcelona. Danish side Brøndby were beaten 6-2 and 5-0. Early meetings with Bayern in September and December 1998 finished 2-2 in Munich and 1-1 in Manchester. After a 3-1 aggregate win over Inter Milan in the quarter-finals, the supreme performance came in Turin in the second leg of the semi-final. Two goals down, United won 3-2 against Juventus, progressing 4-3 on aggregate. Including a pre-qualifying round against Poland's LKS Lodz, United scored thirty-one goals in thirteen games, averaging more goals per game than any Champions League winner between the tournament's redesign in 1992 and Pep Guardiola's Barcelona in 2009.

Amid this front-footed approach, Ferguson made an essential concession to respect the firepower of European opponents. 'In the Premier League, Sir Alex was happy for everyone to get into the box, so we were countered quite a lot in the league against good teams,' said Neville. 'In Europe he modified it. One of the things he introduced in 1999 was specifically to stop us being counter-attacked. If Becks had the ball on the right and was about to cross, I was allowed to support and go as far as I wanted. But on the opposite side, if Giggsy was high up the pitch, Scholes and Keane had to stay outside the box and left-back Denis Irwin tucked inside to make sure we had numbers back. If Scholes went into the box, Giggsy had to hang back to help Keane. That way, Sir Alex ensured there were always two outside the box to stop any counter-attack. That made it less cavalier than we generally looked.'

Whatever the intentions defensively, it did not always work that year as many United games turned into end-to-end goalfests. United kept conceding early. They did so in the group stages in Barcelona and Munich, and in the semi-final second leg against Juventus. Giving up sixteen goals across the competition means that as well as one of the most potent attacks, they had one of the worst defensive records of any European champion.

The bad habit continued to the final, the difference in Barcelona being that it did not lead to a thrilling spectacle – at least not until the last ten minutes.

The dynamic was determined by the timing of Basler's goal, which ideally served Bayern coach Ottmar Hitzfeld's plan. The Germans approached the match as if accepting they were technically inferior to United, presuming their best chance of victory to be scoring first and shutting down the game. To be blunt, Hitzfeld's mindset reminded me of an underdog trying to achieve a shock result.

Bayern's line-up was full of power and athleticism more than finesse. Midfielder Jens Jeremies summed them up. He was a destroyer and dis-ruptor, there to fill spaces and prevent United's creative players receiving possession in threatening areas. Stefan Effenberg was another imposing central midfielder capable of going box to box. The veteran Matthäus, who at this stage of his career usually played as sweeper, kept switching between filling in as an extra defender when United had the ball and taking an orthodox midfield position when his side had it. Up front, Bayern relied on old-school target man Carsten Jancker, with Basler and Alexander Zickler as wide supporting strikers.

'Basler, Zickler and Jancker were big lads,' Neville recalled. 'The 4-3-3 they went with was a good idea against us, because we were so strong in wide areas. We had been successful all season because of that. In the quarter-final versus Milan, Becks and Giggsy caused big problems. It was the same in the semi-final against Juventus.'

Tactically, Hitzfeld was seconds away from nullifying what had been Europe's most lethal attack, Yorke and Cole especially quiet.

I played in many games where the manager's strategy was similar to Hitzfeld's, especially in Europe. When you face a side with the capacity to hurt you from so many angles, you must be compact. Wide midfielders help full-backs, central midfielders rarely commit into advanced positions, and occasionally one will be given the duty of tracking the most dangerous creative player, as Jeremies was with Beckham. In such a system, you need a dependable striker who can hold the ball and relieve pressure, preferably assisted by a pacey support act who will cause carnage on the break. As a defender, you camp on the edge of the penalty area and set the puzzle for the attacking side probing for chances. The longer the game proceeds, the more frustrated the team monopolizing possession without reward gets. When you emerge with a narrow win, it is not especially pleasing on the eye, but you come off the pitch content with a professional day's work and couldn't care less whether neutrals were entertained.

This timeless tactic is why most games are won by the team scoring first. Regular studies have shown that 70 per cent of football matches in the Premier League and Champions League are won by the team that does so.*

Bayern can argue they would have merited victory for carrying out their manager's instructions. I would not dispute that goalkeeper Oliver Kahn was not required to make many saves until the dying moments.

Had Bayern seen it through, I am sure Ferguson would have shaken hands and accepted that his players did not find a way on the night. United were below their best. That is why so many still mistakenly believe they deserved to lose.

---

* https://www.pinnacle.com/en/betting-articles/Soccer/first-goal-predict-champions-league-results/8WP2B3A6KUL6JGAB

For all that, the more I observed how Bayern played, the less I could comprehend how anyone can argue that the German champions played well, let alone dominated. Their best player was substitute Mehmet Scholl, and he was only on for the last nineteen minutes.

Do not misunderstand my assertion. I am not suggesting Bayern would have been lucky winners. What I am arguing against is the idea it is one of the great Champions League injustices that they lost.

Anyone studying the match statistics will say it is a stretch for me to argue that United deserved victory. My response to that is this: those same statistics offer no support for the prevailing view that Bayern were more worthy champions.

The teams had fifteen shots apiece, United having two more on target, and Ferguson's side forced five more corners. In the first half, United had 57 per cent possession to Bayern's 43 per cent, which is a massive difference in a cup final. How do we equate that fact with Matthäus's 'one-way traffic' claim? Although this sizeable gap reduced after the second half, that was because Bayern had more of the ball when the game opened up near full time. The analysis by sports data analysts Opta revealed that the 'expected goals' – a measure of the quality of the chances and assists a team had in a particular match – gave United a total of 2.26, compared to Bayern's 1.54.

United's problems trying to make the most of their possession stemmed from Keane's and Scholes's absence, which unbalanced the tried and trusted central four. The United XI had never started together before and would never do so again. Midfield was completely reconstructed. Giggs, usually on the left, moved to the right to accommodate Jesper Blomqvist. The game passed the Swede by as he failed to offer any attacking threat. On my recording, his likely substitution was predicted after thirty-three minutes by the ITV co-commentator Ron Atkinson, the manager Ferguson replaced at Old Trafford in 1986. Beckham, usually on the right, moved into the centre alongside Nicky Butt.

'When Becks was in the middle he ran everywhere and pinged it all around the pitch,' Neville said. 'Sir Alex knew Becks would work hard, but he would not play the 10-yard pass if he saw the killer ball over the top. He always wanted to play the Hollywood pass, so Sir Alex's concern was, would we get enough midfield combinations?

'When Becks was out wide he had that ability to get it in those areas where he could whip it right into the striker's feet. It was such a weapon.' As an opposition defender I have plenty of bad memories of that. He was a killer, and every United corner or set-piece near the penalty area brought anticipation of a chance or a goal.

United inevitably lost potency because of these enforced changes.

But whatever the tactical implications of moving Beckham into the middle, I want to emphasize how outstanding he was in his deeper midfield role. He thrived with the responsibility, the accuracy of his passing and the energy he provided driving United on until the end.

'When you do not have someone like Roy in the team, that changes how you play and the responsibilities of each player,' Beckham told me. 'We all had to step up. When the manager asked me to play there, I was excited. Even though my favourite position was on the right, I loved playing central midfield. I knew I was going to get on the ball more and would be able to get around the pitch. On the right, I had more limited touches.'

Was this a position he craved more often?

'No,' he replied. 'I knew my place. You know what the gaffer is like! I knew what his answer would be. You were just happy to be in the team. I was never going to go to him and say "Can I play in the centre today?" because we had Roy, Scholesy and Nicky Butt who were all great midfielders. I never expected to get in front of them. I was happy on the right, and as well as I played in the middle it was never a discussion.'

Beckham's contribution to United's European success en route to Barcelona and in the final itself should not be underestimated. I believe it is. He was the Champions League's stellar performer in 1999. That justly won recognition at the time. Beckham almost won the Ballon d'Or and FIFA Player of the Year, finishing second to Barcelona's Rivaldo in both. Rather than sympathize with Beckham for just missing out, some supporters queried why he was picked above other United players.

That view prevails. Whenever United fans talk about 1999, I rarely, if ever, hear Beckham's performance in the Nou Camp mentioned. Schmeichel, Stam, Keane and Yorke are name-checked as the season's most influential players. Keane's semi-final display in the Stadio delle Alpi has become part of United folklore and is celebrated as the chief reason United won that year's competition. 'Roy's performance in Juventus is what he was all about. We looked down and out and he pulled us through,' Beckham reiterated. He is being too modest about his own role that night, and over the campaign. His numbers show that no one was more instrumental than him.

During the group stages, Beckham was responsible for assists away in Munich and Barcelona, earning United a point. He gave a virtuoso performance at home to Barcelona, scoring a 25-yard free-kick and providing the crosses for United's two goals in the 3-3 draw. His two crosses for Yorke gave United a critical 2-0 first-leg lead over Inter Milan in the quarter-final. It was a Beckham cross which led to Giggs's equalizer against Juventus in the first leg of the semi-final, and a Beckham corner to Keane kick-started the comeback when United were 2-0 down in Italy. Combined with both goals in the final, that means Beckham was directly involved in six of United's last nine in that year's competition.

'I can see you were right at the top of your game in that run and the best player on the pitch in the final,' I told him.

'It was one of the best seasons of my career,' he acknowledged.

So why is this rarely the main focus?

Partly because there is more drama in celebrating the goalscorers in the Nou Camp, especially as they came off the bench. It should not go unnoticed that the man who took the corners was the first Sheringham and Solskjaer ran to.

I also believe it is because Beckham's celebrity – or the public reaction to it after his marriage to Spice Girl Victoria Adams – is unfairly referenced when judgement on his footballing ability ought to be based solely on performances. In the late nineties and at the start of the new millennium, the tip of the football pyramid was occupied by legendary midfielders Zinedine Zidane, Luís Figo and Ronaldinho; Beckham was rightly among the host of great players in the tier below. Perhaps he did not have the same connection to the hardcore United fans as local boy Scholes and the anti-establishment, outspoken Keane.

The truth is, this has led to Beckham being underrated, critics too quick to debate rather than acknowledge how good he was.

'I had that from early in my career,' he told me. 'Once I met Victoria at twenty-one and headed towards my peak, it meant people started to question, not my ability, but my professionalism. The people who mattered, those I respected more than anyone in the game, saw the reality. Ask the gaffer, Roy Keane, Steve Bruce, Bryan Robson, and all my teammates what they saw. They would never question my professionalism. The people who matter to me are those I played with, and those who understand the game. It means more coming from Roy, Gaz or people like yourself. They are the people who will want to speak about my football. Roy will say "no one could ever doubt his commitment to the team". That is enough for me. All those who say "he was talked about more for being famous off the pitch than his ability on the pitch" mean nothing to me. There is no one more honest than Keaney. He may not have agreed with the lifestyle I was perceived to have off the pitch – and it was a lot of perception because it was never all red carpets every week like some people seemed to believe – but it was always about what I did on the training ground, and what I produced in the matches. I was never questioned by any professional or manager on that.'

Let's get it right. In his prime, David Beckham was one of the best midfielders England has ever produced. The consistency of his crossing, passing and long-range shooting – that ability repeatedly to locate the 6-yard box or top corner at the biggest moments in some of the biggest games – was peerless among our generation.

His two assists alone should have won him man of the match in 1999, but there was far more to his Nou Camp performance.

The background to Beckham's 1998/99 season is noteworthy. He was made a scapegoat and vilified by media and rival fans following

England's round of sixteen defeat to Argentina in the 1998 World Cup having been sent off for kicking out at Diego Simeone. United's first away game of the Premier League campaign was at West Ham. Fans were burning effigies of him. Stones and bottles were thrown at the United coach. Beckham's every touch was jeered, the abuse going way beyond football rivalry. It was shameful at the time, and looks even more so now, when you realize how little action was taken by the Football Association to protect a young player who would go on to captain his country.

'Going into that season off the back of that World Cup, I never felt I had anything to prove,' said Beckham. 'That kind of thing did not come into my head. It was only when I looked back I began to see how big a year that was for me. It was such a disappointment with England and getting abused at West Ham the way I was. Even if I did not think I was proving people wrong, it was obviously something I had to do because people doubted me. Maybe they were not doubting my football ability, but my temperament. They doubted whether I could continue to play my football at the right level, and some were even asking if I could continue to play for England. If I had thought about it more then, it would have been on my mind too much and maybe I would not have had the season I did.'

Holding aloft the trophies eleven months after his ordeal in St Etienne made for a symbolic response. Having come through that experience, leadership qualities were coming to the fore.

'In a lot of our games, I would get Becks going,' Neville said. 'At the end of that Champions League run, it was the other way round. In the semi, when we were 2-0 down to Juventus, I was down and Becks was shouting at me, "Come on, we are going to win this!" It was exactly the same in the final.'

'That happened naturally,' said Beckham. 'I did not necessarily think to myself "we are going through a bad time, I need to step up". I was not thinking "I am the one who can change things, I am the one who has to make a difference" in response to a particular situation. I tended to play that way all the time. I was brought up to play that way from playing Sunday League, through to youth teams and working with Eric Harrison and then Nobby Stiles at United's academy.

'Throughout that season there were occasions when we were not playing that well but there was always someone who would step up. We had so many players who could do that. If I was not playing well on the right, Gary probably was, or you would have Roy or Scholesy and the rest.'

Beckham's excellence ensured there were conspicuous warnings for Bayern throughout the final. I never felt they survived so long because of the quality of individual performances. With the honourable exception of centre-back Samuel Kuffour, few of the Bayern players shone. For such an imposing side there was no ferocity to Bayern's tackling. There was one booking in the match, for Effenberg after an hour.

Effenberg had no influence, and at thirty-eight, Matthäus was understandably a shadow of what he had been as a midfielder. That is why he was generally a sweeper that season, and despite a positional switch for the final his instinct was always to help his defenders rather than threaten or penetrate with his passing and shooting in the way he did in his prime. He did not have the same capacity to get around the pitch and dominate.

Although Jeremies constantly pursued Beckham, he was nowhere near him, failing to prevent the United man dictating in midfield. Beckham delivered numerous passes from deep to his forwards and wide men which should have been used more productively. United were not playing badly. They were lacking the attacking spark they had in previous rounds. This would have all been forgotten or considered irrelevant had Bayern won. I had not realized until rewatching the match how much it has been ignored since they lost.

What pushed Bayern on was their slender advantage, allied to United's anxiety chasing the game. That emanated from United's poor start, when Bayern's initial ease with their environment contrasted with their opponents' nervousness.

The opening goal came when Ronny Johnsen was adjudged to have fouled Jancker on the edge of United's penalty area, which was a harsh decision by Italian referee Pierluigi Collina. Jancker hit the turf after no more than a shoulder barge. Nevertheless, Johnsen was caught out of position by a looping pass from Zickler.

Basler's free-kick to put Bayern ahead was strange rather than spectacular. It was struck low and hard, beating Schmeichel in such a way that most viewers presumed it had been deflected. United's problem was their wall. Schmeichel positioned six defenders to block the shot, but Babbel took a position on the far left of it, as the United keeper saw it. That meant instead of standing alongside his teammates, Butt was impeded by the Bayern player. Under today's rules, this would not be allowed. Babbel is there to create a gap for the shot, ready to back into the rest of the wall and make the opening for his teammate. When Basler motioned to shoot, Butt desperately attempted to get around Babbel. He was too late.

Schmeichel's positioning looked wrong. He was standing in the middle of his goal anticipating that a direct shot on target would hit the defenders, thus presuming Basler would try to clip it over the wall into the top corner. Basler side-footed powerfully to the goalkeeper's left and Schmeichel was unsighted so he barely moved.

Considering his experience, the stand-in captain playing his last United game, Schmeichel looked like a rookie in those first ten minutes. His kicking was haphazard as he kept finding the stands, and he seemed to be doing everything at twice the necessary speed. Three minutes after the goal he rushed out of his penalty area and almost collided with Johnsen, which would have led to a comical second for Bayern.

United chased the game with a haste that gave the impression they had only a few minutes left to equalize. Bayern benefited, limiting clear-cut chances. That is why Bayern fans and players maintain they were comfortable and there was nothing to indicate what was coming. 'Everything started well,' said Babbel. 'We dominated them and I was just thinking "cruise the game out".'

But as the finishing line approached, the roles switched from the start of the match. Bayern were getting visibly twitchy, including the centre-backs, who had seemed most calm until those last ten minutes. They had good cause to worry.

Even though they were pursuing a historic treble like United (they had already won the Bundesliga), Bayern were carrying scars into Europe.

This was their first appearance in a final since 1987 when, 1-0 up against Porto with thirteen minutes remaining, they lost 2-1. Matthäus was in the Bayern line-up that night, too, seeking the only major trophy that had eluded him. It must have been on his mind.

Despite domestic success, all Bayern's teams in the eighties and nineties were in the shadow of the side skippered by Franz Beckenbauer, which won a hat-trick of European Cups between 1973 and 1976. The weight of history took its toll.

'I couldn't enjoy the game because I was just thinking "don't do a stupid mistake, don't do anything silly",' Babbel confessed. 'That was my biggest problem. I was so fucked in my head because of that. It was really sad because I never felt like that in all the other finals. If we played in the German cup or the Europa League, which we won with Bayern Munich, I never had this problem. I never felt like that with the German national team when we won the European Championship [in 1996]. I was focused, yes, but I enjoyed the game and the experience. That Champions League final was the only game in my career when I felt this way. I should have been telling myself, "Hey, come on, we will win this. I am better than the guy I am playing against, Blomqvist. I will beat him. I will make him make mistakes because I am too good on this day." That wasn't my thinking because it was always my biggest dream to win the Champions League. That was because, for me, it was the biggest trophy that you can win.'

It's the fear of losing I have discussed at length elsewhere in the book. Although United did not create clear chances until the end, what Bayern's players experienced in 1999 was exactly the same as what Liverpool's players went through during the final few minutes against

Arsenal at Anfield in 1989. Players began following the ball rather than keeping the team shape, taking unusual positions and making rash decisions in possession they would not have done in a less stressful fixture.

Even Matthäus was guilty of that before his substitution. On 65 minutes, he was running down the left wing, attacking Neville, only to cross wastefully into the penalty area. He told his manager he had no energy left and was subbed shortly after. 'The fact I was substituted was maybe a signal to our opponents,' Matthäus observed. 'By replacing a personality like myself they gained in confidence. Maybe we should have done things differently, including my substitution. I was exhausted and signalled to come off.'

'Of course, at that moment I was thinking, "What the hell is he doing? Why is he going out?"' said Babbel. 'He said he was tired and couldn't play any more and didn't want to do a stupid mistake, because normally if you're tired that is when it happens, you know? Now I understand it. But it was a problem because until then Man United had not had a chance; we were solid at the back.'

What Bayern lost was the experience of the man who might have guided them away from the ensuing chaos, giving onfield instructions and reassuring anxious teammates.

It took seventy minutes for United's strike partners to work in tandem and create an opening, Yorke's free header from Neville's long throw enabling Cole to attempt an ambitious overhead kick. Bayern's marking was poor, but they escaped.

By then, United had made their first change.

Enter Teddy Sheringham.

The previous two years had brought an assortment of emotions for the United striker. When I spoke to him, he admitted that the final ten days of the season camouflaged what had been his most difficult spell at the club.

Despite his healthy return of fourteen goals, United had failed to win a major trophy in Sheringham's first season following his move from Spurs. 'I was made a bit of a scapegoat,' he said. 'We were twelve points clear and winning easily and then had injuries to Giggs, Keane and Pallister. That is what hurt us, but Fergie brought Yorkie in for the start of the [1998/99] season. I could have left, but I still felt good enough and thought I could prove my worth.

'What happened at the end of the season was quite surreal. When people talk about 1999, they think I had a great season. They think I must have scored about fifteen or so goals. I only scored five. But the last two are the most important you can score, in the FA Cup and Champions League finals.'

Even that majestic final ten days did not run as smoothly as it seems. 'I was shocked to start the last game of the Premier League season against Tottenham,' said Sheringham. 'But when I was booked just before half-time, the manager told me he could not take a risk and took me off. So I went from that high of being picked for what was by then the biggest game of the season to being gutted at being taken off at half-time.'

As time was United's enemy inside the Nou Camp, Sheringham was one of the few United players content to see Bayern retain their lead early in the second half. 'The manager told me at half-time if it stayed the same, I would be on in the next fifteen minutes. Obviously, I was hoping that would happen.'

Until his introduction, Sheringham's sole contribution was directing a verbal volley at a couple of the Bayern players while he was warming up, requiring Collina's intervention. 'One of the Germans was blowing kisses to his fans, so I had a word. "What you fucking playing at? Who do you think you are?" That is how I remember it, anyway. I thought they were showing off a bit.'

When Sheringham replaced Blomqvist, his impact was initially negative. United temporarily changed to a diamond formation. Sheringham joined Cole up front, Yorke dropping deep behind them. It did not work, leading to Bayern's most encouraging attacking spell.

What happened between the 73rd and 84th minutes is the reason the 'smash and grab' theory lingers, and why those who have never revisited the 1999 final believe Bayern outplayed United.

Scholl replaced Zickler in the 71st minute. Two minutes later, a poor Sheringham pass upfield allowed Bayern to counter-attack, United's midfield and defence exposed as Effenberg forced Schmeichel into his first meaningful save, pushing an attempted chip over the crossbar.

United's next sigh of relief came on 79 minutes, when Basler's run fed Scholl and his beautiful chip beat Schmeichel who could only stand and watch as it rebounded off the post and into his arms.

In the 84th minute, another Scholl attempt was pushed wide, and within a minute Jancker hit the crossbar with an overhead from close range as United failed to clear a Bayern corner. These were great individual efforts which have since been described as 'great chances'. There is a difference between wonderful team play regularly opening a side up and a forward almost scoring out of nothing.

By now the game was open. Ferguson ditched the diamond and sent on Solskjaer to replace Cole, with Yorke moving from the centre to the right and Giggs in his more comfortable position of left wing. The extensive list of chances for United as the ninety-minute mark approached created the sense that a goal was coming.

Eighty-seven minutes: Stam's long ball into the box was directed to Sheringham. Kuffour made a terrible, panicky challenge, missed his header, and the ball fell to Solskjaer. Thomas Linke was not close enough to the Norwegian. Solskjaer flicked back to Sheringham, who dragged his shot at Bayern keeper Kahn. Kahn picked up the ball and kicked long, directly back to United, who instantly attacked again.

Eighty-eight minutes: Beckham's diagonal pass found Yorke in space in the penalty area. Yorke headed towards Sheringham. He was unable to make the distance for what would have been an easy opportunity.

Eighty-nine minutes: Neville made good progress on the right wing and crossed for Yorke, who was again unmarked but miskicked from close range.

Eighty-nine minutes: Solskjaer headed straight at Kahn after a Giggs cross found him unmarked between the two Bayern centre-backs.

'They are now creating chances for fun,' said commentator Clive Tyldesley.

Ninety minutes: Babbel underhit a backpass and Linke was forced to concede a throw-in under pressure from Solskjaer. Giggs was about to take it quickly when he was ordered to wait. Neville had the clarity of thought to sprint across the pitch from right-back to the left wing and take a long throw-in. 'It was just an instinctive reaction,' said Neville. 'I saw it and thought we just have to get the ball into the box somehow.'

On such small details, the course of history changes.

Kuffour headed the throw clear from his 6-yard box, but only to Beckham. He embarked on a superb run and released it to Neville, still on the left, whose cross with his unfavoured foot was blocked by Effenberg for a United corner.

Both Neville and Beckham have assured me United's encouraging onslaught came when Beckham moved to his familiar right wing. I kept rewinding and rewatching to see this positional switch. It did not happen, as far as I am concerned. Beckham was still more central, as likely on the left as the right, as demonstrated by the build-up to the equalizer.

For all his fine work in midfield, Beckham's phenomenal execution of his set-piece skills won the game. He took all twelve of United's corners in the Nou Camp, six in each half. United scored from two of them. Conceivably, they could have scored from five. There was nothing unpredictable about the chances he created in injury-time.

'I practised corners as much as free-kicks,' said Beckham. 'We would do a lot of set-pieces, and since I was a kid I always tried whipping into the right position. When I broke into the United senior team Peter Schmeichel was perfect for me in training. He would kill me if I put it into the wrong area. That helped me in my career. I always practised.'

United also had recent history winning cup finals late on courtesy of a Beckham corner. 'The FA Cup final in 1996 against your lot when Eric scored,' he recalled with a laugh. 'The gaffer had turned to [assistant manager] Brian Kidd just before I took that one and said, "If he puts that into David James's arms once more he is coming off."'

The message was clear to Bayern. First, a United corner was perilous at any time. Second, a United corner when your defenders' concentration levels were not 100 per cent was catastrophic.

When Beckham delivered his eleventh corner of the 1999 Champions League final, Schmeichel had taken it upon himself to run the length of the pitch into the penalty area. His challenge on centre-back Linke proved a helpful distraction, stopping the centre-half making a simple header. The loose ball fell to Thorsten Fink, the man who replaced Matthäus. He miskicked his attempted clearance, so it found its way to Giggs on the edge of the box, the position he had been taking all season to halt counter-attacks at their source. His scuffed shot dropped to Sheringham, whose shinned strike made it 1-1.

'I was thinking, "Oh no, not extra-time, because I'm so tired. I can't play any more because I can't enjoy it any more,"' said Babbel. 'I wasn't physically tired, I was mentally tired.'

Amid his relief, Neville felt the same. 'I was fucked. My legs had gone ten days before. I was really tired and thinking how I would get through extra-time. That is no fun as a defender.'

There were twenty-five seconds between Bayern restarting and conceding another corner. You will never see a more vivid example of a team crumbling under pressure, which is astonishing given German football's reputation for possessing mentally strong players. What any side in their situation must do is reassess, try to keep the ball for the next minute and kill momentum. Usually, both teams are content to take the additional thirty minutes of extra-time. What Bayern did from their kick-off, immediately handing the ball back to their rejuvenated opponents, is extraordinary in the circumstances. Jeremies passed it wide left where Scholl hammered an aimless high ball towards the United defence, Stam winning a header and Giggs shrugging off Effenberg to collect the rebound. When Irwin played down the line towards Solskjaer on the United left, Babbel and right centre-back Linke were out of position. Solskjaer had only Kuffour for company. This makes for staggering viewing, the Norwegian having the kind of space you would imagine on a counter-attack. He turned and won the final corner. Bayern's players look like they were in a trance, watching rather than participating.

Beckham's twelfth corner-kick could not have been placed any better. Linke's mind was obviously scrambled as he was 5 yards away from Sheringham when the striker had a free header, glancing into the 6-yard box. Solskjaer was the predator on the spot to divert past Kahn as Tyldesley exclaimed, 'United have won it!'

'I broke the cardinal rule of commentary,' Clive admitted. 'I called the winner across the line before they'd got there, but it was as dramatic and emotional a five minutes of football theatre as I've ever seen.'

'It was bedlam,' said Neville. 'It all happened so quickly. I was on the floor looking at the sky thinking, "What just fucking happened?" I was nowhere near the celebrations.'

Collina ended the game almost immediately. There is no worse way to lose a final. There will never be a better way to win one, with too little time to digest the magnitude of the moment, or allow the jitters to affect your own team's defence.

'I said to Ole, "You do not realize what you have just done. It will live for ever,"' said Neville. 'I knew the history – Matt Busby's birthday, the treble, the perfect storm. I did not go to sleep that night. I never wanted the day to end. I knew the moment would never come again.'

Only the coldest heart could not be affected by the image of Bayern's Kuffour in tears banging the floor in frustration, while his teammates stood around paralysed in shock. Those scenes won the sympathy of neutrals, and probably contributed to the idea that Bayern are the most unfortunate losers in the competition's history.

'It is not that we lost the game,' said Babbel. 'We can lose against Man United, of course. It was the way it happened which was so hard. It was not normal. I was mentally fucked for a few weeks after. Straight after the game it was like someone died. Silence. No one was speaking because everyone was shocked. Not only the players; the coaching team, the staff, the big legends like Uli Hoeness, [Karl-Heinz] Rummenigge. No one could understand what happened. If you lose in the last two minutes of a game, it's the worst thing that can happen to you as a sports guy.'

Worse still, Bayern had a prearranged post-match dinner to attend. 'About one thousand people were there, fans and sponsors,' said Babbel. 'The first minute was quiet. Then more silence. And then – I don't know why – after a while six or seven players decided to start celebrating like it was a party, dancing on the tables; Mario Basler was there, Jens Jeremies was there, Mehmet Scholl was there, Alex Zickler, Carsten Jancker . . . I had never experienced anything like it before. It was the best party of my life. It was unbelievable. You know we lost the game, a massive game in a way normally you can't explain, and then you have a party. The best party ever in my life. It was unbelievable. It carried on until six o'clock in the morning. Everyone was pissed.'

Maybe that contributed to their German cup defeat to Werder Bremen two weeks later.

Perhaps this togetherness stirred Bayern's recovery to become European champions in 2001, overcoming Valencia on penalties, a run which included a quarter-final triumph over United. Seven players who were involved against United in 1999 featured in that victorious chase for redemption.

Manchester United and Bayern Munich are among a handful of clubs that will always define themselves by European Cup success. The competition is intertwined with United's heritage and fundamental to why the club became so globally popular, going back to the tragic events of the Munich air disaster in 1958, when eight of Busby's young side lost their lives returning from a European tie. There is something about holding that particular trophy which makes you instantly realize you are touching history. At certain clubs you are doing more by honouring the legacy of legends and creating one of your own.

'We knew what we had just done, but the enormity of it really sank in a few weeks later – the games we played, how we won them,' said Beckham. 'We were all so young, growing up under that manager, and achieving what we did was so big. Mentally and physically we were exhausted but we realized nothing we did, with the exception of winning the World Cup with England, could have bettered it. Even if we had won another treble, it would not have been better. And doing it for the team I supported, with friends I had known since I moved to Manchester when I was fourteen, made it more special.

'The gaffer would not let us get carried away. We were so dominant because he did not want gloating for long. He wanted us to go and do it again. He never wanted anyone feeling too comfortable. That was one of his greatest qualities as a manager. He wanted you to enjoy the moment and get more. In my mid-forties, I can see it was the best time of my career.'

If there is any regret for the United class of '99, it is that they failed to build on their European breakthrough, instead reverting to their habit of losing winnable ties in the knockout stages.

'After we lost to Bayer Leverkusen in the semi-final in 2002, Keano referred to people stepping off the gas and talking about Rolexes,' said Neville. 'After winning it, we almost forgot how hard it was. We didn't invest big after winning the '99 treble. We were a worse team a year after because we lost Schmeichel. We should have brought in a couple of players, but Sir Alex had a problem because who do you bring in who can replace the heart of that team? Who challenges that? Whoever joined was going to have to be prepared to sit on the bench.'

United beat Chelsea on penalties to reclaim the Champions League in 2008, and were unlucky to face one of the greatest club teams ever, Pep Guardiola's Barcelona, in the 2009 and 2011 finals. Most agree the United side, with Rooney, Cristiano Ronaldo and Carlos Tevez, was the best of Ferguson's reign.

'I always feel I am a bit harsh on that '99 side when comparing them to the other teams Sir Alex built,' said Neville. 'Between 1996 and 1999 we won three league titles, two FA Cups and the Champions League, but other United teams, like the Cantona team, are remembered more fondly. Now I see Sir Alex recreated what Sir Matt had done. We had eight out of eighteen in the squad that were home-grown. That is the pinnacle for any club, having your academy lads come through like that. Sir Alex split up the 1994 team, selling Paul Ince, Paul Parker and Mark Hughes to give us our chance. He was justified by that European Cup win.'

As well as their skill and ability, I applaud the character of United's '99 side. One of the most understated qualities in the greatest teams is the force of its personality, while one of the most overstated is occasional strokes of good fortune. These attributes are not unrelated. It is no coincidence that the sides with the will to win no matter what the circumstances often benefit from the rub of the green at critical moments in a match or season.

For all the credit that is afforded the most successful teams, it is uncanny how often detractors attempt to demean their achievements by referencing luck. This certainly dominates plenty of the analysis of United's 1999 treble, greatly influenced by memories of the Champions League final.

It is nonsense.

Luck inevitably has a supporting role in success, especially one so rare as winning three major trophies in a season. Anyone who has played sport to an elite level understands there are incidents which can turn a game or a cup run, and United had many of them in 1999. In my experience, luck's role is vastly overblown, especially in the context of last-minute equalizers or winners.

Obviously you can score flukey goals in football, or you can suffer from a poor refereeing decision or a freak injury, wrecking your chances. But no trophy lift can ever be deemed a fluke given the preparation and application required to put you into a position to win, regardless of how you get across the line.

When a player such as David Beckham has dedicated years to perfecting his dead-ball technique, and delivers the optimum performance at the eleventh hour in the biggest game of his career, how can this be characterized as luck?

I have never understood why scoring late is regularly described in terms of being fortuitous. It is good timing, not good luck. When a team makes a habit of scoring late, it tells you everything about their mentality. United made it their forte.

'Sir Alex would say, "You are a crazy team, you lot,"' Neville recalled. 'It felt like we were bored in the first part of a season until it got serious, and we were bored in the first part of a match until we had to play. He always said he knew we would score goals. "Even if we have ten minutes to go, we will score," he would tell us.'

It is no coincidence so many clubs with average teams and underperforming managers consistently decry their misfortune, while hinting that any fortune going spare falls the way of better sides. There is a logic behind that.

I suffered during United's treble run in February 1999, part of the Liverpool side ahead in the FA Cup fourth round at Old Trafford until the 88th minute when Yorke equalized and Solskjaer scored the injury-time winner.

'Typical, lucky United,' we all cursed on the coach home to Merseyside.

It was my worst defeat in football until that point.

The timing hurt more, and there is a sense of fate working against you when you are so close. Then you think back and remember how long we were holding on to our lead. Keane hit the post twice before the equalizer, David James made numerous saves, and Solskjaer was on the pitch because Ferguson took off Irwin, gambling with only three defenders for the last ten minutes. You reluctantly admit the game was heading that way, United's players eventually taking advantage of our inability to see it through when the pressure intensified in front of a hostile home crowd. Neville told me it was the turning point of United's treble season, which made me feel even worse.

When we improved at Liverpool, such last-minute hardships

occurred less often. Two years later we were inflicting them on Arsenal and Alavés to complete a cup treble of our own.

United did it so often throughout Ferguson's reign that there was an expectation towards the end of games in which they were behind that they would always create a chance or score the goal to get them out of trouble. This took residence in the heads of their opponents and became a self-fulfilling prophecy. If all else failed heading to the latter stages of a match, United had 'Fergie Time' as the ultimate psychological weapon to test the nerves and resolve of opponents while they pushed on, buoyed by how often they found a way to save or win matches. The challenge was on those trying to protect a win or a draw to show they had the mental capacity as much as ability to see it through. If they failed, they had to look at themselves rather than the referee who added an extra minute or two of injury-time.

Look for the greatest sides who dominate in an era, in any team sport, and you are guaranteed to find numerous examples when they were fighting against the clock and still found a way to win. Manchester United always seemed to have that ability under Sir Alex Ferguson, and the Nou Camp typified it more than any other game for which he was in charge.

When people recall the immediate aftermath, they most often quote Ferguson's awestruck pitchside response to ITV reporter Gary Newbon: 'Football, bloody 'ell.'

What is forgotten is what he said next: 'They never give in. That's what won it.'

That is why I believe it fitting to leave the last word to the 1999 Champions League final's true man of the match.

'You create your own luck,' said Beckham. 'I never believed we were lucky in any sense to win that game.'

8

Wednesday, 3 April 1996

1995/96 FA PREMIER LEAGUE
Anfield

LIVERPOOL 4 – 3 NEWCASTLE UNITED

Fowler *2, 55*
Collymore *68, 90+2*

Ferdinand *10*
Ginola *14*
Asprilla *57*

'I would rather just miss out chasing the ghosts of Shankly, Paisley, Dalglish and Rush than win the Premier League backed by a shitload of money'

– Stan Collymore

ONE OF LIVERPOOL'S WORST SIGNINGS never played for the club. He was never unveiled at a press conference, nor did he participate in a training session. In fact, he spent only a couple of hours with Roy Evans's squad in the spring of 1996, oblivious to the reputational damage this brief association would cause.

He never wore the shirt. He designed the cream-coloured FA Cup final suits.

The culprit was Italian fashion designer Giorgio Armani, and his single, fateful Anfield contribution was presenting his catalogue before Liverpool's Wembley date with Manchester United.

The clash between football's old and new world at Anfield in the 1990s is encapsulated by the image of the suave catwalk choreographer in what was then still a ramshackle wooden hut at Melwood. 'I shit you not, Armani was standing there in the Melwood canteen with two lackeys going through the colour range,' said Stan Collymore. 'David James had a deal with them at the time, and some of the players were not averse to wearing garish outfits. Even the captain John Barnes would sometimes turn up in a canary suit, so there was some excitement when a couple of players saw cream ones. No one gave it a second thought. We were thinking, "We are going to win the FA Cup. Who is going to give a fuck about the suits?"'

With that calamitous decision preceding a dire final, Evans's Liverpool squad was immortalized for possessing more style than substance, forever associated with the demeaning boyband tag of the Spice Boys which they have resented ever since.

'How does it feel to be seen as one of the poster boys for that?' I asked Collymore in the midst of a lengthy chat about the defining period of his Liverpool career.

'I take that as a stick to beat us for not having the ultra-professionalism needed to win the trophies that were within our grasp,' he replied, while insisting on a non-negotiable condition: 'As long as it is shared. We all take the blame. From the top down.'

For better and worse, labels stick in football, memories framed by events which may be more representative of a fleeting moment than an era. Sometimes, a career can be deceptively reduced to a single game, a winning goal or a terrible mistake.

Win, and warts are hidden and lapses forgiven. Fail, and you are always reminded of what might have been minor blemishes.

No Liverpool side understands that better than that of the mid-nineties, their credibility undermined by a fashion statement that would have been considered daft but trivial had they gone on to beat Manchester United at Wembley, or won a league title or European trophy.

Evans's side assembled in a period when young players were characterized as seeing their jerseys as means to secure celebrity status, acquire advertising endorsements and get invited to the right parties on the arms of pop star girlfriends. This was hardly exclusive to Anfield. United's superstar midfielder David Beckham signed an Armani contract and actually married a Spice Girl, yet he and his United teammates carry none of the same baggage because of one all-encompassing fact.

They won, and kept on winning.

Nothing they did or said off the pitch could eclipse that part of their story.

Between 1995 and 1998, Evans's side lifted a League Cup, reached the FA Cup final, a European semi-final, another League Cup semi-final, and were involved in two title races. All of this is overshadowed.

'We are remembered for losing an FA Cup final and wearing those suits,' Robbie Fowler despaired. 'If we had won the game they would never be mentioned, but we know how the football world works. All of a sudden that was it. I am not sure if that was the start of the Spice Boys thing, but it was ridiculous. Someone mentioned it and it stuck, and it has been hard to get away from it.'

The crossroads for that Liverpool team was the climax to the 1995/96 season, when they had a chance to achieve an FA Cup and Premier League double. On Sunday, 31 March, they beat Aston Villa 3-0 at Old Trafford in the FA Cup semi-final. Protecting an unbeaten twenty-two-match league run, the following Wednesday they welcomed title rivals Newcastle United to Anfield for a game many consider the Premier League's greatest ever.

It is certainly one of the most curious, because although they have so much in common, the Newcastle team that lost is revered more than the Liverpool side that won. That contradiction fascinates me as much as the tactical overview.

Newcastle's players look back upon that game and the season as north-east legends who fell agonizingly short in their title bid, the Anfield defeat the psychological wound that lingered most. We remember Kevin Keegan's Newcastle for their swagger. We think of them as an attacking side known as 'the Entertainers', coming close to the championship playing with gusto and ambition. There is no condemnation for being unable to make that final step, only sympathy and commendation for their efforts.

Their players reminisce about the most exciting time in the club's modern history. 'You had [David] Ginola on the left, [Keith] Gillespie on the right, Peter Beardsley just behind me, Rob Lee,' Les Ferdinand, the striker who joined Newcastle in the summer of 1995, told me. 'It was just raining chances, every game. I used to say to the wingers, "Don't look for me, just put the ball in the box and I'll go and attack it." I knew it was coming in, cut-back after cut-back after cut-back. I got chance after chance, especially at the start of the season.'

That Newcastle's sense of adventure is considered their undoing adds to their appeal, as if their failure was heroic.

For a couple of years in the mid-nineties, Newcastle could justly claim to be everyone's second team as they took on Manchester United playing in a manner that enchanted neutrals. Theirs is a romantic story. We still think of Keegan's philosophy as centred around attack to the detriment of defence, his pursuit of goals leading him to reinforce his side with maverick South American striker Faustino Asprilla halfway through a title bid when a commanding centre-back and a few pragmatic, scruffy wins would have made the difference.

'The context is really important,' said Martin Hardy, the *Times*' north-east journalist whose book *Touching Distance* honoured Newcastle's title bid. 'In three years, Newcastle went from looking like they may go to the [old] Third Division to the top of the Premier League.

'The ground got rebuilt, Newcastle started signing big players, and Kevin Keegan was saying, "Right, we're going to try and win the title this season." Newcastle hadn't come that close to winning the title since 1927, so it'd never happened in anybody's lifetime. Liverpool fans grew up winning the title, Newcastle fans grew up in the Second Division or getting relegated or scrambling around mid-table and selling their best players. It was just a magic time, especially when you think of the chaos at the club ever since.'

Keegan, like Evans, was mentored by the Anfield god Bill Shankly, so naturally each side's approach mirrored the other. Yet history has afforded Evans's team none of the same charm.

With respect to Newcastle, that is because the expectations, standards and responsibilities of being a Liverpool player are incomparable. There is nowhere to hide when you are caught between seventies and eighties legends who produced one of the greatest eras in football history, and the team of the 2000s which, while unable to take the Premier League, regularly won big honours.

I made my Liverpool debut under Evans in January 1997, nine months after the Newcastle game. The team into which I was introduced – alongside Fowler, Collymore, Barnes, James, Steve McManaman and Jamie Redknapp – had more natural talent than those with which I later lifted trophies under Gérard Houllier and Rafa Benítez. The finest

Liverpool teams I played in were as inconsistent over a thirty-eight-game Premier League season, but we won six major trophies between 2001 and 2006, including the UEFA Cup and the Champions League, because we possessed a quality lacking in the mid-nineties side – what I would describe as a collective winning mentality. We had the ability to drag ourselves across the line even when not at our best.

The distinction was not the ability of the players, and we reached so many finals you can forget about suggesting it was all down to being lucky at the right time. There has to be another reason for it, and I can only talk about what I witnessed and experienced.

In terms of mentality and professionalism, the Liverpool of the 2000s was superior to the team in which I made my debut, the changes implemented by Houllier and Benítez transforming how the players approached training and executed tactical instructions.

I write that as an observation based on my career rather than an intended criticism of Evans, a man for whom I have only respect. Roy is one of the greatest Anfield servants as a coach and assistant manager during Liverpool's heyday in the 1970s and 1980s, deservedly promoted to the role of manager. The fact is, English football was undergoing radical change after the formation of the Premier League in 1992, increased revenues from TV deals generating more commercial opportunities (some would say distractions) off the pitch and meaning that players started to earn millions rather than thousands. In the midst of unfavourable comparisons to the managerial legends who came before and while going head-to-head with a genius such as Sir Alex Ferguson, it was an unenviable task for any Liverpool manager trying to stick with the tried and trusted old ways.

The methods of the previous decade – when Bob Paisley, Joe Fagan and Kenny Dalglish empowered and trusted a dressing room of senior players and proven winners to manage themselves as much as be coached – were flawed by the time Evans was in charge, especially as the game had moved on to the point where star signings were as likely to take career advice from agents, financial advisers and PR consultants as coaches.

Evans's immediate predecessor, Graeme Souness, attempted to manage the club in a stricter manner and met with resistance for changing too much, too soon. A more amiable man-management style was welcomed upon Evans's appointment in 1994.

John Barnes signed for Liverpool in 1987 and was sharing captaincy duties with Ian Rush by 1996. He recognized that the club was struggling to come to terms with the shifting dynamic. 'When I came to Liverpool, I did not learn anything technically,' he said. 'I learned how Liverpool played, but as a footballer I learned about the mentality of having to win. You had to have that to be a Liverpool player. The older players ruled the dressing room, Kenny Dalglish and Graeme Souness the prime examples in the mid-eighties. When Ian Rush and Ronnie Whelan were young, do you think they could ever say anything to Dalglish and Souness? That changed in the mid-nineties because the older players like Steve McMahon, Whelan and Jan Molby were the last of the great mid-eighties side to go. By the mid-nineties it was the younger players who were of more value to the clubs than senior professionals. The Bosman rule [allowing players to see out their contracts and leave on free transfers] meant you had to protect their value and give the best of them bigger contracts. It meant they had more of the power than some of the older players. Liverpool did not go and buy senior players to replace the older ones who left, so who were they going to learn the Liverpool way from? I am not talking about tactically or technically. I am talking psychologically.'

By 1996, Barnes and Rush were the only players left from the great 1980s side, and the only ones with experience of what was needed to win championships. But Barnes says he never felt like he could fully assert his influence. 'Look, for a long time at the club during its successful years players would go out and get pissed. But when it came to training and matches, they did everything properly. There were never any excuses. Monday to Friday you had to be on it because that was where you won the game on Saturday. The attitude had to be right. You could not be brilliant against some teams and not deliver the same performance against others. I will give you an example. Ian Rush never scored against Manchester United for the first ten years of his career. It did not matter. It was about winning every game, not just big games. Every game was a big game. I understood that more when I joined the club in 1987, and I learned all that from the players there. By the time I was the captain I was frustrated. In training there was a lot of messing around, fucking around all the time. How could I bollock them? It was, "What does Barnesy know?" People thought I was moaning.'

Some of the younger players in the squad at the time disagree with this interpretation. I doubt there is anyone more hurt by it than Fowler.

I have never believed Robbie's reputation was damaged in the same way as some of his nineties teammates'. Fowler scored thirty-six goals in the 1995/96 season and was immune from criticism from The Kop for the side's shortcomings. His performances during that period were extraordinary, and he was also part of the side that went on to win trophies under Houllier. When your nickname is 'God', it is a fair assumption your legendary status will remain intact.

He takes exception to criticism of his mindset.

'I remember an argument with Jason McAteer because he said we didn't have the mentality,' Fowler recalled. 'I was, "Hang on, you can question your own, but you can't question mine or everyone else's." I argued my case. Everyone is different. Everyone reacts differently in training, to results and training sessions. There was nothing wrong with my attitude. I went out there wanting to do well in every single game and believing I would.

'What happens when you get an adverse result is people look for a reason or a scapegoat, someone to blame, any excuse other than the football. You played under Rafa when the side lost one game and finished second and people were looking for daft reasons then, too. Sometimes because it is such a good team people want to question you, your abilities or what you did right and wrong. Regardless of what we were like, there were other teams a bit better than us. There was some messing about, but we were professional, and we did what we needed to do to prepare for games. What we lacked – and I have seen this with Liverpool teams over the years – is consistency. But when you look at it, we lost only two of our last twenty games that season. We lost the league because of a bad run the previous November.'

My view is that every team is a reflection of the personality of the manager, whether it is the free-spirited Evans and Keegan or a disciplinarian such as Ferguson. What you see on the pitch is an extension of what is happening on a day-to-day basis, whether that is in how a team is set up or in how individuals apply themselves minute to minute, game to game.

'I know Robbie gets the hump about it all, but the reality is what it is. It has to come from the top. You and I know that,' agreed Collymore, who signed for Liverpool for a British record £8.5 million in the summer of 1995. 'We have played under managers who give you that look which tells you if you dick about again, that's it. There was as much talent in our Liverpool team as there was in that Manchester United team, so it is clear what the difference was. Ultra-discipline. Managers have different styles. Roy was brought up in the boot room and there was a system in place that had worked for the club so it is natural you are going to stick with that; but when the person at the top of the organization perhaps gives you that little bit of leeway, there is no doubt to a greater or lesser degree . . . well, we all took the piss. Whether that was Robbie and Macca [Steve McManaman], whether it was me, whether it was Jamie [Redknapp], whether it was Barnesy or Rushie and other senior players. We all have to accept our share of the responsibility.

'A lot of the Spice Boys stuff alluded to a group of lads going out partying. At the same time, the "Class of '92" at United were not angels. They wanted what all young lads did, to play great football and then enjoy themselves after. Fergie was pulling Lee Sharpe and Ryan Giggs out of parties. Some of the older professionals at United, legends like Bryan Robson, liked to go out and have a drink. There was not a great difference between them and us. If we went to London we would see them in the same places. But Fergie set parameters. It was a case of, "you can have the first one free, but after that you are out". We never had that.

'The managerial staff at Liverpool were dealing with a group of modern players, a bit cocky, a bit flighty with wages going through the roof, but they never wanted to babysit anyone because that was the attitude that had been there since Dalglish and Souness were running the dressing room. What we had was a lot of young lads, four years after the start of the Premier League, on good money and all the lads' mags and *GQ* ringing us up on a daily basis. There was a lot of innocence around it. We did not know what the drill was. We were thinking we could play football and do all the other stuff as well.'

As a brilliant but flawed striker, Collymore was an appropriate match-winner for this gloriously imperfect match against Newcastle – two swashbuckling title challengers exposing each other's deficiencies. Evans described it as 'kamikaze', the game shaping football fans' view of how the 1995/96 title was won and lost with negative images of these two teams' defences.

The critical appraisal of this game homes in on the reason neither won the Premier League. Equally, it is clear to see why they were contenders. As a package, this match is considered exceptional with good reason. It is worth reiterating how technically impressive it was.

'I said at the time it was the best game I have ever seen,' said Andy Gray, co-commentator for Sky Sports on the night. 'Since then I must have seen thousands of games and I still haven't seen one to beat it for ninety minutes. When you look at the gluepot of a pitch and the skill involved with these players, a goal in the first minute and a winner in the last minute, it was everything you want football to be.'

At times the attacking quality was astounding. There were forty-one shots. A typical Premier League game in 2020 averages twenty-four. David Ginola's performance was world-class, McManaman's, Ferdinand's, Fowler's and Collymore's likewise. Beardsley, once of Liverpool but by now back at Newcastle, and Liverpool's Barnes were destructive when given time on the ball. Any defence in the world would have struggled to keep a clean sheet against those line-ups on that particular night.

As with any goals conceded, areas of weakness can be highlighted. Many are obvious. But even when using this match as an example of why both sides were so vulnerable, in the context of the season it is not as black and white as those Newcastle jerseys.

The preconception is that Manchester United won the league in 1995/96 because they were less flamboyant in attack and possessed a superior defence. It might surprise some of you to learn that Ferguson's side scored more league goals than the free-spirited strikers of Newcastle and Liverpool that season. It might surprise you even more to know that Newcastle, the team that apparently could not defend, had conceded two fewer than Manchester United on the day they travelled to Anfield. Their defence leaked at the same rate as the champions' for the remaining games, so the four they gave up at Anfield were an anomaly. Liverpool's defensive record was also superior to Manchester United's and would remain so until the end of that campaign.

So, what was the difference? We see it at Anfield with two sides who are superb with the ball and vulnerable without it. Against most teams in the Premier League that season that wasn't a problem for Liverpool and Newcastle as they were in possession most of the time. It became an issue on those occasions when they needed collectively to dig in. How often do we mention this in a title run-in when pressure builds? That there are certain matches in which you need to grind out victory, fighting through difficult moments and edging ahead before seeing the game out?

That comes from attitude and talent. You need to be mentally tuned and well rehearsed to make the switch from piling forward to working as a unit closing down spaces, identifying and nullifying threats.

'If you cannot score, make sure you do not concede' is a timeless message, but evidently not at Anfield in April 1996. Every time one side gets the ball, they look as though they are trying to score rather than work out their opponent, slow the tempo and control the game. They are like boxers constantly looking for the knockout punch rather than jabbing and probing for weaknesses, waiting for the right time to strike.

That meant Liverpool v. Newcastle turned into a game of perpetual counter-attack, Keegan's men only identifiable as the away side because of the venue rather than the direction of the match.

Newcastle had the courage and ability to come from behind and led twice, but the longer the game progressed the more you sensed they might succumb because it was not in their nature to resist and allow the opposition to dominate possession. 'Keegan's philosophy was always "they'll score but we'll score two; they'll score two, we'll score three", and that's the way we approached the Liverpool game,' said Ferdinand.

Liverpool had the same strength and flaw.

'My feeling at the time was, if we do not play well, we will not win the game,' said Barnes. 'That has to be because of a soft mentality. Between 1994 and 1997 there were lots of occasions when we were playing well and scoring goals, and I would be looking at Manchester United and thinking, "Sometimes they are playing shit, winning 1-0 and getting the job done." Winning 4-3 is not what being champions is all about. Champions get the job done when they are not at their best. We were not too soft physically. We were too soft mentally.'

The statistics behind that season support Barnes's view. Liverpool lost only seven of their thirty-eight league games, but they included away defeats to the teams that finished twelfth, thirteenth, fourteenth and sixteenth. They dropped a further ten points to sides finishing fourteenth or lower. United's six losses included those at Anfield, Highbury, White Hart Lane and Leeds's Elland Road. All traditionally tough games. They also lost their first game of the season at Aston Villa, who finished fourth that season. Only The Dell in Southampton, itself a notoriously troublesome venue, represented a real shock. Newcastle had similar consistency to United until 21 February when they began a horrendous run of four losses in six games, squandering the twelve-point lead they had four weeks earlier.

By the time they arrived at Anfield, Keegan's side were three points behind United, Ferguson's side in the midst of a season-defining run of narrow victories. Four of their five 1-0 wins in eight games between 4 March and 18 April were courtesy of Eric Cantona winners. That is where the title was won and lost, and it comes back to the mentality issue, Ferguson fine-tuning a group of players to attain a base of consistency which meant they knew how to win ugly as well as gloriously. Their experience of previous title climaxes obviously helped.

'The consistency of Man Utd that year was frightening,' said Fowler. 'They had the right balance when to defend and attack, knowing how to see out games. In March they played Newcastle, QPR, Arsenal and Tottenham and they won three and drew one, 1-0, 1-0, 1-0 and 1-1. So when you are looking for individual brilliance from players and you have the likes of Steve Bruce and Gary Pallister at the back, that is where consistency comes from. Knowing when it is just about the result. We did not have that. We were gung-ho.'

These are not 'small details' or 'lucky breaks' as many like to suggest when reassessing success and failure. They cut to the heart of why certain teams always find themselves participating in rather than watching trophy presentations.

'Liverpool and Newcastle were both scoring the goals per game that a title-winning team needs, and the stats say we were OK defensively,' said Collymore. 'But when you look at the great sides – and let's take the current Liverpool under Jürgen Klopp as an example – there is something about them where they will score a couple of goals and you then get the feeling if they need to keep a clean sheet, they will. I never had that feeling playing for Liverpool. There was no confidence when we looked around that we could say to each other, "We are 1-0 up, can we defend for our lives for the next seventy minutes?" That is what undid us.

'The really classic example was the first Newcastle game at St James's Park earlier in the season. I have never played in a game at any level, whether at youth or senior, where one team was so dominant, yet we lost 2-1. After the game Roy and Ronnie Moran said, "If you keep playing like that you will not be far away." For me, it was odd. It said to the team we were going to win more than we were going to lose, but it was a back-slapping move. As opposed to teams who lose 2-1 who might have said, "That is not fucking good enough. We have come here, had 70 per cent of the ball and mullered them. We should not be getting beat." We should have been able to go places and play shit and win.'

This game shines because where most managers study the opponent and make plans to deal with obvious threats, it looks like Keegan and Evans backed their attackers to outscore the others. It means the most gifted players had space to thrive.

'I was thinking when I was out there, "Whoever's watching, it's one hell of a fucking game of football tonight,"' said Ferdinand. 'End to end, both teams committed to playing on the front foot.'

The speed and tone were set from the first minutes when Fowler scored with a brilliant downward header from Collymore's left-wing cross. Collymore's contribution is spectacular, dismissively evading Newcastle right-back Steve Watson's attempts at a diving tackle and comfortably shrugging off Beardsley before whipping the ball from the byline near the corner flag directly to his strike partner. 'I always knew where Robbie would be,' said Collymore. 'I knew if I put it into an area, he would get on the end of it.'

Fowler relished having a partner who could deliver from wide areas. 'I am not saying Stan was the best I played with, but he was the best partnership,' said Fowler. 'I got a lot more space because of him.'

Newcastle's immediate response was impressive, pressuring Liverpool's defenders on the edge of their penalty area and scoring twice before the quarter-hour mark to take a 2-1 lead. The pace was unrelenting. The defending was abject.

Asprilla's nimble footwork in the penalty area terrorized Neil Ruddock with a nutmeg in the build-up to Ferdinand's equalizer, and James's attempted save was poor. From a defensive perspective, everything was wrong. Asprilla should not have been allowed to make progress towards the byline to cross, and Ferdinand should have been prevented from turning and shooting by Mark Wright, who had lost his man near the 6-yard box and seemed off-balance. Even then, the shot was not powerful enough to beat a keeper of James's quality, albeit from close range.

Ferdinand was the creator of Newcastle's second, finding space near the centre circle to see and deliver a wonderful pass with the outside of his right foot. Not for the first time on the night, Liverpool's high defensive line was a mess.

Liverpool played a 3-5-2 pushing wing-backs into attacking areas. Evans had introduced it at the start of the 1994/95 season. The system became fashionable, with England adopting it for Euro 96. 'It was to accommodate three centre-backs, and because we had full-backs who wanted to attack and play more like wingers,' explained Barnes. 'Jason McAteer was a midfielder playing wing-back. That made us such an attacking team because, with an extra centre-back, we did not have any defensive midfielders. Jamie [Redknapp] and I were in the middle. It never necessarily worked for us defensively because we had defenders who were so narrow, so when the full-backs pushed on, our right- and left-sided centre-backs were uncomfortable being dragged into wide areas. That meant there was a lot of space to attack us out wide.'

Against David Ginola, that was asking for trouble. McAteer had a fine game going forward. I would imagine he never had a tougher evening defensively trying to stop the charismatic French winger. Ginola had an ability to receive the ball with a defender at his back and turn in a single movement, his balance and touch taking him away before the full-back could react. The danger was obvious in the first few minutes. The closer McAteer got to his back, the more vulnerable he was to being turned; holding off and allowing Ginola to turn without a challenge was even more of a risk, as he was able to face McAteer one-on-one and, so good with both feet, was capable of dribbling either side of his marker.

When Ferdinand sent Ginola through on the left, the issue with how Liverpool executed their formation was apparent. McAteer was out of position upfield, which may not have been so big a problem had one of the three centre-backs been close enough to the wing to cover for him. Instead, there was barely any distance between Liverpool's three centre-halves, all of them occupying positions in the middle you would expect in a flat back four rather than a 3-5-2. There were less than 10 yards between Wright, Ruddock and John Scales, the latter pair effectively side by side.

'There are different ways of playing a back three,' said Barnes. 'For it to work at its best, it has to be mobile. When England used it that summer, it was completely different. The two wide centre-backs were usually full-backs, Stuart Pearce and Gary Neville, with Steve McManaman and Darren Anderton on the wings.'

A full-back playing centre-back would be more instinctively aware of the threat of wide midfielders and be in a position to help his wing-back. McAteer had no such assistance when he made his error for the second goal. When Ginola received Ferdinand's pass, he faced no obstacle other than beating James, which he did easily in front of The Kop.

There was no sense of the visitors sitting back and protecting their lead as the chances kept coming, Newcastle the superior side until half-time. Barnes was fortunate not to concede a penalty to Asprilla and James made amends for his earlier mistake by saving from Beardsley.

One of James's most positive contributions came two minutes into the second half when Rob Lee should have extended Newcastle's lead, dashing from midfield as Liverpool's centre-backs were opened up again. Lee seemed to hesitate or lose confidence just as he came face to face with James in the centre of the penalty area, his shot too close to the goalkeeper. This was one of many moments which in normal circumstances you could describe as a game-changer. But there were so many in this match.

For all Newcastle's enduring threat, the dominant player in the second half was McManaman, the unorthodox playmaker at the heart of all Liverpool's best attacking work.

McManaman's position in that Liverpool team was unique, neither a winger, a number 10 nor a traditional attacking midfielder. He had a licence to be a bit of everything, the 3-5-2 system built to grant him freedom to roam. He would receive the ball in deep midfield areas and his first instinct was to dribble into the opposition half before he looked up in search of a cutting pass. I think his ability was underrated and underappreciated at Liverpool, opposing managers often designating a man-marker to shadow him.

'I agree,' said Fowler. 'He was phenomenal. He does not get the recognition and adulation he deserves. He glided effortlessly past people and he was one of those players who was actually quicker running with the ball. He would go past players like they were not there. I got a lot of praise because of my goals, but Stevie was unbelievable that year.'

To illustrate my point about how and why some players catch the imagination of their fan base more than others, Liverpool's supporters do not idolize McManaman in the way Newcastle's do Ginola. That can only be a consequence of the image surrounding the mid-nineties team, and the manner of McManaman's departure three years later.

McManaman won the FA Cup and League Cup with Liverpool and went on to win two La Liga titles and two Champions Leagues at Real Madrid, making him the most successful overseas English player. The Kop, unaccustomed to seeing one of their home-grown graduates seek a move away from Anfield, held that against him because when his contract expired, his exit on a free transfer cost Liverpool millions. It means McManaman is categorized a little like Michael Owen, who followed him to Spain for a fraction of his value, albeit Michael gets more stick because he ended up playing in Manchester for United rather than City.

McManaman never suffered the abuse Michael got, but his career seems to be looked upon lukewarmly by Liverpool supporters. That is equally wrong given how good he was for seven years, an academy product who cost nothing and who represented a sense of hope during a difficult period when the big-money signings were not delivering anywhere near as much. It has always angered me when players who joined Liverpool for big money and who contributed much less than the home-grown players who were lured to Europe's biggest clubs receive tremendous ovations from Anfield on their return compared to the ambivalent or hostile reception given those who did more in a red shirt.

McManaman was at his peak for this match, his understanding with Fowler leading to the equalizer ten minutes into the second half. As with Fowler's first, the build-up play is sensational, with McAteer picking out McManaman, who was free on Liverpool's right. In keeping with the night, with one pass McManaman was in position to face Newcastle centre-back Philippe Albert in an area on the wing where you would expect him to be crowded out by the left-back John Beresford and a wide midfielder. After a few shuffles he paused and picked out Fowler, whose first-time finish, placing the ball with the outside of his left foot past Pavel Srníček, was breathtaking.

By now, the defending from both teams had become a horror show.

Newcastle regained the lead two minutes later, their third typical of how easy it was for the teams to cut through each other. Beardsley was in his own half but bypassed Liverpool midfielders with no more than a 6-yard pass to Lee, who sent Asprilla beyond a misshapen backline in which Steve Harkness, a half-time substitute for Mark Wright, was trying to play offside as Scales hung back. Asprilla's finish was made easier by the onrushing James, who because he was outside his penalty area opted to try to make a save with his head. That bizarre image summed up the haphazard period of play.

There could have been five goals in the first fifteen minutes of the second half, Barnes shaking his head at the sense of disorder which was thrilling to watch but exasperating to play in. 'I remember speaking to Rob Lee as the game was going on: "All we're doing here is running up and down." Newcastle would attack so I would run back to try and help the defence. Then our front five would pick it up and run to the other end so Lee and David Batty were running back. By the time we got there, either someone had scored, or it had been played back up front. It was like a basketball game because it was all happening so quickly. A nightmare.'

During the final half-hour there was momentum in one direction, Liverpool's chances more frequent. McAteer was prominent as an attacking force, his right-wing deliveries especially effective with Beresford in a lone battle to stop him. That source fed Collymore for the 68th-minute equalizer, Newcastle's inability to monitor the striker's positioning on the left proving their downfall.

Liverpool's attacking duo were worth fifty-five goals that season, Collymore's ability to drift wide continually providing the service for Fowler. That may have been a happy accident rather than a preconceived plan given that when Collymore signed he was initially paired with Rush; Fowler began that season as the back-up. 'I knew I would have to adapt to the Liverpool style, and they would have to adapt to me, which is fair enough, but I didn't realize how much,' explained Collymore. 'In my first game against Sheffield Wednesday, even though I scored the winner, I have to be honest and say I did not see the ball for sixty minutes. The vast amount of ball I would get at Forest, over the top, getting the ball to me quickly on the half turn and running at people, was Steve McManaman's role. I had to adapt my game because I was not the primary goalscorer any more, and I was seeing less of the ball than at Forest. I had to move left and right and find different spaces far more. So the relationship with Robbie had to develop. By the end of the season I had fifteen assists and nineteen goals. As a strike partnership it was "A" grade. What helped is I played as a wide man in the reserves when I was at Crystal Palace at the start of my career. When I made my debut for Palace, I was the tallest winger in football.'

Newcastle's selection made them especially vulnerable on the left because Beardsley, who spent his entire career as a deep striker, played an unfamiliar right midfield position to accommodate Asprilla.

Asprilla's role in the title run-in proved divisive, not because anyone doubted the quality of the Colombian, but because his arrival from Parma two months earlier for £6.7 million coincided with Newcastle's worst run of results. Keegan's men were flying with Gillespie and Ginola as wingers and there did not appear to be any creativity or goalscoring issues, so there are those who still query why Keegan made such a major signing.

'We lost a game at Arsenal in the League Cup in January and I will never forget Kevin came in and ranted at us,' Ferdinand recalled. 'Everything went quiet and everyone was still sitting there, and I thought, "Well, tell you what, someone's got to make a move," so I got up and I walked into the shower. Kevin followed me in and said, "I know what's happened here. We're expecting you to score a goal every game. They're putting too much pressure on you so I'm gonna get someone to help you." That was the first talk I heard about him getting another centre-forward. The next week there was talk about Asprilla coming in, but then after the first talks it looked like it was not going to happen. He went back to Italy. Then all of a sudden it was resurrected.'

Batty also signed from Blackburn for £3.75 million in February 1996, which shows Keegan was aware of the need to add defensive balance to his midfield having reinforced his attack.

The issue in the closing stages at Anfield is not so much that Asprilla was in the side. He was magnificent. It was more significant that Gillespie was out, an unused substitute that night. The lack of a right-sided midfielder with the awareness to watch and stop Collymore was fatal.

'Gillespie was injured in December so was out of the team for a while, so Kevin moved Peter [Beardsley] to the right,' Ferdinand recalled. 'As good a professional as Peter was, he was never going to be disciplined to play the role like Keith. He naturally got sucked into playing in the middle. When you watch the game there are times when I am playing in the right-back position because we had a void down that side. That was where the balance changed. In the early part of the season, I don't think I ever saw our 18-yard box other than when I had to go back for a corner. I never had to get back over the halfway line. When Asprilla came in, my natural instinct was to try and help in that situation. So I think the imbalance was moving Peter out there. I remember talking to Liverpool players after the game and they said they knew they were going to have situations where they were one-on-one with our full-backs.'

Liverpool's last two goals can be attributed to this, especially when

Rush's introduction for wing-back Rob Jones meant Collymore ended the game as an out-and-out left-winger.

Collymore's injury-time winner is one of the most replayed goals in Premier League history. It is also one of the most underrated. Amid so much focus on the drama of the moment and what it meant for the title race, the quality of the goal itself has been overlooked.

Watch again that calm, composed exchange of passes between Barnes and Rush on the edge of the Newcastle United penalty area, while Collymore cleverly loiters on the left, waiting to pounce. No Newcastle player is near him. Beardsley is not even in the picture, which underlines Ferdinand's point about the loss of balance, although he winces at his own role. Having been denied by James when he could have made it 4-3, Ferdinand feels he could have done more to stop the build-up to the winner.

'If you look at the start of it, I closed John Scales on the wrong side, allowing him to come into the pitch,' he said. 'If I had arced my run, I would have made him go backwards. Instead, I forced him into going in midfield with the ball and running, which meant he could give it to Barnes who ran on from there. You look back on that as a player. As much as everyone says it was a great game, you never think it was great when you have lost it.'

Barnes says that he found himself so far up the pitch in a last-ditch attempt to contribute in attack. 'The one-two with Rushie is probably the first time I got forward. Stan's goal came from me being frustrated because I was running up and down and not getting the ball, so I thought, "I am going to have to do something here." I wanted to feel involved. Newcastle were organized going forward but at the back, like us that night, they were a shambles.'

Unmarked, Collymore took control with an exquisite first touch before unleashing a vicious shot, beating Srníček at his near post.

It looked like he had shifted the momentum in the title race. He had. Liverpool defeated Newcastle in a classic game, but Manchester United ultimately won.

'I would have traded that goal for an FA Cup win, League Cup or the Cup Winners' Cup, when we lost finals and semis,' said Collymore. 'As a player you want to compete for things, and we did. But we always fell away.'

Was this really where it ended for Newcastle?

'There are particular games in a season, particular points in a season, where if you win, it pushes you on,' says Ferdinand. 'I think if we'd have won that game, we would've gone on and won the title. I was convinced of that. I think losing that game in the way that we did kind of knocked the stuffing out of us. We went to Blackburn the weekend after and lost in exactly the same way, ahead until the closing stages and then losing to a last-minute goal. The feeling was starting to creep in where, after we were getting a bit of the rub of the green in the early part of the season, that had now abandoned us and too many of us lost form at the wrong time.'

If the Liverpool defeat offered a convenient cover story for those presenting Newcastle as stumblers under pressure, Keegan's demeanour, starting with him forlornly draped over an advertising board at Anfield as Collymore celebrated in front of The Kop, fuelled it.

When Alex Ferguson suggested some clubs were trying harder against Manchester United than Newcastle, Keegan reacted. 'I've kept really quiet, but I'll tell you something, he went down in my estimation when he said that,' he said. 'We have not resorted to that. You can tell him now: we're still fighting for this title. And I'll tell you, honestly, I will love it if we beat them. Love it.'

Keegan's emotion showed what pressure can do, even to a manager accustomed to winning titles and European Cups as a player. Ferguson helped tip Keegan over the edge, feeding the idea of him winning the managerial 'mind games', but the damage was done two months before that public feud.

'It was more the pressure inside Newcastle than what Ferguson was pushing,' said Martin Hardy. 'The pressure was cranked up so much and they didn't know how to handle it. When you haven't been there, you have no experience. In the dressing room, only Peter Beardsley and then David Batty had been through that situation. In the same way, the city didn't know how to react either. There was a bit of naivety. The amount of pressure that was inside the city was phenomenal and Kevin carried all that, so when you see him slumped, I still find that quite a sad image.

'The Liverpool game was like Marvin Hagler v. Thomas Hearns, punch after punch after punch after punch until someone got knocked out. Terry McDermott said something changed in Kevin that night. Maybe it was the idealism that was knocked out of him.'

What could have been a bold first title bid ahead of a fresh assault the following season proved the highlight of Keegan's reign. There was no reason it should have been, given that he added Manchester United's number one target, Alan Shearer, for a world record £15 million from Blackburn in July 1996.

There were echoes of Liverpool's nineties issues with that deal, what seemed the solution to one problem leading to unforeseen others. While welcoming Shearer's arrival, there were implications for Ferdinand as Keegan left him in no doubt who the senior partner would be in their relationship. 'Kevin told me Shearer had asked for my number 9 shirt,' said Ferdinand. 'He said the reason he asked was because he had worn the number 9 all his life. I said, "Well, I've worn the number 9 all my life." Kevin also said the number never bothered him during his career, which I might have believed but for the fact he had a chain around his neck with the number 7 he wore at all his clubs on it.

'I never had a problem with Alan, and he thanked me for it. But when I asked for the number 23 because I was a Michael Jordan fan, the board said I had to have between 1 and 11. I was like, "Are you taking the fucking piss? You took a number between 1 and 11 off me." Then they sold Lee Clark to Sunderland, so that's the only reason I ended up in the number 10.'

Shearer's arrival did not elevate Newcastle to the next level and Keegan quit in January 1997 suggesting he had 'taken the club as far as he can'. Newcastle have never challenged for the title, or even threatened to, since. That is why Newcastle fans look back so wistfully on this time, craving the return of those days.

So much around this game chimes with the era – the Premier League in its infancy and the broadcasters thirsting for fixtures to match the hype surrounding English football, especially in the build-up to a major international tournament on home soil. When we say Liverpool v. Newcastle was one of the greatest Premier League games, what we really mean is it was one of the greatest to have been screened live, with all the razzmatazz that came with it, the spectacle and drama aligning with the fact that it had a major influence on the title's destiny. This level of entertainment was precisely why Sky paid so much for the rights to English football in 1992, and why they have continued to do so ever since. This is where they could see that investment paying dividends, especially as such games attracted a global following, and more overseas talent was enticed to England by the style and rewards on offer.

'This game typified exactly what the Premier League was originally set up and designed to do,' said Andy Gray, one of the broadcasting pioneers at the league's conception. 'We wanted the cream of world football watching and then joining the cream of British football. With that, it brought a level of professionalism that we hadn't really seen in the old First Division and the foreign influence – more foreign players and more foreign coaches.'

Liverpool v. Newcastle demonstrated why English football was more marketable and a lure for sponsors and, dare one say it, fashion designers wanting to be associated with the brand.

At Anfield, where The Kop still clings to the Shankly values, it was inevitable that adaptation would not be entirely comfortable. As my conversations with the Liverpool players of that time indicate, there is wariness and weariness when they look back. Teams that won nothing and competed less frequently are respected more than those in the mid-nineties.

Collymore, James, Phil Babb, Ruddock and McAteer certainly come into that category, given they were either sold or dropped over the coming seasons. It makes the question about any regrets they have pertinent, but not as easy to answer as some presume. Collymore accepts his Anfield career is thought unsuccessful while those who achieved no more or less at Newcastle under Keegan, or at Leeds when they challenged for the title and made the latter stages of the Champions League at the start of the millennium, are spoken about warmly during regular nostalgia trips.

'In Liverpool, the bar is set high,' he said. 'The day after we lost to Manchester United in the FA Cup final we actually had a bus parade and people still turned up. There was one bloke standing on the side of the street who had a banner which said "Fuck off, you lot are a disgrace". With that, you see the difference between Liverpool, Manchester United, maybe Arsenal, and other clubs in England. But do you know what, Jamie? I would rather stick my neck out and play for a club of Liverpool's size, know what it feels like and be deemed a failure, than succeed at a club where you did not have that same level of pressure and expectation every single day.

'I do not mean this as disrespect to Alan Shearer, but there is a difference going from Southend to Forest and Liverpool, than from Southampton to Blackburn to Newcastle. Even at Nottingham Forest the expectations were very high because the memories of winning two European Cups were still fresh in the early 1990s. You had to live up to the standards set by Cloughie's great side. At Liverpool it is another level completely. I would rather try to live up to that pedigree and have that pressure. I would rather just miss out chasing the ghosts of Shankly, Paisley, Dalglish and Rush than win the Premier League backed by a shitload of money where you are following Simon Garner [Blackburn's record goalscorer].

'One day someone will come along and create a new club, with no history, no supporters but lots of money where the best players in the world play in a completely synthetic environment and win the title. As a player, you tell me where is the value in being part of that? If you do it wearing the shirt of a striker who has not played since before the Second World War, rather than the weight of the pressure of wearing Roger Hunt's number 8 jersey? It really means something to play for and have played for Liverpool. Manchester City's players are great, serial winners, but does it mean more winning with a quarter-empty stadium, or what those Liverpool players have experienced under Klopp playing in front of those fans, knowing you have walked the path of Dalglish or Rush? For me, it is a no-brainer.'

I have often asked myself what I would have been like had I been a little older, broken into the Liverpool side a couple of years sooner, and found myself in the situation of those players, especially in the build-up to the 1996 FA Cup final. As a teenager trying to fit into the dressing room I would have had no choice but to go along with what everyone wanted. By the time I was a senior pro I could be more emphatic. There is no way Steven Gerrard or I would have even considered turning up for a cup final in anything but a traditional dark suit. And there is no way Houllier or Benítez would have allowed it.

Why does it matter so much? Because the incident presents an open goal for those wishing to portray players as losing touch with the culture of their club and its working-class fan base, adding more pressure than is needed. As an experienced player, you learn to think ahead, imagining the consequences of all outcomes.

If you wear cream suits before an FA Cup final, you have to win. Losing unnecessarily increases the chances you are still going to be asked about it for the next thirty years.

'We didn't see it,' said Collymore. 'We just thought we looked cool as fuck. We thought we were being cutting-edge. Then Fergie says he knew as soon as he saw us they would win because we were not taking it seriously enough. The reality of that is it is absurd, but when the opposition manager is able to use something like that with his own players and say to them "That lot have turned up here looking like a fucking jazz band", these little things make a difference. Then it takes on a life of its own.'

I witnessed the growing sense of disconnection between players and supporters as Roy Evans tried to take the next steps. A week after my Liverpool debut in 1997 we suffered another significant FA Cup defeat, knocked out 3-2 by Chelsea at Stamford Bridge having been two up at half-time. I was on the bench for the next game at Derby County, where a group of disenchanted Liverpool supporters turned up at the hotel wearing T-shirts with a message.

'Loadsamoney, no medals', they read.

Was it fair the players were mocked in that way? No, but the scars were self-inflicted.

Evans would later react to accusations that Liverpool lacked physicality and drive by replacing Barnes with Paul Ince. As with Collymore's signing two years earlier, no sooner had one piece of the jigsaw slotted in than a final piece was missing elsewhere.

'When people looked for excuses they came up with the idea we were a physically soft team,' said Barnes. 'A physically soft team with Neil Ruddock and Mark Wright at centre-back? Come on. So then they said we did not have enough steel in midfield, which worked against me. Eventually I was made a scapegoat. There was more to it than that. Incey came and nothing changed. That Liverpool side had as much quality as any I played with, not the mentality, and that Newcastle game epitomized it. We won and thought we were going to win the league. What happened? We lost the next game against Coventry City.'

Liverpool finished fourth, third, fourth and third in successive years under Evans. His Liverpool came close. Very close. As this season proved, close is acceptable at most clubs. Close makes you a legend at Newcastle United.

Close is nowhere near enough at Liverpool Football Club.

9

Sunday, 13 May 2012

2011/12 FA PREMIER LEAGUE
The Etihad Stadium

MANCHESTER CITY 3 – 2 QPR

Zabaleta *39*	Cissé *48*
Džeko *90+2*	Mackie *66*
Agüero *90+4*	

'It was like waking from surgery'
— *Vincent Kompany*

THERE ARE TIMES DURING THE greatest games when you can feel rising tension. You could distinctly hear it inside the Etihad Stadium on the afternoon of 13 May 2012 – an incessant murmur of pain from the stands as Manchester City took hold of, fumbled and finally grabbed the Premier League title.

'Ninety-three minutes of suffering' was how Vincent Kompany described it to me. That sounds a downbeat recollection of the day which irreversibly changed the history of the club he skippered.

Kompany was responding to the question I asked in the introduction of this book, which I put to many interviewees: 'Have you ever rewatched your greatest game in its entirety?'

'No,' he said. 'I will watch the moments. Never the full game. It still comes back as a nightmare, even though I know there is an unbelievable ending.'

I appreciate Vincent's eagerness to skip the prolonged periods of despondency as City toed the cliff edge before overcoming Queens Park Rangers, instead editing and fast-forwarding to what is generally known as 'the Agüero moment' in added time.

It trivializes Sergio Agüero's goal to say it won a football match. It may even do so to say it secured a league title. But certainly the Argentinian changed how we think about the club. There is the perception of Manchester City before Agüero shot at QPR keeper Paddy Kenny, and the Manchester City we have become accustomed to since.

The collective anguish in the minutes preceding Agüero's momentous strike still makes for harrowing viewing and listening. The more the camera panned on the crowd, the greater the torment. Supporters were appealing for rather than encouraging City's forty-four goal attempts, wailing in despair when moves broke down, pleading with accelerating desperation for positivity. With each of QPR's fifty-seven defensive clearances, City's fans' spirit sapped. When Jamie Mackie headed QPR 2-1 up in the 66th minute, some fans were in tears. One was shown frantically kicking his seat in exasperation as the latest City attack fizzled out. The majority stood in a tortured trance, arms folded, as if morbidly enduring their ordeal through loyalty to the badge rather than faith that the situation would be salvaged.

I do not believe I have seen defeatism envelop a stadium or manager so prematurely.

At its most theatrical, this fatalism infected manager Roberto Mancini, who rather than provide a calming, reassuring presence on the touchline reacted to QPR's second goal by rushing from his bench, pointing at several of his players and shouting 'Fuck you, fuck you and fuck you' at whomever he deemed fit to berate. This went way beyond anxiety or panic. This was an extreme, communal psychological implosion.

Even when accounting for the prize on the line, in most cases a home side finding itself one goal down against a relegation-threatened opponent reduced to ten men for over half an hour recognizes there is enough time to react. How could a team with so much in its favour find itself in the grip of such institutionalized dread?

There are certain clubs whose belief is culturally embedded because they can lean on days when the cruellest setbacks proved temporary rather than terminal; for them, a dire situation is an obstacle to overcome rather than a signal to surrender. There are others so accustomed to fiasco, it is as if they need to learn that the art of winning involves dealing with mishaps. Until then, they can never escape their cycle of gloom.

Even at the gateway to glory, with all their class players, the likelihood that they were here to stay challenging at the top of English football under the world's wealthiest owners, and having taken the significant first step of winning the 2011 FA Cup, Manchester City needed to unload the weight of past misfortunes.

'The fans had a feeling that anything that could go wrong for the club, would,' Joe Royle, the former City striker and manager, explained to me. 'When you thought it could not get any worse, it did. And when something was going well, it would not last.'

He coined a colourful phrase for this variation on what we generally know as 'Sod's Law'. 'I called it Cityitis,' he said. 'I noticed it when I was a City player. There was a kind of pessimism around, where if we were 3-0 up the fans would say, "Get one more and we will be safe." Rodney Marsh used to say there was no club better at making a sow's ear out of a silk purse.'

Royle's funny and astute observation was as informative as it got as to why, aside from the obvious and understandable fear of surrendering the first chance of a league title in forty-four years to rivals Manchester United, the fans became so distraught, so soon.

When Royle became manager in February 1998, Manchester City had been relegated from the Premier League and were fighting against dropping into what is now called League One, the third tier of English football. Royle was well acquainted with a legacy of melancholy. 'Before I got back there as manager, there was the famous game in 1996 when the lads were keeping the ball at the corner flag thinking they were safe from relegation by drawing 2-2 with Liverpool on the final day of the Premier League season,' he said, working his way through an extensive list of meltdowns.

As Steve Lomas kept the ball from a Liverpool side uninterested as they looked ahead to participating in the following week's FA Cup final, a frantic Niall Quinn, subbed earlier in the game, rushed down the touchline to tell teammates they had to score again. City went down on goal difference by playing for a draw in a game they had to win.

Four months into his job, Royle was close to ensuring City did not descend further. Winning their penultimate game against direct rivals in their relegation struggle would have kept them up, but they drew 2-2 after a farcical own-goal by midfielder Jamie Pollock. Pollock beat his goalkeeper, Martyn Margetson, having skilfully lobbed the ball over striker Mike Sheron and perfectly placed a header which arced beyond the advancing number 1 – a goal that was somehow both sublime and ridiculous.

The opponents that day at Maine Road? QPR. City won their final game 5-2 at Stoke City, but it was not enough. Royle's side dropped into the third tier of the Football League, Division Two, a point behind the Londoners.

'There were so many examples of hard luck stories,' said Royle. 'There was a game against Liverpool when we were both going for the title in 1977. I scored to put us 1-0 up, and we were looking comfortable. Then Dave Watson scored an own-goal, heading past Joe Corrigan in the 89th minute. We lost the title to Liverpool by one point.'

While I was well aware of some of the worst modern cases of Cityitis, others were so absurd they needed fact-checking. In 1989, City were a win from guaranteeing promotion to England's top flight, leading Bournemouth 3-0 in their penultimate game. Manager Mel Machin thought he would relax his players by asking comedian and City fan Eddie Large to conduct the half-time team talk by impersonating Deputy Dawg, Frank Carson and Cliff Richard. The game ended 3-3, City fortunate to go up a week later with an 86th-minute equalizer by Trevor Morley at Bradford City.

Even the most celebrated honours were accompanied by rueful perspectives under the tagline 'Typical City'. Manchester City won the FA Cup in 1956; Manchester United went one better and won the English title. Manchester City won the English title in 1968; Manchester United went one better eighteen days later and became the first English side to win the European Cup.

Among City's most dubious records is being the sole top-flight champions to be relegated a year later, which the club somehow managed in 1938 despite scoring eighty times – the only occasion in English history a side has gone down as the division's leading scorers.

Rather than seeing Royle's 'Cityitis' branding in derogatory terms, in the late nineties City fans embraced it as a form of gallows humour, especially as they dropped down divisions while their neighbours at Old Trafford dominated English football and pursued the Champions League.

'City fans adopted a song which they began singing at places like Port Vale and York City during our time in Division Two,' said Royle. 'Wherever we played you would hear them singing "We're not really here". There was a kind of "this really can't be happening" idea. The fans still sing it now. I think it is a reminder of what they went through, and there is a real sense of pride at how they stuck by the team and their club through it all.'

The Division Two play-off final of 1999 was the first step up the leagues under Royle, the comeback win against Gillingham often cited alongside the 2012 title in the list of the club's greatest moments. City were two down in the 90th minute when Kevin Horlock and Paul Dickov sent the game into extra-time, Royle's side winning the penalty shoot-out to get back into Division One (now the Championship). A year later they were promoted into the Premier League.

'After the Gillingham game, I thought that broke the ice,' said Royle.

Off the pitch, spectacular reversals in fortune could be traced earlier, to November 1995, when Manchester was awarded the 2002 Commonwealth Games. Host venue City of Manchester Stadium was subsequently leased to the club by Manchester City Council, providing the sky blue half of the region a ready-made 50,000-capacity venue. That made City attractive to overseas investors eager to buy into English football, so although there was one more Premier League relegation and promotion in the early noughties, the first global takeover of the club by former Thai prime minister Thaksin Shinawatra in 2007 offered hope for a more stable future – initially at least. Sven Göran-Eriksson's first job upon leaving as England coach was at City, between 2007 and 2008.

The club established itself as a mid-table Premier League side, dreaming of breaking into the top six, but there was no sense of threat to our top-four status whenever Liverpool played City. During that time, I saw them as a club which might recruit stars already past their peak, such as Steve McManaman following his departure from Real Madrid. If City unearthed a gem from their academy he was likely to look elsewhere to fulfil ambitions to play in the Champions League, as proved the case with Shaun Wright-Phillips moving to Chelsea in 2005. There was no hint of a reawakening as a major force in English football, although Vincent Kompany saw unfulfilled potential.

'I did not need convincing to go to City,' Kompany recalled. 'I had an issue with the president at my club Hamburg surrounding my involve-ment in the 2008 Olympics, and I told him I was desperate to move. Literally, the first bid was Man City. City had some great players around that time Nicolas Anelka, Robbie Fowler – and they had some veteran superstars, if you like. The manager was Mark Hughes then, and when I met him, I had a good feeling.'

Kompany signed on 22 August 2008. His timing was as impeccable as one of his best tackles. Nine days later Sheikh Mansour bin Zayed Al Nahyan's Abu Dhabi Group shook up the Premier League and the sporting world, purchasing the club on 1 September.

This was English football's greatest lottery win, eclipsing Roman Abramovich's Chelsea buyout five years earlier. Many will argue that this, not Agüero's goal in 2012, was the real game-changer. Money laid the foundation and made success possible – some might say inevitable – but the cultural transformation from aspirational wannabes constantly fearing the worst to proven winners anticipating the best would take time. It always needs more than the signing of cheques.

Brian Marwood, managing director of City Football Group, joined in 2009, initially under the title 'football administrator' – effectively the Director of Football overseeing transfer activity. 'Positions of that kind are the norm now,' he told me. 'In English football back then, it was akin to being a tax collector or traffic warden. The industry has matured and changed.' He was convinced to leave his sports marketing job at Nike after meeting City chairman Khaldoon Al Mubarak, sure that the

Premier League was about to experience a powershift. 'When I heard his vision, not just with football but the city of Manchester, and the whole structure of the club, I was blown away. You are always sceptical because at that time there were a lot of clubs who had gone through difficult times with foreign owners. The sense of expectation on the pitch was always there, but this ran deeper.'

City's transfer statements became progressively louder, Sir Alex Ferguson famously dubbing them 'the noisy neighbours' when Carlos Tevez crossed the Manchester divide in 2009, part of a £100 million spree that added Gareth Barry, Joleon Lescott and Kolo Touré.

'In those early years we still felt we were far away behind United,' said Marwood. 'I used to work between three sites: the Platt Lane Academy complex, the former training ground at Carrington and the office at the stadium. I would make a point of trying to drive past Old Trafford because I saw it as a statue to success. It was a daily reminder of how much we had to improve; a personal motivation for how we were going to get closer to this amazing club which had done so much in English, European and global football.

'People forget now, but we were getting ridiculed. People were saying they had seen these kinds of projects before and it would all end in tears. Then Sir Alex came out with that famous quote and it fuelled us more.'

I wanted to know how the United players felt about this growing rivalry, which in the past had been a parochial squabble rather than about league titles. 'The "Welcome to Manchester" poster!' Wayne Rooney immediately reacted. (City announced Tevez's signing with a prominent display for those arriving into the city.) 'I thought it was more the diehard fans calling them "cheeky bastards" than the players. The way I saw the Tevez deal, it was Man United's fault. We should have signed Tevez on a permanent deal when we had the chance. What was it, £20 million? There seemed to be issues with his agent, but you could not allow a player like Tevez, at his peak, to go to your rival. He was a brilliant player. He was massive for them, and there were games he dragged City through. He was on a mission. I think the goals he scored at the end helped win them the league, didn't they? So, I suppose it was karma.

'Until then, I never felt the Manchester derby was the same as the Merseyside derby. I still think the big game for United fans is always Liverpool, but that was especially true during my first six or seven years I was at United because City were not really doing anything. For me, the derbies were big, but not the same as Liverpool v. Everton or United v. Liverpool.'

In 2010, City completed two of their most important deals. Yaya Touré joined from Barcelona and David Silva, one of my favourite Premier League footballers, from Valencia.

'David nearly didn't happen,' Marwood told me. 'We initially wanted Yoann Gourcuff, a player we were watching who had done really well at Bordeaux and broken into the France team. We did not know David was available. Then Valencia had financial issues and we heard they were open to selling. We had a comprehensive dossier on David and knew he was the one. We took a tremendous amount of criticism for spending £24 million on him, then for paying so much for Yaya, who was twenty-seven by then. But we were playing catch-up. We had to invest and sometimes pay more than other clubs were prepared to, in order to convince them to come to Manchester City and prove we were true to our word about competing at the highest level.'

Mancini's appointment helped, the Italian replacing Hughes in December 2009. He had won three league titles with Inter Milan. 'There was a feeling we needed European experience and knowledge and tactics,' said Marwood. 'Roberto was available and he intrigued us. He had been successful working at a big club, and he had discipline. I do not think it is a secret we did not see eye to eye on many things. He rocked the boat and was ready to upset people, but that is what the club needed at the time. He pushed everyone to their limits, and that was what it was all about for getting to the next level.'

Under Mancini, City did not strike me as a flamboyant side. Playing against them, I always felt it was individual quality that might overwhelm you. What Mancini introduced was structure and balance at both ends of the pitch.

'Mancini gave me an unbelievable understanding of defensive duties,' said Kompany. 'I really enjoyed defending under him. We became a band of brothers as a defensive unit, determined to keep clean sheets. What I would say, it was not as detailed as it became later under Pep [Guardiola]. We played on the natural strength of the top-class players we had. We were not a machine yet. Far from it.'

City closed the gap on the pitch in stages, securing Champions League qualification in the same week they won the 2011 FA Cup, their first major trophy since the League Cup in 1976. Heading into the following season, they were ready, the statistics showing they excelled in attack and defence in 2011/12. Mancini's side scored ninety-three, more than any other side that year, and conceded the fewest, just twenty-nine. When they defeated Norwich City 5-1 on 3 December, City had scored three or more in eleven of their first fourteen games, winning twelve and drawing two. Strangely, they had failed to keep a clean sheet in eleven of those fixtures, a trend reversed as the season progressed.

The classic spine of Mancini's title-winning team was in place, with England number one Joe Hart, Kompany, by now emerging as one of the Premier League's best-ever centre-backs, the creative and physical midfield power and skill of Touré – free to express himself, complemented by the more disciplined Gareth Barry – and the lethal Agüero.

Agüero's arrival from Atlético Madrid for £35 million in the summer of 2011 was the final piece, taking the strike force up several notches. He, Edin Džeko and the maverick Mario Balotelli contributed fifty Premier League goals in that campaign, their most spectacular combination coming in their first Premier League Manchester derby together. The trio scored five between them in a 6-1 win at Old Trafford – the most emphatic of City's early statements of intent.

'I would always say the change in mentality happened the previous year when we beat Manchester United at Wembley in the FA Cup semi-final,' said Kompany. 'That was a really massive moment. We had so much respect for Sir Alex Ferguson, and I looked at players like Rio Ferdinand and all the big names they had and knew how good we had to be to beat them. They were a really strong United side. To get through that, we knew something was changing. I always think of that as the first time we could say to the fans, "It is not going to be a 'Typical City' any more." The 6-1 win at Old Trafford I see more in isolation. To the fans, that felt like winning a trophy mid-season, but I do think we had already sent a positive message about what we were capable of.'

Marwood thinks another cup tie with United, in January 2010, was as significant. 'We narrowly lost in the League Cup semi-final over two legs, but we beat them in the home game. It was that night that I felt a change,' he said. 'I was looking out of the window from my office at the stadium and there was such a buzz. Until then, people were struggling to believe that we could get to that highest level. It is hard for people to believe until they have experiences of those moments in time. The place was rammed from four p.m. You could sense people thinking, "This is what it could be like." That was a milestone. We lost the tie, but it felt like we were growing up. The green shoots were there.'

City still had to overcome the capacity for making life more difficult than necessary, though. In the midst of their title bid, Tevez did not feature for City between 27 September and 21 March after being placed on 'gardening leave' for failing to come on as a substitute in a Champions League tie at Bayern Munich. Initially the spat with Mancini did not derail their challenge, but by the time Tevez returned, United led by a point. By 8 April, when City lost 1-0 at Arsenal, that had extended to eight, most pundits declaring the title race over. 'The end is nigh for Mancini's men' read the headline in the *Manchester Evening News*, the early drafts of the season review now focusing on the self-destructive tendencies of Balotelli, sent off in the defeat at the Emirates, and whether City's manager had over-indulged the erratic Italian.

Marwood and chairman Khaldoon headed for the dressing room post-match to try to lift spirits. 'I saw my job as supporting the people we had put in place,' said Marwood. 'I wanted to reassure people, the players and staff – don't worry. You could see they were deflated and could see it slipping away. The chairman sat Roberto down. The manager was very emotional and was upset. The chairman said do not worry, stay calm and do the right things. "What do you need, what can we do to help?" We felt it was not a time for divisions. A change of direction followed that game.'

Had City not won the league that season, I have no doubt Tevez's and Balotelli's roles would have been written into the club's self-sabotage chronicle.

Instead, it was United who choked in their final six games. 'What made the biggest difference was after being eight points clear we drew 4-4 with Everton when we were winning 4-2 with a few minutes to go,' said Rooney. 'And we lost to Wigan and at City away. In four games over nineteen days we got four points from twelve. That cost us.' Most pertinent was City's 1-0 win at the Etihad thanks to Kompany's 45th-minute header. That meant that by the final day, superior goal difference put the title back in City's hands.

'To be honest, we all thought City would smash QPR,' Rooney recalled.

City's long-suffering supporters evidently still needed convincing. 'Everything was nervous that day, nothing was normal,' said Kompany. 'You know yourself that what you want as a player, even when you know it is a big game, is normality. Come in, do the job you have done all season, no problem, and take care of business. As soon as we got to the stadium, everything felt different. You sensed it, even when the people were welcoming you. It was a different atmosphere.'

Studying the match programme, City may have been tentatively encouraged by the familiar faces in the QPR line-up. As well as ex-manager Hughes and coach Eddie Niedzwiecki, their squad included former City idol Wright-Phillips, ex-midfielder Joey Barton and Academy graduate Nedum Onuoha. Reserve keeper Brian Murphy was another ex-City trainee. But QPR could not allow themselves to be guests at a title party. They needed a point to guarantee Premier League survival, otherwise they would go down if Bolton Wanderers beat Stoke City.

The only way QPR saw themselves getting anything from the game was by playing defensively, and although statistics can sometimes deceive, they did not that afternoon. City had 938 touches of the ball (seventy-six of which were in the opposition penalty area) compared to QPR's 375, and had 81.3 per cent possession – the fourth-highest since Premier League records were kept.

I played in many games like this for Liverpool and England, part of a defence with no defending to do for eighty-nine, even ninety minutes, facing a side which would not yield to countless attacks.

I absolutely hated them.

No matter how accustomed to it you were and how much you knew what might happen without an early goal, you could always fall into the same trap.

Clarity of task in a well-organized defence means the experience is uncomplicated in endurance mode. You know your job, appreciating all help received blocking any gaps, generally with four orthodox defenders, four midfielders operating in their own half, and at least one striker dedicated to closing down the opposition midfielders, seeing counter-attacking as a bonus. When you are in the team dominating the ball but failing to create chances, one of the greatest threats is demoralization, which leads to other problems affecting concentration.

Because the attacking balance is so one-sided, everyone watching presumes that victory for those pushing forward should be a formality, and is usually critical if dominance in possession is not quickly reflected in the score. All they see is the side failing to get through 'not playing well', using a series of negative images to explain their attacking shortcomings: they are too impatient, lack imagination, need to increase the tempo, or require the manager to rethink the formation. When a side dominates but fails to score, the post-match conclusion is always the same.

'They played shit today.'

On the flipside, a team in a rearguard action is described as 'brave' and 'heroic' for their stubbornness and success in implementing a one-dimensional plan.

All that might end up being true, but when you take on any well-coached team with a reasonable skill level which is demonstrating zero attacking ambition, it should not be ignored how tactically problematic it is for the only team proactively trying to score. I am amazed how often it is. The defending side feeds on the growing exasperation, recognizing that urgency and desperation might eventually affect decision-making.

Sometimes, being the dominant home side in these situations can be a hindrance. So much of City v. QPR reminds me of Liverpool's home game with Chelsea towards the end of the 2013/14 season. On that day, José Mourinho made it a strategy to use to his advantage the yearning of The Kop for Brendan Rodgers' title-chasing Liverpool side to blitz their opponent, intuitively understanding that if his players took any opportunity to slow down the game it would have a negative impact on the atmosphere, turning hope into dismay, influencing the players' judgement and increasing the likelihood of an error.

Mourinho was subsequently, and fairly, hailed for his cunning in Chelsea's 2-0 win. What he did was textbook spoiling. Managers always do it when they feel their best chance of success is to 'keep it tight at the back' for as long as possible, play down the clock and provoke frustration.

Mark Hughes almost pulled off exactly the same trick at the Etihad two years earlier.

When Barton went down and required treatment after a head collision with Barry after 18 minutes, it already looked like time-wasting. 'It was,' Joey admitted. 'We were thinking of a draw and knew they needed to win and would be desperate, so it could be used to our advantage. We knew United were in Sunderland and people in the stadium would have an eye on that score. We were obviously the same thinking about Bolton at Stoke.'

Barton and Barry became embroiled in a running battle for the rest of the first half, occasionally 'leaving one on' each other, as the saying goes – a polite term for when a player has no qualms about kicking a shin or ankle when fairly winning the ball. Barton had made some well-publicized critical comments about Barry after the 2010 World Cup. He provocatively claimed that Barry 'had a good agent' for securing his City transfer and described his rival's midfield performance when England were comprehensively beaten by Germany as 'like the tortoise versus the hare'. 'He was the guy who was in the England squad and got his big move,' said Barton. 'I always used stuff like that to motivate me. It was not personal. I know Gareth is a good guy.'

A scrappy, belligerent game was the opposite of what City desired. The City of Mancini was not as adept at solving the riddle of the defensive block as the one we have seen in the Premier League under Guardiola. Few teams are.

There is no coach better than Guardiola at working out how to overcome the sort of barricade QPR erected, making the parameters of the Etihad pitch seem wider in 2020 than they appeared in 2012. That is partially due to Guardiola's use of wingers such as Raheem Sterling, or previously Leroy Sané. Guardiola always wants players capable of dismantling a defensive structure with dribbling, pace and movement, dragging full-backs and midfielders out of position to open space for his creators.

Mancini's City team did not have that profile.

In Guardiola's 4-3-3, the magician Silva became a central midfielder. Under Mancini, Silva and Samir Nasri switched between wide areas in a 4-4-2, and their natural tendency was to drift inside to combine with Touré.

'Until Pep came, I always thought of Silva and Samir as our main creative weapons,' explained Kompany. 'David loved cutting in from the right on his left foot, and Samir cutting in from the left with his right foot. We had a lot of great striking options – Sergio, Carlos Tevez, Edin Džeko, Mario Balotelli – and then Yaya driving us from the middle.'

In the first half, every City attack was through a central zone. On 52 seconds, a freeze-frame of the pitch showed Silva, Nasri, Agüero and Tevez forming a perfect but unhelpful square on the edge of QPR's penalty area.

Knowing how 'narrow' City played, Hughes instructed his defenders and midfielders to keep the pitch as 'small' as possible. Full-backs and wide midfielders could force their direct opponents to run or pass infield, denying them width. Silva and Nasri needed no encouragement to do this anyway, so QPR allowed them into a congested zone where it was harder to put together passing combinations, and the skilful providers were outnumbered.

QPR's back four retreated as far to the edge of the box as possible to guarantee that a hopeful ball over the top would not find a target, but not so deep as to make them vulnerable to aerial balls which might only require a flicked header to trouble goalkeeper Kenny. The centre-backs had responsibility for keeping that balance. QPR's defenders, Clint Hill and Anton Ferdinand, were outstanding.

City's trepidation surfaced quickly because it was obvious QPR were not going to be shrugged aside, the home side with no fluidity or penetration as they repeated the same move. They continued to run into a cul-de-sac, feeding the ball into the feet of Agüero and Tevez on the edge of the penalty area, hoping their trickery would allow them to turn their man and test Kenny. They could not get through because if Ferdinand or Hill did not intervene, Barton and central midfielder Shaun Derry pounced, or striker Bobby Zamora was on the edge of his penalty area to make a challenge. QPR kept nine players in and around their box, leaving my former Liverpool teammate Djibril Cissé alone up front to chase clearances.

For thirty-eight minutes, City could only muster a couple of lame attempts from distance of no concern to Kenny. Blend this with the fans' responses to the key fixtures elsewhere – QPR fans had begun to celebrate upon hearing that Jon Walters had scored for Stoke after 13 minutes while City supporters absorbed Rooney's goal at the Stadium of Light after 20 – and fingernails were already on the buffet.

City's difficulties were aggravated by Touré suffering a hamstring injury on 34 minutes. His discomfort was immediately apparent, but he was urged to carry on by Mancini and his coaching staff. Yaya could barely move. He still had a final contribution in him, though – an assist in City's opening goal six minutes before half-time. That should have changed everything.

City's marauding full-backs were the obvious response to the deep defensive block. In a game of attack versus defence, from the outset the onus was on Pablo Zabaleta and Gaël Clichy to scurry down their touchline and provide width.

As with all City's first-half attacks, the move for the opening goal began with City's midfield four in a rigid, straight line, barely 15 yards between them. Clichy and Zabaleta offered a passing option out wide, Silva picking out the Argentinian in an advanced crossing position. Zabaleta had one target in the box, Tevez, so his delivery was easily intercepted by Hill.

Fortunately for City, Hill's block bounced 20 yards straight back to Zabaleta. From there, he played a 6-yard pass to Silva, and Touré momentarily overcame his hamstring problem, sprinting into the QPR penalty area. Whatever possessed him to do that, it gave the attack its impetus as he was unmarked when receiving the ball from Silva.

Zabaleta made a critical decision. Most full-backs would start an overlapping, semi-circular run around the back of QPR's defence to put themselves in a position to cross across goal towards a predatory striker. Instead, Zabaleta darted diagonally, straight at and beyond Touré towards the 6-yard box. This inspired improvisation meant he could gather Touré's subtle pass in his stride and shoot. When he did, he was in the position of a number 9, not a full-back.

This was the only time QPR were caught out in the first half, Zabaleta's spontaneity their undoing. The visitors could still consider themselves unlucky. The shot was not great. Kenny should have saved it, the ball bouncing off the top of his gloves before looping into the far corner.

City's relief was palpable, although while Zabaleta dashed to the corner flag to be hugged by teammates, Touré could be spotted hobbling along, unable to join the celebrations having aggravated his hamstring problem. He was substituted for Nigel de Jong, and his composure was missed.

Nevertheless, City scoring first ought to have made the rest of the game a procession. By then, the match stats provided by Premier League analysts Opta offered no hope to QPR or Manchester United fans. In the sixteen minutes before half-time, City had 84 per cent possession. QPR had not yet touched the ball in City's penalty area, their one attempt a Cissé free-kick that gently rolled into Hart's arms. In a game where their only chance of scoring appeared to be from a set-piece, QPR had not had a corner. They would never have one.

All Hughes could tell his players at half-time was to stick to their plan, keep it at 1-0, and hope the result in Stoke favoured them, or alternatively that the tenseness of City's players would force a mistake.

He could not have imagined how soon into the second half City would oblige.

There are two headers in this game by Lescott worthy of scrutiny, the first of which was catastrophic. It can only be attributed to a brain freeze by a player who had had nothing to do for forty-eight minutes, lulled into believing there was minimal attacking threat.

QPR's equalizer was also the first sign of what City lost in Touré. His replacement de Jong, a fine player, squandered possession in midfield with an innocuous but aimless header towards Onuoha. This was not so bad; a minor detail. It just feels like something you rarely, if ever, would have seen Touré do. You can imagine Yaya taking a similar ball on his chest, calming the play and passing to a nearby teammate.

Onuoha passed wide to Wright-Phillips who did no more than kick high and long towards City's defence, where Lescott was waiting to deal with a situation he would have encountered a thousand times in his career. The City centre-back misjudged the ball's flight, his body position too far forward so that when he attacked it, it deflected off the back of his head towards his own penalty area. He could only turn in horror when the ball fell perfectly to Cissé, who had only Hart to beat.

The finish was typical of Djibril. He was not one for finesse when he could put his laces through it. At that point, QPR needed a point because Bolton had gone 2-1 up at Stoke.

City's fans had felt assured for just nine minutes of open play between Zabaleta's and Cissé's goals. Now they needed a saviour. Before they found one, it looked like a pantomime villain might suffice.

Joey Barton reflects upon the moment 'all hell broke loose' in the 54th minute with typical candour. 'I always say I am the only City player to never get a medal,' he joked. 'Their heads had gone at that point. If I had not been sent off, no way would they have won.'

What lit the bonfire seems run-of-the-mill on first viewing, Barton and Tevez tussling off the ball and City's striker falling to the ground. Barton maintains that, initially at least, they were as guilty as each other. 'The cameras do not do it justice. I blocked Tevez from a throw-in a few seconds earlier and he got frustrated. Nothing major, but when he got the chance he clipped me. I looked around and no one saw it, so I thought "cheeky bastard" and had a pop back. Tevez hit the ground. Then I saw the linesman flagging and thought, "OK, I have been collared here but they must have seen both of us, not just me." Turns out he saw the first bit, kept watching, and then saw Tevez drop to the ground. He screamed, fell to the floor and played the game.'

Upon seeing the replay, referee Mike Dean's decision to show Barton a red card is obviously right. Tevez was elbowed in the face. What does surprise me is how certain the linesman Andy Garratt was to instruct Dean to take action. Garratt was at the opposite side of the pitch.

'Yeah, the linesman was flagging and from nowhere,' said Barton.

That does not excuse what happened next.

'Bobby Zamora came up to me and said, "Joey, you are going. Take one of their players with you." So I thought the best thing for the team was to try to even it up. When the Tevez thing happened, Agüero ran straight to the referee, so I kneed him for grassing me up. Then Lescott and Kompany came over so I had a pop at them. I think they were wise to me. A few of their players were shouting for everyone to stay calm. In the end I got done three times for one sending off. An initial three-game ban, then another four games for the second kick, and then another five games for the way I left the pitch to take me to twelve games. I have been sent off many times in my career, but never reacted like that. And then that helps them later with all the added time. It seemed a good idea at the time. Not the best in hindsight . . .'

Barton never played another Premier League game for QPR as the disciplinary charges mounted. The fact, until that day at least, he still had a soft spot for his former club added to the inferno. 'I still get United fans saying "You got sent off because you wanted City to win the league" and City fans saying thanks,' he told me. 'I am like, "You're joking, aren't you? Do you think I would get a twelve-game ban for that?" I was gutted by what happened. Don't get me wrong, I was at City for nine years and when it was obvious the title was between them and United a few months earlier I wanted them to win the league. Then I saw the fixture list and was thinking, "What if I play well and help stop them winning it?" Every time I went back to City I saw people I respected. I had friends there. But we went there needing a result and were fighting for our lives, so it was a weird one for me. I wanted to stay up for QPR so all the City feelings were out of the window that afternoon.

'What flipped me over the edge was when the coach pulled in and we saw balloons and banners saying "Premier League Champions". I was like, "They think they have won already?" A lot of lads saw that so the team talk was done. We thought it was disrespectful to park the coach right there. It probably was not meant that way, but we used it to get into the zone.'

Referee Dean halted play to deal with Barton after 53 minutes and 34 seconds, restarting three minutes and forty-seven seconds later – worth keeping in mind given how much injury-time was added.

Aside from the obvious numerical disadvantage, Barton's exit made no difference to QPR's approach, although it prompted Hughes to replace goalscorer Cissé with Armand Traoré, a player more suited to tracking back along the left wing. That forced Wright-Phillips into central midfield.

Whatever the defensive intentions, Traoré helped QPR take an improbable lead just six minutes after coming on.

Every time Kenny caught a City cross he was looking to kick long and get the ball as far away from his penalty area as possible. It was the only way QPR could get the ball out of their half, and more often than not even this seemed counter-productive, resulting in the home side immediately retrieving possession and piling forward again. In the 66th minute, Kenny's release finally found one of his own players, helped by Traoré's pace giving him an advantage in a foot race with Kompany. With Zabaleta spending more time resembling a right-winger, there was space beyond him which Traoré exploited. Seeing the danger, Kompany had a decision and opted to hurtle into the tackle near the halfway line. He could not get there in time, so when Traoré nudged the ball forward he was clear and Kompany out of the game.

Now Lescott had to consider whether to keep his central position or run to the ball and man. Initially, he began a sprint towards Traoré. Then he changed his mind. He was never going to make the ground and prevent a cross. That momentary indecision cost him a yard.

With Kompany and Lescott having vacated their central positions, left-back Clichy had to cover at the heart of City's defence and follow QPR striker Zamora, who made an intelligent run into the middle, dragging the full-back with him. That meant QPR right midfielder Mackie, who sprinted the length of the field to join the attack, had the freedom of Manchester at the far post where Clichy would normally be. Traoré picked him out, and Mackie's header was into the surface, taking a bounce before finding the opposite corner.

This was QPR's second touch in City's penalty area. There would be no third.

'Typical City,' said commentator Martin Tyler.

Headlines prepared.

Mancini's hysteria when Mackie scores looks funny in retrospect, rampaging around his technical area and engaging in a manic scape-goat hunt, his finger wagging at his players, ditching the overcoat and sky blue and white scarf he'd been clinging to as a lucky omen. Had City not come back, the debrief would not have viewed such conduct sympa-thetically. So many managers who have been runners-up in title races have been mocked for (as the chant goes) 'cracking up' in the final straight. None of them displayed the symptoms of the triumphant coach of 2012.

'That was a dark moment,' said Kompany. Then he paused. I could tell he was choosing his next words carefully. 'Mancini did not mind a bit of drama in his coaching style, let's put it that way,' he added. 'That would sometimes happen in certain situations. In training, or games, that is how he was. That moment brought out the most acute version of that because it was such a stupid moment, giving the title away at home against QPR. Most people felt the same as he did. He could not keep it in.'

Although Barton was now watching the rest of the game on a Sky TV monitor along with pitchside reporter Geoff Shreeves in the players' tunnel, he says that from the early stages he was taken aback by the City manager's demeanour. 'I have always felt Mancini lost his job that day. I know he stayed for another year, but I don't think it was easily forgotten. What he was saying to players was outrageous. He was leathering them all, calling them motherfuckers for how they were playing. Obviously I knew a couple of the City lads, and to this day some of them do not like talking about what happened, especially how Mancini was nailing them. It brings out so much emotion they cannot compute.'

Mancini reacted more proactively with a couple of substitutions, but there is no particularly identifiable structure to how City went about retrieving the situation. The first change was Džeko replacing Barry on 69 minutes, so in theory City reverted to 4-3-3, Agüero, Tevez and Džeko the strikers until Balotelli replaced Tevez on 75 minutes. The reality was 2-1-7, with the full-backs as high as possible up the pitch, fed by Silva and Nasri who were constantly supplying Clichy and Zabaleta.

QPR were comfortable dealing with any cross into their penalty area until Džeko's introduction. Given how the game had gone until that point – and Džeko's subsequent impact – I cannot help but think he should have been introduced earlier.

Between his arrival and his equalizer, including eleven corners, City attempted an extraordinary forty crosses, seventeen of which were from either Zabaleta (ten) or Clichy (seven). That is a cross every fifty-five seconds, with Hill most often making a headed clearance. City were so entrenched in the opposition half, Hart was near the centre circle and took three throw-ins after QPR kicked out of play.

No sooner was Džeko on than there was a replica of the situation from which he would later score. As Silva took a corner on the City right, Džeko and designated marker Onuoha grappled in the 6-yard box, exactly as they would in injury-time. Silva's 71st-minute set-piece was slightly overhit so went beyond Džeko and Onuoha, although Tevez's back-post header forced Kenny into a fingertip save.

QPR's defenders were so deep, and Kenny was so disinclined to come off his line and try to catch, the set-piece threat was enhanced by Džeko. He made the corners tougher to defend when Silva and Nasri got it right. Mancini could see this, now growing enraged when deliveries were off target, or because his players were not attacking the set-pieces with enough purpose.

The pressure on QPR's defence was unrelenting, but as time became the enemy, players fell into the trap of shooting on sight within 25 yards of goal. Silva, Balotelli and de Jong did so, occasionally lucky when wasteful attempts deflected for another set-play.

Kompany, in a last desperate act, was thinking of becoming a fourth striker, but that did not happen until after the equalizer. 'Before Džeko scored I cannot remember that last push,' he admitted. 'The centre-backs were still doing the job of getting the ball back to the midfielders and strikers. We had nothing else to do. That meant I had a lot of thinking time. I just wanted to give it to David and Samir as quickly as I could so they would use their quality. Then a few things went through my mind, the biggest of which was, "How stupid is this?" There was a point at which I was thinking how we will have to put on a brave face, come out with a strong message and say, "We will win it next year."'

As the captain was mentally preparing for a defiant post-match interview, the board went up for five minutes of injury-time.

In Sunderland, the game was about to finish, the messages being communicated by the United supporters, players increasingly aware that the podium might have to be hastily prepared at the Stadium of Light. 'We didn't know any score from City at half-time,' said Rooney. 'The manager would have known but he did not let staff get a message to any of the players. He wanted all our focus on our game. It was only when we heard all our fans cheering twice in the second half that we thought, "QPR must be scoring here. Something is going on." When our game was over someone told us it was 2-1 to QPR, so we were on the pitch knowing their game was not finished and as it stands, we have won the league. Inside I was buzzing but not celebrating yet because we did not know. Then all of a sudden the Sunderland fans started cheering, so I thought, "Shit, they must have equalized."'

One minute and fourteen seconds of injury-time had been played when Silva's nineteenth and last corner finally found its mark. Džeko connected, overpowering Onuoha, with Kenny again so rooted to his line he was virtually behind it when trying to make the save.

'When Edin scored, it was like waking from surgery,' said Kompany. 'I can only compare it to a feeling like you have been knocked out and then woken up. I was just thinking, "Game on."'

There were 126 seconds between Džeko's equalizer and Agüero's winner, the goal timed at 93 minutes and 20 seconds.

My first observation about that concerns QPR's kick-off, which they struck high and long down the field so they could retain their defensive shape, despite inviting City to attack again. QPR were still secure with a point, the result at Stoke favouring them: QPR fans had been celebrating again on 75 minutes when hearing news of the latest Stoke goal, a Walters penalty.

'When Džeko equalized, I knew we were still safe because of the Bolton score,' said Barton. 'Some of the lads knew, but others didn't. Some were thumping the pitch thinking "we have been sent down". It was chaos followed by pandemonium. Then City attacked again. For everyone in the ground there ended up being a moment when it went from a funeral to a wedding in the space of two seconds. Because I could see both games on the monitor, I went from thinking I had caused our relegation to buzzing.'

Wright-Phillips had not stopped fighting for QPR's cause, chasing and winning a throw-in inside City's half which could have given his defence a chance to push out and slow the game down heading towards the fourth minute of added time. Instead, Onuoha threw down the line and Lescott made his second significant header of the game. From Onuoha's throw-in, striker Jay Bothroyd, a 76th-minute substitute for Bobby Zamora, did not offer much of a challenge and Lescott was clear minded enough to nod a deliberate pass infield to de Jong, who had the space to drive on.

Kompany was now centre-forward, more advanced than Agüero, who made the best decision of his life to drop deeper to receive the ball from de Jong in front of the packed penalty area. At the start of the game Agüero was receiving passes with his back to the QPR blockade. Now he was running at it, looking for a passing combination.

He still played the same pass City had attempted and failed with over the previous ninety-three minutes. But there were three key differences.

First, Agüero was running with the ball from a deeper position looking for a 'give and go'.

Second, the receiver in the number 9 position, Balotelli, had the strength to hold the ball, turn and return it to Agüero, stretching his leg to divert it into his run.

Third, Kompany was in the penalty area distracting defender Taye Taiwo, who would normally have had only Agüero sprinting at him in mind. Rather than standing still, as a centre-half unaccustomed to evading a marker in the penalty area might do, Kompany cleverly ran away to make space for the incoming striker. Taiwo reacted, and then realized that would create space for Agüero. Caught in two minds, he was off-balance. The defence opened up for the first time.

Agüero saw the gap and did what world-class strikers do.

In the archives, Kompany will never be credited for the assist – a huge injustice. That is why statistics are often flawed. What Kompany did was as vital as Balotelli's return pass.

'I try to be as humble as I can be,' Kompany said. 'It is the one moment I keep claiming for myself because I know what I did. The ball coming to me was not an option, so when I saw Kun making the run I thought, "I have to move." I was emotionally drained, but yes, I did think about running across the box in the opposite way. You can see the left-back [Taiwo] make the move to follow me and then double back to try and stop Kun, but he is too late and Kun gets through. That little hesitation? I want to claim that one. When Kun shot, I was praying. I saw him hit it and thought, "Please don't be a rebound landing on my knee or shin." I was following it in, so all my instincts were right.'

Agüero ended a forty-four-year title wait with the forty-fourth goal attempt. It was not quite the last kick of the game. Bothroyd and Derry restarted by kicking into touch and Clichy took a throw-in to Hart before referee Mike Dean called time and heartbreak took a rapid 140-mile detour to the Stadium of Light, where United's players, wondering and wandering around, absorbed their disappointment from the faces of their travelling fans.

'After the first cheers from the Sunderland fans there was a second one almost immediately,' said Rooney. 'It felt like it was the same, as though it must have been for the same goal. I thought their fans must be winding us up, but then one of our staff said it was 3-2 to City. It was horrible. The worst feeling. Before the game we were not expecting anything. Then you hear it is 2-1, and then to score like they did . . . It is the worst I have felt in the dressing room, everyone quiet. Horrible. I would rather City had won 5-0.'

Agüero's goal is worthy of comparison with Michael Thomas's at

Anfield in 1989 for its financial and dramatic impact. For Brian Marwood, there was a welcome sense of déjà vu. 'I was involved that night as part of the Arsenal squad too, although injured so I couldn't play,' he said.

The idea of the Premier League gathered pace on the back of Arsenal's title win that night, capturing the imagination of the armchair viewer, prompting Sky Sports to pay £300 million for televised rights ahead of English football's relaunch in 1992. In its twentieth year, the top division and Sky had its equivalent just as negotiations were concluding for the next broadcast deal. On 13 June 2012, exactly a month after City's title win, the Premier League confirmed a Sky and BT Sport contract worth £3 billion – a 70 per cent rise on the previous arrangement.

'No wonder the Premier League chief executive Richard Scudamore had such a beaming smile,' joked Tyler, whose work that day elevated him to the distinguished list of broadcasters whose unscripted exclamations have captured a defining moment in our nation's football history.

Great games are often accompanied by perfect soundtracks. Think of Geoff Hurst's hat-trick goal in the 1966 World Cup final, and Kenneth Wolstenholme is in your head. Clive Tyldesley's commentary will always be synonymous with the Nou Camp in 1999 and Istanbul in 2005. Arsenal fans call one of their podcasts 'It's Up for Grabs Now' in honour of Brian Moore at Anfield in 1989. Whenever I think of Steven Gerrard scoring against Olympiakos in the Champions League in 2004 I hear Andy Gray shouting 'Yer beauty!', even though I was on the pitch, sprinting to my captain to celebrate near the Kop corner flag at the time.

Perhaps these goals are so monumental: no matter what is said it is destined to be carved into our consciousness. I am not so sure. There are plenty of extraordinary moments when I barely remember who was on the microphone.

In the broadcast age, there will always be two aspects to experiences we cherish: what we hear can leave as deep an impression as what we see.

Martin is one of the most modest fellas I know, but I have done him a disservice by referencing City's 'Agüero moment' earlier in this chapter. Whenever it is spoken or written about there is intentional emphasis on the striker's surname. It is really the 'Agüero-oooo moment' because that is how Tyler expressed the thrill and magnitude of what was about to transpire.

Having made the switch from playing into broadcasting myself, what impresses me as much is what Martin did not say. There was a pause between Agüero scoring and scampering around the pitch and Martin's iconic commentary line 'I swear you will never see anything like this again', which makes it resonate stronger.

'I was sure when Agüero took the touch he would score,' Martin told me. 'What struck me in that millisecond when he did was the noise. Mark Hughes later said it was the loudest he had ever heard a stadium. If I had said anything, I do not think it would have been heard.

'For what happened next, I think a lot of the credit should go to the director, Tony Mills. The shots he captured told the story. Think of the decision to cut to show Joe Hart's reaction as the celebrations started. To me, that is as much part of the broadcast as anything I said. Joe is running around like a headless chicken, no teammate near him to jump on, not knowing whether to believe it has happened. That is an extraordinary image which really caught a million-to-one moment. There were camera shots like that all around.

'So, I think the words that then came from me reflected that. I was as amazed as anyone that I was there to see it, knew I had never seen the like before and would never do so again. I always say the skill is not commentating, it is being there so you are in a position to have the microphone in your hand to call it.

'When the trophy presentation was made I had tears in my eyes. Not because I am a City fan, but because I was present at one of the greatest footballing dramas and lucky enough to have the microphone. That was very emotional.'

Given that he mentioned several times before injury-time that a City title win from such a perilous position would be extraordinary, I wondered if he secretly had a line prepared?

'No,' he replied, 'because nobody expected the game to turn out as it did. That is the joy of the job. If you think it through too much, you can overthink it. None of the most famous climaxes to games could have been imagined. I think that is why some of those famous commentaries stand out. Think of 1966. Who could have imagined there would be people on the pitch thinking it was all over that day at Wembley? And then at that exact moment Geoff Hurst blasts into the top corner?

'This is not false modesty. I had no idea my Agüero commentary had any impact. The game did that. Agüero did that. I felt lucky not to have messed it up. It was only when we all assembled for our traditional end-of-season meal a few hours later in a restaurant in Manchester I could hear everyone replaying it on their mobile phones. Yes, I was choked up. A really big day had gone OK.

'The following pre-season I saw the Reading manager, Brian McDermott. He was talking to some journalists and shouted over, "At least you didn't fuck it up!" I liked that. I am proud of it. It is something to be remembered.'

McDermott's observation could be equally applied to City.

Tyler's co-commentator that day was the former City striker Niall Quinn, the man who sixteen years earlier was begging players to stop keeping the ball at the corner flag thinking they were safe from relegation. The symmetry of City dismantling their reputation for debacles was inescapable.

'That was such a weird day,' said Marwood. 'We were fighting that "Typical City" idea that was in the air, never more apparent than in the 89th minute. At the moment your body just goes numb. I remember sitting there thinking, "I cannot believe this is happening, that we have put ourselves in such a position, with such a strong side, and now . . ." Then it all happened. Now I look around the club and cannot help but be proud of everything we started, whether it is the training ground, sports science departments, the Academy, or our support for the women's game. When I see people walking into our new training camp today, I wish they could have seen it during those first days before we left Carrington and how far we have come. They might appreciate it even more.'

'The club has gone intergalactic now,' said Joe Royle, although he believes there are aspects of the City he managed which remain. 'The owners have never forgotten the players and staff who came before. They have been very good that way, keeping that sense of community. They have always been good to me whenever I have returned. I still find it a very warm club.'

Vincent Kompany added a further three league titles (one under Manuel Pellegrini in 2014, two under Guardiola in 2018 and 2019), contributing his own title-deciding screamer against Leicester City – an unforgettable farewell gift – before moving into management with Anderlecht. 'I could have carried on for another year but it felt like the right time,' he said. 'Rather like David Silva when he decided to move on, I did not want to stretch the last drips. We are seeing the end of the first era now with players like Zabaleta, Yaya, myself and Silva more recently leaving, but the torch is carried on. Kevin De Bruyne is carrying the new era with Ederson and Aymeric Laporte – solid characters.'

Although there is an inevitable focus on the wealth which funded and sustains success, Kompany insists the club's hierarchy oversaw the transformation with studiousness and care, not simply big spending. 'City is one of the luckiest clubs in world football to have that ownership group come in, settle and put down roots in Manchester,' he said. 'It is phenomenal. They have ambition, yes, but what is also important is their leadership style. The owners had a vision but we had to jump through a lot of stages to get there.

'The first time you meet chairman Khaldoon you get a good vibe. It is the calmness of the owners that realizes the objectives. The rules are simple. Every department has to perform. But if you perform and you are loyal, the club is loyal to you. That is rare at a football club. When you have been through so many identity crises it is very difficult to find a new way and not dismiss the past. They have done that so well.'

The years between 2008 and 2012 announced the regeneration of a football club. Agüero's goal completed a more profound rebirth, City never again to be described or ridiculed as downtrodden losers, or with cause to be concerned that their achievements would be eclipsed by illustrious neighbours. What was 'Typical City' in 2012 is something else entirely today.

If Cityitis still exists in any form, it defines their transformation into serial winners courtesy of a stupendous swing of Sergio Agüero's right foot.

10

Saturday, 28 May 2011

2011 UEFA CHAMPIONS LEAGUE FINAL
Wembley Stadium

BARCELONA 3 – 1 MANCHESTER UNITED

Pedro *27*   Rooney *34*
Messi *54*
Villa *69*

'It was one of the most complete games we ever played'

– Xavi Hernández

Wayne Rooney spent most of his Manchester United career facing teams who believed they were chasing a lost cause.

Ahead of the 2011 Champions League final against Barcelona, that role was reversed.

'I did not think we had any chance of beating them,' he told me. 'Even when we made it 1-1 before half-time, there was no other game I played for Manchester United where we were one down, equalized, and I was on the pitch thinking, "There is no way we can win the game." It was a case of "let's just see how it goes" because we were playing the team which, in my opinion, is the best there has been.'

I partly agree with Wayne. Pep Guardiola's Barcelona between 2008 and 2012 was the greatest club team ever. Over four years they won fourteen of the nineteen trophies available, including two Champions Leagues, three La Liga titles, and two FIFA Club World Cups. In the same period, Guardiola gave debuts to twenty-two academy players, ensuring his success was rooted in the distinctive Barça way.

To those who witnessed it, the 2011 Champions League final at Wembley was the pinnacle – a flawless exhibition of pass-and-move football which has inspired coaching seminars ever since.

If Guardiola composed the symphonies, Xavi Hernández was his principal conductor. I had the pleasure of reassessing the 2011 final with the midfielder who would be my first pick in any world XI. 'The Wembley final was one of the best matches of that generation of players, without doubt,' Xavi told me. 'It was one of the best games in the history of Barça.'

What a team it was.

Xavi is the finest Spanish midfielder of all time. Andrés Iniesta is not far behind. Sergio Busquets completed a midfield trio which is the gold standard for productivity with the ball and dynamism without it.

And then there is Lionel Messi. The greatest footballer of his generation.

Beyond the exceptional individual quality, what Barcelona collectively represented between 2008 and 2012 defined modern football.

There are great teams who are supremely successful by wearing the current football fashion better than the rest. They create dynasties without necessarily introducing new or radical ideas. I put Bob Paisley's Liverpool of the 1970s and 1980s and Ferguson's United in that category. More recently, I see Zinedine Zidane's Real Madrid in the same way.

Then there are great teams that win as pioneers, such as the Ajax side featuring the likes of Johan Cruyff, Johan Neeskens and Ruud Krol that lifted the European Cup on three consecutive occasions from 1971 to 1973, and Arrigo Sacchi's AC Milan in the 1980s. They changed the game.

Guardiola's Barcelona had the same weighty influence. His Barça were descendants of the Total Football ideal most associated with Ajax and the Dutch national team in the 1970s. Manager Rinus Michels created a form of play in which every player looked like they would excel in any position, fuelled by Cruyff's attacking genius. Michels took his Ajax blueprint to the Nou Camp in 1971, Cruyff joining him there two years later.

The Spanish club's identity evolved when Cruyff returned as coach between 1988 and 1996, mentoring the young Guardiola and, alongside assistant Carles Rexach, solidifying their principles from the youth levels upwards, creating passing shapes across the pitch to ensure wherever his sides had the ball, they could always outnumber the opponent. Long, aimless clearances were forbidden, Cruyff saying he would prefer to lose playing the 'right way' than win sacrificing style. His 'Dream Team', in which Guardiola played in midfield, won the club's first European Cup at Wembley in 1992.

'Johan is the most influential person in recent football history,' Xavi explained. 'To define the Barça style and Cruyff's influence, it is important to understand Johan's idea of having the ball, of being the instigator of the match, attacking, putting on a show, playing in triangle formation, and understanding that there's always a player who is free and you must find him, and from there, being better than your opponent. Barça has incorporated his football philosophy, and I believe that football worldwide is taking a similar route.

'Cruyff's idea was that it was important to put on a show and enjoy the game. From there, more chances of winning are created through controlling the ball. The style of the game can't be lost, because we believe in it, we train that way, and we want to compete with that idea in mind. When you win it's doubly satisfying because you have controlled the game, beaten your opponent, and you feel the hero in the victory.'

While Cruyff was an artist able to verbally convey the creative patterns he expected from players, another Ajax and Barça coach who later succeeded him, Louis van Gaal, gave it a scientific base. His players were informed which positions they ought to be in via charts and diagrams.

The Barça philosophy was set in stone by the time Guardiola succeeded one of the members of Van Gaal's 1995 Champions League-winning team at Ajax, Frank Rijkaard, in 2008. Guardiola elevated it to supreme heights, merging the poetry of Cruyff and the science of Van Gaal with an unparalleled attention to detail to create the purest expression of Barça football yet.

'We shouldn't forget Rijkaard and Van Gaal, who were both influenced by Cruyff, and the offensive style, but Pep pushed the envelope a little bit further, and provided a more tactical approach,' said Xavi.

The Spanish media gave it the catchy name *tiki-taka*. That branding was not universally popular in Catalonia as it oversimplified the idea of a 'short, passing game'. 'It's not passing for passing's sake,' Guardiola responded, insisting that every interaction served a clear purpose.

The genius of it is it looks so easy, players retaining possession for extended periods with 6-yard passes and patiently manoeuvring from a defensive into an attacking position. And yet it requires a complexity which only the most technically and mentally gifted players can harness.

Most players are coached to see the pitch in terms of defensive, midfield and attacking zones. When you watched Guardiola's Barcelona, it was as if they saw the field in square inches, and knew to the exact millimetre where they should be in every conceivable attacking and defensive scenario, with and without possession.

Thierry Henry, who left Arsenal for Barcelona in 2007, once explained to me that he had to adjust his mindset to the likelihood he would not receive a pass for prolonged spells. His movements off the ball at the Nou Camp were increasingly about creating a diversion for teammates to take advantage. That applied to every player, so they worked in collaboration to ensure a minimum of two passing options for a teammate. The most immediate and obvious evolution under Guardiola was that ball retention started with the goalkeeper. Barça's number 1, Victor Valdés, became the first outfield defender, expected to kick short to centre-backs in unorthodox positions wide on the edge of his penalty area.

No side had ever imposed this concept in such a meticulously prepared and trophy-laden way before 2008.

Journalist Graham Hunter, author of *Barça: The Making of the Greatest Team in the World*, researched the level of sophistication. 'Some players had never been trained in the mental discipline of positional play, which demanded the patience of a Buddhist monk,' he told me. 'The idea is to keep your position irrespective of your brain telling you to do the opposite. Pep, this untried manager who had just been promoted from managing the Barça "B" team when Cruyff singled him out as his heir, would literally take these world-class players by the shoulders and tell them where to stand. Pep's intensity and demands for standards were so revolutionary, after his first pre-season training camp held at St Andrews in Scotland in 2008 a lot of players wanted to leave.

'Look, I don't need to tell you this as you are someone who has played at the elite level, but if the other team has the ball and you see a situation where a teammate needs help on the pitch, what is the instinct of most top-class footballers? It is to go and help him out, right? To not do so is counter-intuitive.

'With Pep, you must leave that job to whoever has already been designated responsibility, and always stick to your position. Multiply that by the number of situations a player finds himself in over ninety minutes, each told to be within a certain space of each other at all times, and you are basically telling players, some of whom have already won everything in the game, to relearn the rules of football.

'They all knew how to play. Now they were all given an understanding of the game. There is a difference between being told what to do and doing it and understanding and doing it. Those players who could not understand it, or chose not to, were turfed out quickly. That included some top-class players like Zlatan Ibrahimović.'

Throughout our game's history many teams have 'played out from the back', but not with all eleven players so elaborately choreographed. And certainly not with such accuracy, pace or energy over ninety minutes. Under Guardiola, Barça became as impressive at closing spaces and crowding out the opposition to retrieve the ball in attacking areas.

When ex-players say the principles of 'pressing' and 'playing between the lines' between the traditional four defenders, four midfielders and two strikers always existed, they are right in theory, but fundamentally wrong in suggesting it was practised like this. It is correct that identifiable patterns are as perceptible during previous decades, but it is incomparable to this Barça team or many elite teams since. The change is far-reaching when judged directly against games in the eighties, nineties and even the early noughties.

It has been instructive rewatching matches and seeing how much has advanced since Pep's Barça emerged in 2008, his ideas circulating across the world. I retired relatively recently, in 2013, and the attacking ambition demanded of coaches from fans and media has substantially changed. Players are expected to be braver on the ball and be capable of and willing to make riskier passes. That necessitates a more technically proficient brand of football.

In the past we used terms such as 'dropping into the pockets between defence and midfield' when identifying the role of individual players in specific positions at a given moment. I know from my own experiences that the coaching was never so precise as with Guardiola's Barcelona. If, to give a specific example, the second striker in any side I was in was permitted to roam freely, it was not my duty or that of every one of my teammates (including the keeper) to assume a predetermined place on the pitch which constantly adjusted as the attack developed.

Generally, whenever my managers focused on organization, the clearest and more detailed emphasis was on where we should stand or run when our opponents had the ball. To me, team structure was about defence and knowing how to withstand attacks. As a centre-back, I either stood near an opposing striker near the halfway line if we were playing a 'high line' of defence, or 15 to 20 yards further back if we were constructing a more cautious 'low block' nearer the edge of our penalty area.

Defending in football is black and white in that way, easier to understand and operate. There are basics which are non-negotiable about where you go when the opponent has possession. It does not require amazing tactics to demand that ten players get behind the ball and stand on the goal side of the player they are marking. That's why the first measure of improvement when teams appoint a new manager tends to be the increasing number of clean sheets.

Any competent coach should be able to train a Premier League-standard team to defend properly. That is not especially impressive. The hardest thing in the game is scoring goals without compromising that defensive organization.

Through different eras, most coaches believed that to be related to the instinctive ability of strikers. In working towards the final third of the pitch there was less precision to a team's architecture until relatively recently. When it comes to attacking, there remains a broad sense of goals being a consequence of individual flair, off-the-cuff skill and accurate shooting. That is why the creative players, or those with ability to score regularly, are usually the best paid and most expensive.

'If only I had a twenty- or thirty-goal-a-season striker' is an often heard lament by coaches seeking the 'X Factor' signing who will take their team to the next level. How are prolific finishers described? 'They are natural goalscorers. You cannot coach or teach that.' You never hear the same about the best defenders, do you? When a back four excels, it is usually – rightly – attributed to training-ground drills.

All the offensive players I worked with, certainly under my most successful managers Gérard Houllier and Rafa Benítez, were under no illusions about their defensive responsibilities during training sessions. Defenders did not receive the same level of specialist advice about attacking. Whenever we practised offensive patterns – repeating set routines to free the front players, such as Michael Owen, Steven Gerrard or Fernando Torres – such workouts tended to begin with the ball already deep in opposition territory, not working it from goalkeeper to centre-forward. If striker coaches were invited to join training sessions, they focused on improving the skills of individuals with tailored shooting drills, not by engaging with all ten outfield players. The forwards headed off to a different part of the training ground to receive hints on how best to beat a goalkeeper. As a number 9, you either had it or you didn't. If the manager did not have such a player, he was soon asking the board to sign a substantial cheque.

Guardiola has done more than anyone to demonstrate how the creation of goalscoring opportunities can be as much a part of high-intensity, collective training manoeuvres as defending, so the offensive threat of players who did not previously score or create that often can be developed. That still requires and facilitates spontaneity – how could it not when Guardiola's teams possess players of Messi's or Kevin De Bruyne's class? – and he still spends big for the most talented players, but there is a theory to how his teams play.

Analyse how Barcelona and Manchester City attack under Guardiola and you can see the hours of training-ground rehearsal. He embraces the responsibility of educating his players in how to get the ball through the thirds of a pitch, from the keeper through midfield to the edge of the opponent's penalty area. From there, it is up to them to complete the ball's journey into the back of the net.

Defensive midfielder Javier Mascherano left Liverpool for Barça in 2010 and explained to me the difference in mentality and preparation at the Nou Camp. 'Pep made me see the game with a different vision,' he said. 'At Liverpool, I only thought about the game defensively. I totally disengaged from the offensive part, not seeing that as my function. Pep made me understand that we all had to be part of the construction. No one understands positional play like him. Working with Pep was a huge step in my career.'

Some tactical innovations were drastic. When he won the Champions League in 2009 (also against Manchester United) and 2011, Guardiola did not include a traditional number 9. A new term was invented, 'the false 9', to describe Messi's position, which was more like what we call a number 10. Although it became renowned after Guardiola's use of it, Xavi says this too was first cultivated by Cruyff in the 1990s. 'By using the false 9 we tried to surprise the opponent with a numerical superiority in the midfield,' he said. 'Cruyff used it with [Michael] Laudrup. By drifting back, the false 9 helps midfielders to receive and then run to attack. That's the idea we used with Messi. It's a solution to the defensive playing system of the opponent.'

In 2009, Thierry Henry and Samuel Eto'o were converted from central into wide strikers, switching from the left and the right to feed off Messi's creativity. In 2011, David Villa and Pedro took on those roles.

We cannot ignore that these are players of extraordinary individual talent. Normally it costs millions to create a squad of such startling ability, so Guardiola was blessed to inherit some of the best of all time. Four legends in his side – Messi, Xavi, Iniesta and Busquets – cost no transfer fee. They and centre-back Gerard Piqué (who returned to the Nou Camp after a brief spell at Manchester United) emerged through the Barça youth academy La Masia, already indoctrinated in the Cruyff philosophy. That must not undermine the fact that Guardiola got more from this group than anyone dared imagine upon his promotion to the senior job.

As an attacking force, Barça's productivity rewrote records. In 2009, they became the highest-scoring Champions League winners since the competition's revamp in 1992, scoring thirty-seven times in fifteen games. In 2011, they had already scored twenty-seven in twelve heading to Wembley. Messi had fifty-two in fifty-four appearances.

Facing such a force of nature in the 2009 and 2011 finals, Sir Alex Ferguson, an instinctively adventurous manager, had a dilemma he had rarely encountered during his career.

In 2008, United defeated Rijkaard's Barça in the Champions League semi-final. They did so with Ferguson compromising his attacking values, playing a defensive line-up, surrounding playmakers Xavi, Iniesta and Messi and securing a goalless draw in the Nou Camp in the first leg, before Paul Scholes's spectacular winner after 14 minutes in the return fixture saw United through.

'We won the tie in 2008 by sitting back and frustrating over two legs,' said Rooney. 'In my opinion that was the only way you could beat them. You needed a bit of luck as well, but it worked. I think it made a difference that the assistant, Carlos Queiroz, was still there then [he was replaced as first-team coach by Dutchman René Meulensteen in July 2008]. Carlos was brilliant with Fergie. Whenever the manager was following his instincts and thinking "we're going to attack", Carlos would make him rethink. He was the one who gave us the tactics in 2008 and was the cautious one we needed.'

Queiroz prepared for the 2008 tie by placing a stretching mat in front of United's back four as a guide for centre-midfielders Michael Carrick and Scholes never to allow the gap between them to get too big. The idea was to make the middle so overpopulated, Barça would always be forced wide where they could be contained. It proved a template defensive performance for beating Barça, cramping their style.

Although the Barça of 2007/08 under Rijkaard was not as refined as that in 2008/09 under Guardiola, Ferguson's tactical triumph was rightly lauded. Despite that, the manner of United's win did not sit well with Ferguson. 'He hated playing defensive,' Rooney explained. 'Really hated it. When we got to the final in 2009, he said to us he knew we could beat them playing that way, but then he said, "We are Manchester United and we are not going into the Champions League final to sit back all game. We are going to attack them and do it the right way." We were all sitting there in the team meeting thinking, "Oh fuck." Sir Alex went through their side, saying, "Let's go at them." Then you saw the names like Messi, Eto'o and Henry! I was like, "Fuckin' 'ell, how much pace do you want in one team?" '

In 1999 Ferguson won the Champions League with that 'We are Manchester United' mindset, believing in his side's never-say-die attitude. He was so sure of his team's ability to win on the front foot that his response to assistant Steve McClaren's plea for defensive reorganization after the late equalizer against Bayern Munich in the final was to prophetically declare, 'This game is not going to extra-time.'

But Ferguson was never averse to being defensive when the situation demanded. He often went that way against Arsène Wenger's great title-winning sides at the turn of the millennium, trying to shut down the opponent. I remember Ferguson coming to Anfield on occasions and designating players to man-mark those he deemed the biggest threats. I specifically recall an Anfield meeting in which Steven Gerrard was man-marked by United's Phil Jones – a sign of the respect in which our captain was held when he was at his peak.

In 2009, United went into the Champions League final as European champions. Ask most United fans which is the greatest line-up of Ferguson's reign, and they would most likely pick his 2008 side that won the Premier League and European Cup. No wonder he was determined to defend his crown with attacking flair, especially as Guardiola went into that final with selection problems because of suspensions to full-backs Dani Alves and Eric Abidal, and the absence through injury of centre-back Rafael Márquez. Carles Puyol, usually a central defender, played right-back. Midfielder Yaya Touré was selected in his least preferred position at centre-back. Left-back Sylvinho was past his best at thirty-three, and Iniesta and Henry were carrying thigh and knee injuries respectively.

Rooney says United thought Barça's defence was vulnerable. 'I spoke to Sir Alex before the final and we discussed the fact that they had one of our former players, Gerard Piqué, at centre-half,' he said. 'I used to bully him in training and wanted to play against him. I wanted to be the number 9 with five midfielders. I ended up on the left. But even though we knew their quality in 2009, it was not like the 2011 final before the game because although we knew how good they were, there was still a feeling going into that final we had a genuine chance because we had so much quality in our side. In 2009 we still had Cristiano Ronaldo and Carlos Tevez. If we had played any other team in Europe we would have won the final. By 2011 it was a different feeling. We were on the back end of that era, if you like. Ronaldo and Tevez had gone and Rio [Ferdinand] and [Nemanja] Vidić were a bit older.'

Barcelona won comfortably in Rome with goals from Eto'o and Messi. 'The first goal after ten minutes was a killer,' said Ferguson in the immediate aftermath, explaining the defeat as one side outperforming the other rather than a serious tactical malfunction.

Most reports from 2009 argued that Ferguson picked the wrong line-up, his boldness meaning midfielders Anderson and Carrick were outnumbered by Xavi, Busquets and Iniesta.

In a hint of what impacted his decision two years later, Ferguson suggested that his players had underperformed at the end of a gruelling campaign. 'We didn't play as well as we can, but you have to give Barcelona credit,' he reasoned in the minutes after the final whistle. 'Lionel Messi wasn't the problem. Xavi and Andrés Iniesta kept the ball all night and made it difficult for us. The disappointment was the use of the ball when we got possession. You have to wait minutes to get it back off them. Could be it was an off night. Could be it was a mountain too big to climb. But we've done well, it's been a long season, we've had sixty-six games and you've got to give the players credit for their courage and resilience. Next season we'll be better.'

Michael Owen became a Manchester United player shortly after the final. He told me how on the squad's first day back for pre-season training – the manager having not seen the players since Rome – Ferguson told some of his squad he had watched the final over the summer. The manager jokingly asked Ryan Giggs if he had played against Barça with an injury. Beyond the playfulness, the manager had obviously spent two months stewing on the defeat.

Two years on at Wembley, Ferguson seemed even more convinced that 2009 was just an 'off night' for his players. That prompted him to stick to his ideals and ask his players to try again in a 4-2-3-1 formation, Giggs and Carrick the central midfield pairing and Rooney the number 10 behind striker Javier Hernández. Park Ji-sung and Antonio Valencia were the wide men Ferguson hoped would trouble Barça's full-backs, preventing them playing so far up the pitch.

Nothing Ferguson saw in the first ten minutes at Wembley would have indicated such idealism was spectacularly misplaced. For a brief period, he must have thought it would be rewarded. He saw the United he was accustomed to on European nights at Old Trafford – vibrant, in the face of the opponent, pressing high, forcing mistakes. In the first thirty seconds Park Ji-sung won the ball from right-back Dani Alves and Mascherano ended a counter-attack by nervously clearing straight out. Barça players forbidden from kicking long and high even when under pressure? I don't think so. Rooney and Giggs tried to fill space between Barça's centre-backs and midfielders with some success, harrying keeper Valdés into risky, hurried passes. Barça did not instantly settle into their patient build-up.

'That is the way I remember it, yes,' agreed Xavi. 'During the first minutes we didn't have total control of the game.'

After five minutes, Valdés overhit a pass to left-back Abidal as United's forwards dashed towards the penalty area. 'We wanted to stop them dictating the game like they do by passing the ball sideways,' explained Rooney. 'With many teams we could do it. We did that against Arsenal when they had Mikel Arteta as their deep midfielder. We did it against AC Milan, against [Andrea] Pirlo, and it worked really well.'

As in 2009, United took encouragement from potential weaknesses in Barça's defence. Club captain Puyol had suffered a knee injury a month earlier and failed a fitness test, starting on the bench. Guardiola was forced to gamble in his back four selection.

The most pertinent and poignant move involved Abidal, who was making his first start since being diagnosed and treated for a cancerous tumour on his liver. Abidal played just seventy-one days after a life-saving operation, an incredible feat. That the manager had such faith in him is a tribute to the Frenchman's courage and work ethic. Guardiola kept the information secret from the players until the last moment, unusually for him naming his team in the Wembley changing room. That way, Abidal reserved his adrenalin to get through the game, rather than fretting overnight.

My former Liverpool teammate Mascherano deputized for Puyol. Javier was one of the great central midfielders of his era, but the opposite of what you expect in a centre-half. At Anfield he was a jack-in-the-box, scurrying to win tackles and keep forward momentum, complementing Xabi Alonso and Steven Gerrard. He will not mind me saying he was also one of the smallest of the great footballers I worked with, which is why the cup final previews included numerous discussions about his role. Theoretically, any long, high ball would cause him a problem.

United's keeper Edwin van der Sar kicked long and direct throughout, deliberately targeting Piqué's physicality against Rooney as well as Mascherano. A susceptibility was highlighted in the 8th minute. Van der Sar struck the kind of clearance a tall, commanding centre-back would comfortably head from danger. It was over Mascherano's head. Rooney, who looked sharp, was almost in. Victor Valdés intervened, punching clear from the edge of his penalty area.

'Before the final, I had only played five games at centre-back,' said Mascherano. 'The first time was against Shakhtar Donetsk in the quarter-final. At the beginning, it was not easy. You know if you make a mistake it is a goal. I was able to adapt because the players around me always gave me passing options.

'Defensively, Pep asked his centre-backs to play very high. That was good for me because although the position was different, the zone I was in was the same. We knew Rooney was very clever at getting behind the defensive midfielder so Busquets would need help. By playing high, we were always close to Busquets and had his back. That is one of my big memories of the game. I knew playing against Rooney would be tough, but the team around me gave me confidence.

'What I found different in that position was the challenge of keeping my focus, always living and watching the game, because I did not have so many actions as when in midfield.'

Testing the fitness of Abidal and suitability of Mascherano to play centre-back was an obvious United plan. There was a key stipulation: they needed the ball to enforce it.

After the ten-minute mark, that proved beyond them. United's players were as much spectators as the 87,000 fans inside Wembley, witnesses to a masterclass of ball retention from a team also showing its fleetness at suffocating the opponent and winning it back.

Despite United's energetic start, Rooney sensed early that it would demand a Herculean effort to sustain the required tempo for ninety minutes. The pressing of the front players had to be unrelenting and in unison. He realized the way that United had set up would not work. 'With Barcelona, and how Manchester City are now, the problem you have is they are so patient,' he said. 'They will keep the ball and pass it sideways ten times if necessary, just waiting for when the forward pass is on. So against teams like that, I feel you must defend between the lines. As a forward, you can't just keep pressing them because they will wait, let you get tired and punish you.'

When we see Liverpool do this under Jürgen Klopp, it is not only about their front players. It is as if a starting pistol is fired and everyone takes a predetermined position. United were not so accustomed nor well tuned to playing without possession, so whenever I paused the action to identify where players were moving when Barça played from the back, it was haphazard. Sometimes Giggs was the most advanced player close to centre-half Piqué. This was brave, risky and doomed, because there was no harmony between the ten outfield players.

I spotted multiple examples of United's faulty attempts to press high. When Giggs did it, there was sometimes as much as 25 yards behind him to central midfield partner Carrick. That enabled Barça to bypass Giggs with a short pass. Carrick was therefore constantly outnumbered, Busquets, Iniesta, Xavi and Messi thriving and exploiting the area vacated by Giggs's high press.

The more I watched, the less I understood how Ferguson thought this was the right strategy.

Against that Barça side you had to assume having between 30 and 40 per cent possession. There had to be three key thrusts of the tactical plan.

First, how could you ensure Barça did not turn dominance on the ball into goalscoring opportunities?

Second, how would you instruct your players to win the ball back?

Third, once you had it, how would you create chances of your own?

Question three was irrelevant without answers to one and two.

United were set up so ambitiously, Ferguson seemed to think an open game would create chances at both ends. Big mistake. His players were blockaded everywhere, so even when they did get the ball back they were flustered, rushed into hopeful passes which presented it straight to a Barça player.

'We went into the game knowing we were the better team, but they were stronger physically than us,' said Mascherano. 'All our training was about controlling midfield. We knew we were always going to have one more player in there because they played 4-2-3-1 with two midfielders, Carrick and Giggs, and one second striker, Rooney. We played the midfield three with Messi the false 9, creating that square with Busquets,

Iniesta and Xavi. In this system, the wingers Pedro and Villa were so important keeping their position to ensure United's defence stayed as a back four. Pedro and Villa occupied the full-backs and centre-backs. It meant the centre-backs never knew whether to go to Messi or stay back.'

Within a quarter of an hour, the possession was 66 per cent in Barça's favour and opportunities increased, especially as Messi kept receiving the ball where he most prospered: 40 yards from goal, facing a defence, free to dribble, shoot or pick out Villa and Pedro.

Ferguson saw what was coming on 24 minutes, rushing into the technical area on the sidelines with a face of thunder. What had he expected? That United could press Barça's back four and midfield all night? Either Ferguson underestimated his opponent's greatness or overestimated his team's ability to implement an audacious game plan.

Pedro scored just three minutes later.

It looked so straightforward. United's difficulty began when Van der Sar kicked long and Piqué won a header with Rooney, midway into Barça's half. The thirteen seconds between that and Pedro scoring offer a stark illustration of the United players' confusion. When Piqué won the header, Carrick was shadowing Xavi on the halfway line, poised to compete for any loose or 'second' ball. That showed his and United's intent, the deepest central midfielder 10 yards higher up the pitch than had his instruction been to fulfil a containment role. Xavi was first to Piqué's downward header, so Barça already had three-versus-two in central midfield: Carrick and Giggs against Xavi, Iniesta and Busquets. Xavi nudged the ball a couple of yards back to Iniesta and made a darting run forward. Carrick, rather than following Xavi, felt close enough to Iniesta to press him. A miscalculation hundreds of midfielders made.

'For me, Iniesta is the most talented Spanish player I've ever seen,' said Xavi. 'He has been one of the best partners on the pitch. His ability to keep possession of the ball, win in a one-on-one situation and create opportunities, and recognize the last pass before a goal. He was incredible from when we first saw him play in La Masia when he was thirteen or fourteen. You could already see he could become one of the best players in football history.'

After a quick one-two with Busquets, Iniesta passed forward to Xavi, who was now in space beyond Carrick and Giggs. With four snappy passes of no more than 10 yards, three Barça players against two of United's became one, Xavi, all alone, running against a defence with no midfield shield. Classic Barça.

Giggs chased Xavi but was too far back, meaning that for the first goal there were four attackers – Xavi, Messi, Pedro and Villa – against four United defenders.

For United's centre-backs, Ferdinand and Vidić, the lack of protection from midfield was a nightmare. 'Rio and Vidić were hesitant, in two minds,' said Rooney. 'Sometimes they would push forward, and we were too late, so Messi could turn and get through. I remember Rio speaking to the manager from the pitch, unsure whether he was meant to keep his position or go closer to Messi.'

I find this revelation hard to believe. Everyone knew how and where Messi flourished, so there had to be a preventative measure in place. Such a conversation should have been held in the days, or even weeks, before the final, not during it.

United's issues were exacerbated by their full-backs being similarly confounded by how to deal with the threat of Barça's wide men. '[Left-back] Patrice Evra would run infield to follow Villa or Pedro,' said Rooney. 'He did that a lot where he would end up in front of the centre-backs. That left Vidić and Rio exposed. They were so hard to play against with Villa and Pedro coming inside to pockets. That is why Evra kept getting pulled in, following them.' Evra did this on several occasions, feeling it was his job to track Pedro or Villa whenever they were in his territory.

When it happened for the opening goal, Ferdinand and Vidić were stranded as Pedro first moved infield, taking Evra with him, before changing direction and sprinting wider to the edge of United's penalty area. Having initially pursued Pedro, Evra felt he had to switch his attention to Messi and stayed infield. Right-back Fábio did the same with Villa. When I paused the picture at the moment Xavi released his cute right-foot pass to Pedro for the first goal, Evra and Fábio were effectively in a holding midfield position, so United had a two-man backline and the goalscorer was unmarked.

As Pedro celebrated following an emphatic finish to Van der Sar's left, Vidić turned to Evra to question his left-back's positioning. The movement of Barça's front men had caused chaos. A camera shot showed Rooney with an expression which reminded me of how Sami Hyypiä and I felt when Kaká kept running at us in the first half in Istanbul during the 2005 Champions League final. 'I was thinking, "What the fuck is going on here?"' Wayne said. 'There have only been two occasions in my career when I have been confused on the pitch. That night was the first.

'When we didn't have the ball, Fergie wanted us to get around Bus-quets. When we had it, he wanted us to try to break away. The problem was, whenever I could get goal-side of Busquets, it did not faze him whatsoever. He could pass 5 yards behind you and take you out of the game. I would have preferred to let him have it and drop deeper to help in a midfield three to reduce his passing options, because as soon as they had two-versus-one or three-versus-two on Carrick and Giggs, you ended up outnumbered and confused. Then you get frustrated that you are always chasing. Then you press high and leave more spaces behind, which is exactly what they wanted.'

Follow-up question, then. When was the second time Wayne Rooney felt so helpless?

'When I was back at Everton and we played Pep's Manchester City,' he told me. 'They played a similar system to Barça, with all the mid-fielders and strikers coming inside. They just bamboozled you. Sam Allardyce was manager and we had been playing 4-3-3, with me on the left of the middle three. Then we played Man City at home and the day before the game he told us we were playing 4-4-2. Not with a number 10. With two out-and-out strikers. I was playing centre midfield with

Morgan Schneiderlin against De Bruyne, Silva, Fernandinho, Sterling and Sané. I was like, "What?" I said to Allardyce, "Me and Morgan will be all over the place." He thought we could press them high. It was the same as at Wembley in 2011. I was like, "What am I supposed to do here? Where do you want me to go?" Against City we were 3-0 down at half-time and I was dragged off after 57 minutes. I went off snapping, but when I think back about it now, I couldn't wait to get off given what was happening. So that day in midfield for Everton reminded me of 2011. Their players were so hard to mark, because you could never see them to follow their movement. There was always someone behind you, so small, so sharp and able to get away even if you got close, so you could not get near them.'

For all that, and to United's credit, they equalized thanks to a moment of individual quality from Rooney – United's best player on that Wembley night. It is a special goal, even more so given the circumstances.

Giggs was in an advanced position and offside as he teed Rooney up as the striker followed his own pass into the penalty area. That should not diminish the class of the finish, finding the top corner past Valdés.

This should have been Ferguson's get-out-of-jail card. No manager wants to admit a tactical mistake when losing 1-0 and having to chase a game, but at 1-1 there was an opportunity to reset. United's failure to do so is harder to justify than the starting line-up. Ambition before a game is understandable. Anyone can misread how it will go. You can get carried away by seeing your team blowing most opponents away, or by how sharp they look in training. But when the game is in progress and it is so obvious how it will pan out unless you change? You must respond when it is not working.

As I watched and reached these conclusions, I felt anxious about this chapter. Who am I to question one of the greatest managers of all time? Putting aside the Liverpool v. Manchester United rivalry, I loved Ferguson's competitiveness, and how determined he was to impose his and his team's personality on every match he went into. I simply feel that on this occasion he was mistaken.

Why was Ferguson so emboldened despite the 2009 defeat?

The cup final line-up had worked in the first leg of the semi-final against Schalke, United winning 2-0 in Germany to set up an emphatic 6-1 aggregate victory. United were unbeaten in the competition before Wembley, winning nine of twelve games.

But Schalke were no Barcelona. And no English opponent that season was near them.

In the Premier League, Ferguson's use of Giggs in a creative central midfield role was effective in helping United dominate, and Rooney had flourished as a number 10 behind the pacey Hernández. Yet any scout report must have warned Ferguson of the folly of going toe-to-toe against Barça in 2011. At best, it was naive.

When the line ups were announced before kick-off, even the most optimistic Manchester United fan will have worried. A central midfield partnership of Giggs and Carrick against Barcelona's four-man diamond formation was plainly wrong. With the greatest respect to two great players, even if United had had Roy Keane and Bryan Robson in their prime playing in such a system they could not have dealt with what they were up against without help.

'The truth is that we were surprised that Giggs played in the midfield,' Xavi told me. 'I'm not sure what Ferguson's strategy was. Maybe it was about more ball possession, or about stealing the ball from us. Regardless, we controlled the ball with long periods of possession. We were very technical and that's why I think we were better than Manchester.'

Ferguson's common sense surrendered to romanticism. He was two years from retirement and knew this was one of his last chances to win the Champions League. The game was held at the venue where Sir Matt Busby won United's first European Cup in 1968, and if it was going to signal the beginning of Ferguson's grand farewell on the Continental stage, being part of a thrilling, end-to-end attacking final which he might lose served his legacy more than constructing a turgid, dull match in which his team could compete by stifling flair and representing the antithesis of everything he stood for.

'The truth is we could have played 4-5-1, sat back and defended for ninety minutes and still got beat 3-0 by that Barça side,' said Rooney. 'But I felt that was the only way we were going to win either of those finals, to frustrate them. We almost needed José Mourinho to manage us just for those two games in 2009 and 2011.'

In fairness, Mourinho's adversarial methods were no guarantee of success against Guardiola's Barça either, although they were more likely to cause problems.

On 29 November 2010, Mourinho made the same misjudgement as Ferguson would six months later. Inspired by what had been the greatest start to a managerial career at Real Madrid, Mourinho headed to the Nou Camp for a La Liga fixture believing his side could win an open, attacking game. He played 4-2-3-1 with Mesut Özil as a number 10 and Xabi Alonso and Sami Khedira his deep central midfielders. Barça destroyed Mourinho's side 5-0 in the Nou Camp, a performance which Rooney recalls giving a standing ovation from the comfort of his living room. He says that was the night he declared in favour of Messi ahead of his former United teammate Ronaldo in one of the enduring disputes of our era.

'My missus walked in and I was standing there clapping,' he said. 'She's looking at me thinking, "What are you doing?" I was like, "It's Barcelona. They were just fucking brilliant." That is why when people debate Ronaldo versus Messi you can go either way, but because of those games and having been up close and seen how good he is, I always go with Messi. He is just incredible.'

Mourinho would not make the same error again. His response to the heavy beating when the clubs next met was belligerence, shifting Özil wide to accommodate central defender Pepe in an antagonistic midfield role in a 4-3-3 alongside Alonso and Khedira. Between 16 April and 3 May 2011, Real Madrid and Barcelona played an epic series of 'El Clásicos' comprising a 1-1 draw in La Liga, a Real Madrid victory in the final of the Copa del Rey (the 'King's Cup' – the Spanish equivalent of the FA Cup) and a two-legged Champions League semi-final. Barça emerged

3-1 aggregate winners from a brutal, ill-tempered European tie in which Spanish international teammates resembled sworn enemies. Pepe's 61st-minute sending off in the first leg at the Bernabéu when the score was still goalless swung it Guardiola's way, Barça scoring twice late on, including one of Messi's greatest goals.

Despite ultimate victory, with Barça crowned La Liga champions on 11 May, Guardiola appeared scarred by the battles. Such was the psychological toll as he took on Mourinho on and off the pitch while navigating through the personal politics at his own club that on the eve of the Wembley final his mentor Cruyff suggested it might be Pep's last game in charge three years into the job. Cruyff evidently had personal knowledge of Guardiola's intentions, although it would be twelve more months before Pep left for a year's sabbatical prior to re-emerging at Bayern Munich.

'When Pep said that he was tired and that he needed to rest, I thought it was a shame,' said Xavi. 'But I respected his decision. I remember thinking that he could have continued with that generation of players. He has been the best coach worldwide of the last twelve to fifteen years, that's for sure.'

Perhaps the flawlessness and comfort of the Wembley win eased Pep's state of mind for his additional season. Certainly United never threatened to make the final a war of attrition like Mourinho's Madrid. Spellbindingly good as Barça were, they faced an opponent who enabled them to showcase their brilliance.

It is a valid question as to whether this is really one of the greatest games or should be regarded more as one of the greatest European Cup final performances. I accept that. It would have been more of a spectacle if United had followed Madrid's semi-final blueprint. Nobody of sound judgement would have been critical or considered it a negative had United gone that way at 1-1. Quite the contrary. The manager would have been praised for reacting.

The obvious move was to take off Javier Hernández, a peripheral figure, and replace him with a combative midfielder to at least try to deny

Barça space. I saw no problem with Rooney's position, trying to occupy Busquets. The difficulty was behind Rooney. To prevent being so over-run, United desperately needed an energetic central reinforcement to make it four-versus-four, with Rooney, Giggs, Carrick and one other to mirror the positioning of Busquets, Xavi, Iniesta and Messi. Without that change, United were always going to be a man short.

Midfielders Darren Fletcher and Anderson were on the bench and could have filled this role. Unfortunately, Fletcher was recovering from an illness which kept him out towards the end of that season, otherwise I am sure he would have been involved. Anderson had started the 2009 final but was subbed after 45 minutes. Ferguson must have felt both play-ers could do a job, otherwise why have them in his eighteen-man squad?

Rather than make a change, buoyed by the equalizer he stuck to his original plan. He did not make a substitution until having to chase the game in the 69th minute, winger Nani replacing right-back Fábio. 'The manager felt the Premier League tempo was higher than La Liga so wanted us to keep that,' said Rooney. 'The only change at half-time was he switched Park and Giggs. He wanted Park in the middle for more energy and a bit more bite. But you could have put anyone in there in that system and it would not have worked. We should have played 4-5-1, a flat five in front of the four, and let them have it in front of us and close the space wide. They may not have hurt us so much out there.

'But yeah, some of the decisions around that final were a bit strange. Fábio da Silva played. His brother, Rafael, was a better player. Dimitar Berbatov was not even on the bench. There were a couple of other deci-sions where I wondered what was going on.'

The only noticeable shift at the start of the second half was Barça's.

Into sixth gear!

Minutes 46 to 69 in the 2011 Champions League final are as close as you will see to football perfection. I could dedicate a book each to those who crafted Barça's victory that night – Busquets, Iniesta, Xavi and Messi.

Xavi is my favourite footballer of the last thirty years, a truly unique

midfielder. One of my earliest memories of seeing him was in an England Under-21 match played at Birmingham's St Andrew's stadium in
2001. I was in the senior squad playing at Villa Park the following night,
and watched this small kid dictating the game, so quick and incisive.
No one could touch him as England's juniors, led by Howard Wilkinson, lost 4-0.

The following November I had a closer look in a Champions League
group game at Anfield. Seven months after beating Barcelona over two
legs in the UEFA Cup semi-final, when Xavi was an unused substitute,
we lost 3-1. We were outpassed and outplayed. Xavi was the inspiration,
The Kop applauding Barça's performance. I remember Steven Gerrard
and I walking off the pitch in awe of the Spanish maestro. I had never
seen such a phenomenal midfield display.

In our next meeting, in 2007, we had more success based on a game
plan designed to reduce Xavi's productivity. Under Rafa Benítez, we
were drawn to play Rijkaard's Barça in the Champions League round of
sixteen. Xavi, now heading towards his prime, played in both legs.
Messi, still a teenager, was a winger then. We were under no illusions
about the only way we could win: an unashamed containment policy,
packing midfield, men behind the ball, accepting we would not have
much possession, denying space and time, and using pace up front to
nick a goal from a counter-attack or set-piece.

We won 2-1 in the Nou Camp, later going through on away goals after
a 1-0 defeat at Anfield.

Those games required as much tactical discipline and concentration
as any in my career. Xavi only needed to spot one gap in your defence
over the course of ninety minutes and it might result in an assist. There
was no let-up.

What took Xavi to another dimension is the fact that you already had
to make a concession of some kind before kick-off. You could not stop
him setting the tempo. All you could do was accept he was going to have
most touches of the ball, deliver most passes, and ensure Barça would
force you to spend most of the game chasing and defending.

No matter what the stage, Xavi's ability to orchestrate from midfield continued throughout his senior career. He was named player of the tournament when Spain won Euro 2008. In 2010, he was the heart of Spain's World Cup-winning team with an astonishing 91 per cent success rate in passing over the tournament. He provided two assists in the Euro 2012 final as Spain defended their title, the first time any player had done this in consecutive finals. No matter how big the game, Xavi delivered.

The statistical breakdown of this 2011 final makes for particularly astounding reading. Xavi had the most touches of the ball – 157, twenty-six more than Messi. Xavi completed the most passes – 141, thirty-four more than Iniesta. A statistic displayed on 46 minutes showed Xavi's pass success rate was 95 per cent. In a Champions League final, when nerves are supposed to impact on performance, that is unreal.

'That's what our plan was, to control the game by having the ball,' he told me. 'Iniesta, Busquets and I interacted and understood each other on and off the pitch. We were aware that none of us were the best defenders in the world, but in the end, you defend with the ball. If you have the ball, your opponent doesn't have it. This is one of Cruyff's commandments: long possessions, creation of advantages, and always aiming for the goal. My best partners in my career have been Iniesta, Busquets and Messi.'

Together, Xavi and Iniesta completed 248 passes. As a team, United made 286. As for the passing combinations, Xavi and Iniesta combined sixty times over ninety minutes, topping the list. Contrast that with Manchester United's passing sequences in this game. The two United players who passed to each other the most were Ferdinand and Vidić with sixteen combinations.

Eight Barcelona players had more touches than the most involved United player, Wayne Rooney. Rooney was on the ball sixty times. For perspective, that was thirty-three fewer than Barça right-back Dani Alves.

As for touches in the danger zone, Messi (twelve) had more in the United penalty area than every opposition player combined (ten).

Barça had twenty-three shots to United's five.

By any definition, this was a hammering. The first twenty-four second-half minutes were when Barcelona purred most, pinning United back and scoring the two goals that allowed them to ease to victory.

At the start of the second half, Ferdinand had obviously decided enough was enough in terms of Messi being left alone in front of United's defence. I could see he was trying to push towards him, playing a higher defensive line so that Messi did not have so much time on the ball in the final third. This could work in isolation to halt an attack, but Rio could not sustain it because he knew he would be leaving too much space behind for the speedy Pedro or Villa.

United's 4-2-3-1 was not designed to be compact with defenders, midfielders and attackers close together. So long as Barcelona waited – and they were always prepared to wait – they would benefit from United's imbalance eventually. 'You see the result of this most clearly with our second goal, when the midfield passing makes the space for Messi and he is able to shoot from the edge of the penalty area,' said Mascherano. Yet again it was three versus-two in midfield on the edge of United's penalty area.

Messi's shot on 54 minutes was fierce, but a keeper of Van der Sar's class should have saved it. Regardless of the error, the goal was coming, and it was fitting and inevitable that Messi made the game-changing contribution.

'What can one say about Messi?' said Xavi. 'He is the most decisive player I've ever seen. He's at a different level. An unrivalled player. I said back in 2008 or 2009 that for me he was already the best player in history. He would do what Maradona, Pelé, Cruyff and [Alfredo] Di Stéfano did twenty, thirty and fifty years before, and he still does it. He has been playing this way for fifteen or sixteen years, controlling all aspects of the game – attacking, defending, shooting, and scoring free-kicks and penalties.'

Once Messi struck, for the next fifteen minutes Barça toyed with United, pulling players out of position, creating chances and making a third predictable.

Ferguson's first substitution backfired within seconds as Nani was flummoxed by Messi's genius. The Argentine attempted fifteen dribbles on the night (the entire United team attempted eighteen between them). His most constructive saw him bewilder Nani on United's left and rush at goal before tricking Evra. In the ensuing panic of halting Messi in the 6-yard box, Nani's lame attempt to clear fell straight to Villa on the edge of the penalty area. He controlled and picked his spot in the top corner.

There was not even the hint of a comeback, despite Barça visibly slowing up in the latter stages. A Rooney shot from distance and a strong claim for handball against Villa were the closest United came to setting up a nervous finale.

Once Ferguson replaced an exhausted Carrick on 77 minutes, he could have removed any of his players as an act of charity. He and his teammates looked punch-drunk. Carrick's frustration had been evident when he collected a yellow card after an hour, not for the first time left alone in midfield with no choice but to bring down Iniesta.

Ferguson's scowl had become a gracious smile by full time. 'Nobody's given us a hiding like that, but they deserve it,' he said in his post-match interview. 'In my time as manager, it's the best team I've faced.'

Carles Puyol elevated the emotions by inviting Eric Abidal to collect the Champions League trophy.

'We were clearly superior,' said Xavi, accurately summing things up. 'We had more possession; we created many goal opportunities and deserved the victory. It was one of the most complete games we ever played. Being a final, it was key for us to play our game at our highest level, and we did.'

The mesmerizing manner of Barça's win inspired coaches to spend the next few years trying to imitate their panache, to such an extent that wherever you watch football around the world today you will see centre-halves taking the unorthodox position on the side of their penalty area when a goalkeeper is in possession. It is not enough for keepers merely to save shots any more. They must be adept with feet as well as hands.

Wide strikers are the current fashion, with almost every top side playing 4-3-3. Number 10s are currently an endangered species in the Champions League knockout stage.

Even my referencing positions with numbers shows how Barça helped transform the dialect of football in England. Where once we spoke about attacking and defensive midfielders or strikers, now the jargon is all about number 8s, 6s and 9s. I first noticed this when Benítez brought several coaches from Barça's academy to our youth set-up between 2008 and 2010.

Pep Guardiola is deservedly viewed reverentially as one of the game's revolutionaries; every coach who copies him proves that they believe the Barcelona side between 2008 and 2012 a product of the manager's vision. Pep has always charitably attributed the splendour of his Barça team's football to the qualities of the players. With the quartet of Messi, Xavi, Iniesta and Busquets, anything was possible.

I have referred to this era as that of Guardiola's Barcelona. I asked Mascherano if it is more accurate to see this game as part of the Messi story. Javier said that 2011 was the merging of 'so many extraordinary players in the same place, at the same time, with the ideal coach to develop his ideas of how to play. The midfield three and Messi were born to play for Barcelona. They were all so compatible with each other. That is the hardest thing you will find in football. You will see lots of teams with good players, but they do not always complement each other. They may have some qualities but lack others. But on top of that we had a player in Messi who had everything.'

We all have an idea of what constitutes the 'right' way to play football, and as interviews throughout this book demonstrate, that is itself a contentious term. I do not believe in a right or wrong way because I am not a football snob. I only faced Barcelona twice in knockout football during my career, both times on the winning side and provoking withering, unjust criticism about our defensive tactics.

It was most vociferous after the 2001 UEFA Cup semi-final, which we won 1-0 on aggregate thanks to Gary McAllister's penalty in the second leg at Anfield. The Catalan media destroyed us. The Godfather of beautiful football, Johan Cruyff, gave an interview in which he was scathing about us and Ottmar Hitzfeld's Bayern Munich side, which had recovered from its 1999 Champions League final defeat to Manchester United to win the competition two years later. 'They're all about name and prestige but, in football terms, we're talking about two horrible teams,' Cruyff said. 'You might think I'm exaggerating but in my opinion a team is horrible if they are incapable of stringing three passes together.'

We saw Cruyff's remarks as petulant, disrespectful, and ignorant of how far we had come as a team and club in a short time. Why must everyone see the game in one way? We demonstrated that football is about many qualities, especially when a side is not blessed with the same technical prowess as Barcelona. Nobody at Anfield thought reaching the 2001 UEFA Cup final at Barça's expense was 'horrible', even if we barely touched the ball for 180 minutes.

When Cruyff said he was prepared to lose playing his way rather than win playing another, I believed him and admired his principles while fundamentally disagreeing with him. Do you think I, or any footballer, would rather not have a Champions League or FA Cup final winners' medal because the opposing team played a more attractive brand of football?

'There are two kinds of football – attacking and defensive football,' said Xavi. 'Both can win matches and titles. Of course, with attacking football you can be stopped. A team like Atlético Madrid, who close down defensively, is a good example. Barça were eliminated in the Champions League semi-finals by Inter [in 2010] and Chelsea [in 2012]. But I still believe that offensive football has a better chance of winning.'

For me, Xavi's emphasis on winning is the most important point of his argument. The reason Guardiola played the way he did, and will continue to do so, went beyond style. It is because he correctly assessed it gave him the best chance of success. Who can argue with a manager who at the time of writing has won twenty-nine trophies and is bound to win more?

But I do not for one second believe Guardiola agrees with Cruyff that principles cannot be compromised to win. I recall a game against Everton in October 2016 in which Guardiola sent on centre-back Vincent Kompany to play as an emergency striker for the last four minutes, trying to turn a frustrating draw into a victory by playing long balls in and around the penalty area. I found that reassuring. Not because I am enthusiastic about a primitive brand of football. It is because I am passionate about managers pursuing every angle to get results.

Whatever your belief on how it is achieved, I will always argue that football is and always will be about winning. That was how I was brought up by my dad, Philly, who treated every game in the Sunday League in which he managed as if it was the European Cup final. Anything else is alien to my competitive instincts.

The game is most captivating when there are multiple systems within a league or cup tournament, each evolving through the generations, as I have tried to describe during my analysis of some of the greatest games. Certain basic principles and tactical variations never change.

Every aspiring coach works around limited choices. Will they opt for three, four or five defenders? Is the preference for wingers whose profile is always to attack, or wide midfielders suited to playing centrally and assisting their full-back? Are full-backs encouraged to cross the halfway line or is their job primarily to defend? What is expected from central midfielders? Are they free agents who can go box to box? Creators and goalscorers? Or does the coach prefer combative 'water-carriers' who will cloak his defence, win the ball, harry the opponent and be acclaimed for enforcing tactical discipline? What strikers are the club scouts looking for? Tall, physical target men who are suited to long-ball, direct football? Predators who offer little without the ball, but come alive when there is space to detect in a congested penalty box? Or technical, versatile front men who take as much pleasure from an assist as a goal as they drop deep into the number 10 position?

Pragmatic coaches want elements of all the above so they can consider alternative concepts from one game to the next. Others are fixated on playing one way with a devotion which verges on the religious.

Guardiola is the coach of the modern era attracting most disciples. This has been inspiring and dangerous for those who do not have the raw materials he had at Barcelona and Bayern Munich, and currently has at Manchester City. Managers who try to play the Barça way with footballers of limited ability and goalkeepers who cannot accurately pass to defenders 10 yards away are often accused of favouring style over substance.

'Everyone tries to play out now,' said Rooney. 'Even watching recently promoted teams coming into the Premier League, fighting relegation, 1-0 down, you see they are playing out from the goalkeeper. I am thinking, "Come on, you have to get it forward quicker, get it into the box and give yourself a chance, surely?" It surprised me during my time in the MLS [Major League Soccer]. Every single team was trying to play out from the back. I was thinking, "You are not good enough to do this, so why are you doing it?" The coaches see Guardiola and want to bring that style over. Now don't get me wrong on this. That is brilliant, and it is the football we all want to see. But the most important point is you must be good enough to do it. If you try to play that way without players who can, you are just causing yourself massive problems. If you are a manager, you must know your players. If they are good enough to do it, then yeah, brilliant. If it is not working, there is no shame in going for the front man and going for second balls to get results.'

I believe part of the problem is a misunderstanding of the phrase 'playing direct'. It incorrectly has negative connotations. Direct football does not have to mean a long, hopeful punt in the general direction of a striker. A pinpoint 60- or 70-yard pass to an attacker sprinting into the penalty area to score can be as beautiful as an elegant twenty-five-pass move resulting in a tap-in. In fact, I would describe the former as the best pass in the game. Manchester City goalkeeper Ederson regularly attempts (and succeeds with) perfectly weighted passes to the halfway line and has on occasion passed so long beyond a back four he has sent Sergio Agüero through on goal – so clearly Guardiola agrees.

I love that the game has advanced technically, and the more that can be filtered down the levels, the better. At the highest level, and in international football, these improvements have enhanced the sport. Club owners, supporters and fans are less tolerant of managers whose greatest forte is organizing teams defensively. Any emerging coach hoping to manage an elite club in the future will have to show they are similarly adept at coaching their players to get the ball from one penalty area to the other in a stylish way.

But I have grown to hate hearing managers unveiled at press conferences saying they want to press from the front and play out from the back, as if any pass over 20 yards is prehistoric.

I think coaches fear being labelled as outdated and stroke their egos by allying themselves with the language of Guardiola and Klopp.

If such a side is promoted playing from the back, it is unreasonable to expect the manager to order his players to forget everything and play long-ball football in the Premier League. But mixing it up is more likely to yield positive results for those squads with smaller budgets.

Barcelona between 2008 and 2012 were special for a reason. Can any side seriously plan to imitate them without a massive transfer outlay or four of the best players who ever kicked a football coming through their youth academy at the same time?

Rather than copy, it is vital for clubs to decide upon, understand and be fiercely protective of their own identity, to be aware of trends and what rivals are doing, to be continually observing the emerging coaches so that when the time comes to make a managerial change, the disruption is minimal.

In some cases, such as Everton, I believe that identity was lost at certain points over the last thirty years. Arsenal's shifted in between

George Graham's pragmatism and Arsène Wenger's inventiveness. Manchester City pretty much started from scratch in 2008 and have gone through another major refit under Guardiola. Their challenge will come after he has gone, deciding whether whoever follows him must stick to the same principles.

England have never seemed sure what their identity is; current head coach Gareth Southgate is on a mission to define it.

My own club, Liverpool, had to find a way to reconnect with an identity so distinguishable during the seventies and eighties, a potent mix of high-energy, front-footed football with the shrewdness to kill a game and stifle opponents into submission when necessary. To me, the Liverpool way has always been about 'finding a way to win', preferably in as attractive a manner as possible, but not as a compulsion. It is a way that has made the club European champions six times compared to Barça's five.

Manchester United have recently suffered as Liverpool did in the 1990s and early 2000s, searching for the man who will upgrade and execute the methods of their legendary Scottish coaches.

Barcelona have always stuck to their philosophy. That will never change. Between 2008 and 2012, the ideals of Cruyff and Guardiola fused to prove it is possible to be a football romantic and a winner, setting mind-blowing standards against which all future Nou Camp coaches and players will be judged. As the club's struggles in recent seasons of the Champions League have shown, that legacy can be a blessing and a curse, virtually impossible to replicate, let alone better.

I spoke to Xavi days after the club's heavy Champions League defeat to Bayern Munich in the 2020 quarter-final. The expectation was growing of him leaving his position as coach of Qatari side Al Sadd to fulfil his destiny as the natural successor to Cruyff and Guardiola. 'One day,' he told me. 'I am currently preparing myself for that and it is very exciting. I have to wait for the right situation and timing to go back. It is a dream to train Barça and to win, and that is my objective. I believe that my road map is the right one.'

Xavi's Barça story clearly has more chapters to come. Wherever the script next leads him and Barcelona, Guardiola's side will always deserve to be set apart. Such teams as the 2011 Champions League winners emerge once in a lifetime. For that, all of us who had the pleasure to see them, and every other club hoping to enjoy similar success in the future, should be grateful.

11

Wednesday, 25 May 2005

2005 UEFA CHAMPIONS LEAGUE FINAL
Atatürk Olympic Stadium, Istanbul

AC MILAN   3 – 3   LIVERPOOL

Maldini *1*   Gerrard *54*
Crespo *39, 44*   Šmicer *56*
                           Alonso *60*

Liverpool won *3-2* on penalties

'I needed to see Steven Gerrard with the trophy. I needed it
because I felt I was in some kind of dream. No, not a
dream. A nightmare. I had to convince myself it happened.'

– Hernán Crespo

THE CHAMPIONS LEAGUE FINAL WAS heading towards extra-time when I found myself in a high-stakes poker game with Hernán Crespo.

Andriy Shevchenko shrugged off Dietmar Hamann, skipped past Sami Hyypiä and slid a pass to his Argentine strike partner at an angle in our 6-yard box. Chasing a hat-trick, Crespo had a choice: go for goal or lay into the path of Kaká who, should he score to make it 4-3, would surely win the European Cup for AC Milan.

Sprinting into my defensive position, I too had a dilemma: engage or wait. In my younger, more vulnerable years I might have dashed at the forward and tackled. Now I had the experience to slow down and initiate a bluff. My body position invited a shot while I was primed for my preferred option of challenging Kaká.

Crespo showed his hand. He passed, and I pounced, forcing a fifty-fifty with Kaká in which he shot well over.

I lay on the turf longer than usual and stared beyond Jerzy Dudek's unscathed goal. I was catching my breath. Relieved. Elated. Exhausted.

This stand-off barely lasted a second, so swift that the 69,000 spectators inside the stadium and a TV audience of millions may have missed it.

My mistake, misjudging a header on the halfway line, had set Milan on this attack. Had I not helped retrieve the situation, my role in our defeat would have been torturing me ever since.

Many of my memorable interceptions and tackles, including this one, are described as instinctive, rushed and last-ditch. This wasn't. It was scripted and executed in the moment between Crespo receiving and releasing. Strange as it sounds, to me everything was in slow motion. My heart was pounding but I was not panicked, nor flustered. I was composed and considered.

I played 737 times for Liverpool, winning seven major trophies over sixteen years, but everything preceding and since Istanbul in 2005 is defined by 120 minutes and nine spot-kicks in the Atatürk Stadium. If there is a sequence I would wish to replay to sum up my career, the one of which I am most proud, this is it. Under the circumstances, I consider it my most important piece of defending for Liverpool.

Fluctuating emotions return when I'm reminded of such incidents. Some aspects of that night in Turkey I vividly recalled upon repeat viewing. Others surprised me. Reviewing the footage was like reassembling a jigsaw in which for fifteen years certain pieces had been in the wrong place. These were reconfigured upon seeing the goals conceded and scored, the defensive challenges and muscle spasms endured in extra-time, and all of my frenzied attempts to order midfielders to track back. I was momentarily returned to the edge of our penalty area, constantly straining my rotating neck as Shevchenko, Crespo and Kaká charged on.

There were periods in the first half when I squirmed at how bad we were; in others during the second, we were more accomplished than I thought. A few incidents before the end of full time I would have sworn were in extra-time.

The ambition of our starting line-up still baffles me, the team selected the antithesis of the defensive security, ingeniously organized by Rafa Benítez, which took us to the final. And our escape from what looked like being sporting catastrophe still astounds me.

This was an evening when the small details had alternating traumatic and triumphant consequences for both teams, the cards eventually falling in our favour with Shevchenko's decisively timid penalty aimed directly at Jerzy Dudek.

The quick summary is that Benítez's tactical acumen combined with Steven Gerrard's class and inspiration to pull us from desolation to euphoria. Istanbul was that and far more: skill, courage, character, quick thinking, a never-say-die attitude, luck, canniness, a touch of gamesmanship and several bouts of cramp.

'Leave nothing on the pitch,' they say before a final. Each of us kept that bargain all right.

I know for sure the journey to the winning podium did not start amid the shame and humiliation of being 3-0 down at half-time. Nor with a low-key Champions League qualifier against Austria's AK Graz the previous August, an evening when Michael Owen's omission signalled his Real Madrid transfer. The chain of events takes in the watershed of Benítez's appointment in the summer of 2004 and absorbs Gerrard's numerous history-changing contributions over the preceding two years. The captain's performances in the 2003/04 campaign were as close as you will find to one player single-handedly dragging a team into the Champions League.

My timeline goes further back. It assimilates the 2001 UEFA Cup, part of a cup treble, and the European restoration process triggered by Gérard Houllier, without which Benítez could not have progressed us to the next level.

One of the deceptive consequences of Istanbul, and recent European success under Jürgen Klopp, is that those taking a casual view of Liverpool history seamlessly blend eras into each other, as if the 1990s were a transitional blip before Houllier and Benítez picked up the baton left by the legends of the 1970s and 1980s and off we went again.

This underestimates their achievement.

At the start of the millennium, Liverpool's European success was something to appreciate only in the club's extensive archives. To quote former captain Alan Hansen, by then a respected pundit on BBC television, we were in danger of becoming 'a relic'. Liverpool had made no immediate impression when the Heysel ban was lifted. Between 1991 and 2000, the club spent six seasons in either the European Cup Winners' Cup or UEFA Cup. Losses, mostly early, came against Italy's Genoa, Denmark's Brøndby, Russia's Spartak Moscow, Strasbourg of France, and Spain's Celta Vigo – quite the distance from future knockout victories over Barcelona, Real Madrid, Inter Milan, Roma and Juventus. While the generation before us spoke of the glories of Rome, Paris and Wembley as Bill Shankly, Bob Paisley and Joe Fagan collected European and UEFA Cups, younger fans were talking about a 'legendary Anfield night' against Auxerre in 1991 when Graeme Souness's side overturned a 2-0 first-leg deficit in the second round of the UEFA Cup. The best showing under Roy Evans was a semi-final defeat to Paris St Germain in the Cup Winners' Cup in 1997.

The Liverpool at which I was trying to establish myself at the end of the 1990s, which Houllier left his job as the French Football Federation Technical Director to revive, was at a juncture. The football world had moved on, leaving us trailing on and off the pitch. Our training facility was described as a 'barracks' by Houllier, unfit for purpose, and was subsequently rebuilt. Anfield itself was ageing, the board announcing plans to move to a new stadium in Stanley Park. Chairman David Moores sought external investment from Thailand, Dubai or the United States.

In 1992, the European Cup was rebranded into the more lavish and financially rewarding Champions League. Liverpool did not participate in it for the first nine years of the tournament's renewal, drifting further behind Manchester United and Arsenal as they consumed increasing UEFA and broadcast earnings. Finishing in the Premier League top three and qualifying for the biggest competition in club football was our first priority at the start of a season.

Foreign superstars lured to England wanted to work with Sir Alex Ferguson or Arsène Wenger. Then Roman Abramovich bought Chelsea, making them one of only three clubs to win the English title between 1996 and 2012. We were fighting to keep our best players as much as making world-class signings, even the home-grown superstars like Steve McManaman and Owen, both of whom joined Madrid, and Gerrard, who was the subject of several high-profile bids from Chelsea. Games were played against a backdrop of what they meant for the star players' future rather than the club's.

Houllier and Benítez had to get every deal right because we could not afford expensive mistakes. They also had to diplomatically respect Anfield values while modernizing them, ensuring that the sobering reality of the daunting challenges facing us did not puncture the fans' faith in the glory days returning. There was no such certainty.

Houllier astutely set about that process, building a side to complement the flourishing academy players – myself, Robbie Fowler, Owen and, most important of all, Gerrard. We became a mentally and tactically tougher and more disciplined Liverpool. The 'Spice Boys' reputation was obliterated, the work/life balance of younger players tipped in the right direction.

'Don't go to nightclubs now, buy one when you retire,' Houllier told us.

After a transitional two years, the 2000/01 campaign is still massively underrated. We beat Champions League-calibre teams to win the UEFA Cup: Roma, Porto (who would win the European Cup in 2004) and, most memorably, Barcelona in the semi-final, reviving the majesty of Anfield on those intoxicating midweek nights, and just as importantly repairing the club's competitiveness and self-esteem on the Continental stage.

At that time, I craved the FA Cup more than the other prizes of the cup treble, that being the competition which had more meaning for me – heading to those Wembley finals as a youngster, dreaming of becoming a professional footballer. Houllier and the recently appointed Liverpool chief executive Rick Parry said winning in Europe and finishing in the Champions League mattered most.

They were so right. Without Houllier putting the stamp back on our passport, we would never have been in a position to recruit Benítez, who twice won La Liga with Valencia and had just lifted the UEFA Cup.

After recovering from a near fatal heart attack shortly after the 2001 treble and eventually paying for too many poor transfers, Houllier departed in 2004, but his work ensured the club he left was unrecognizable to that which he had joined. We were not the intimidating and stylish Liverpool of old imposing a cultured, attractive short passing game on overawed European opposition. We were underdogs, resilient and headstrong, scrapping for every point and trophy. Supporters had to adjust. Once on board, they cherished it, The Kop reconnecting with players and managers whom they saw representing their street-fighting identity.

Over time, Benítez enhanced that, his meticulousness, attention to detail and ability to identify tactical nuances mid-game more impressive than any coach I worked with. The better the opponent, the greater his gift for breaking down their strengths and incapacitating them. His training sessions tasked players with operating in specific zones so that attackers and midfielders were the first lines of defence, players having to work selflessly to prioritize clean sheets.

If Houllier was the mentor who turned me into a professional, Benítez was a university professor who made me the player I was. I was ready for the next tier of my education. Rafa was the perfect coach at that stage of my career, his style built around the Arrigo Sacchi model where organization began with the centre-backs.

No sooner had the new manager arrived than he presented me with my first homework assignment: a DVD of the great AC Milan defence of the 1980s, arguably the best back four ever. Franco Baresi, Alessandro Costacurta, Mauro Tassotti and Paolo Maldini are the gold standard. 'Watch them, study them,' Benítez told me as he enrolled me on to a Masters degree in the art of defending.

I was in awe. Still am. Between them, those four played over two thousand games over a combined eighty-three years. Amazing.

I first watched AC Milan in the late 1980s and early 1990s when the side built by Sacchi and later led by Fabio Capello won three European Cups. In my mid-twenties, Baresi became my idol. He was not the tallest of defenders, so was my ideal prototype. He did not just play the game, he read it, organizing those around him so there was a synchronicity when either pushing the defence high or hanging back on the edge of the penalty area. Benítez wanted me to apply this to Liverpool's back four in the way Argentinian centre-back Roberto Ayala had in his Valencia side. No one could ever reach Baresi's level, but I relished the responsibility.

In the Premier League, my first season as an out-and-out centre-back was not successful. After losing Owen we were an unbalanced side, chronically short of goals, with Benítez coming to terms with the differences between English and Spanish football. He needed a year to work that out.

In the winner-takes-all bouts in Europe, where games are slower and more strategic and the intimidation of The Kop could be influential, we were a different animal, capable of executing Benítez's vision regardless of personnel. Players were chess pieces, so at our most effective his invisible hands guided us to the correct sector of the pitch, he and his coaching staff with diagrams for every scenario. If you did not carry out his instructions, he was intolerant. The creative, more free-spirited players sometimes had an issue. His system was about control, not improvisation. Early on he suggested that Gerrard 'ran too much'. It was an analysis, not a complaint. He meant he took up too many positions for an orthodox central midfielder, which naturally left gaps for others to cover. The counter-argument was if Stevie had not been such a player, we would never have qualified for the Champions League in 2004; his habit of dictating events with individual moments of brilliance could supersede any tactical innovations.

I could sit here and write another ten thousand words about formations and match plans, but if Gerrard had not slammed in a 25-yarder past Olympiakos in the 86th minute of the final Champions League group game in December 2004, this chapter would not exist.

Has any goal been so influential on Liverpool's history? Not between 1990 and 2019. Without that 3-1 win taking us into the knockout rounds on goal difference, Gerrard would have left for Chelsea and the next six years during which we were always Champions League contenders probably would not have happened.

We definitely would not have been in Istanbul without Gerrard. The vast difference between the first and second halves of that final also illustrates that without the right set-up to facilitate his talents, he would not have been able to inspire us to win.

Istanbul has something for everyone. You can dine out on the world-class performances of Kaká, Andrea Pirlo, Crespo and Gerrard, or tactical aficionados can feast on the many changes in shape switching momentum. But the most controversial and radical decision did not happen on the night. It occurred sometime between 3 May 2005, when Luis García's contentious goal beat Chelsea in the semi-final, and the hours before we kicked off in the Turkish capital.

Everything Benítez stood for as a coach – his insistence on defensive structure, balance and fortitude, and methodical schemes for how to nullify the opponent's strengths – was compromised by his team selection.

We made the final having not conceded in 297 minutes of European football because of Benítez's expertise and the nous of those of us drawing from our 2001 experience. With and without Gerrard, we had frustrated potent attacks because Rafa kept getting every big call right.

Of all Benítez's tactical triumphs, I defy anyone to find one better than against Juventus in the quarter-final. We led 2-1 heading into the second leg in Turin and secured a 0-0 draw there, despite our captain and Hamann being absent with injury. The midfield three was Antonio Núñez, Igor Biscan and Xabi Alonso. Alonso, returning from injury, had not played or trained with the team for more than one week in the previous three months. Juventus coach Capello used Zlatan Ibrahimović and Alessandro Del Piero as his strikers, with Pavel Nedved floating from the left to be more of a number 10. Using me, Hyypiä and Djimi Traoré as three centre-backs, Benítez confounded Capello. Biscan and Alonso sat deep in front ensuring Nedved was crowded into anonymity, and although the Italians had a couple of dangerous moments, they never created clear chances.

I knew Benítez was a shrewd strategist when he arrived. Turin confirmed it.

In the semi-final against the 4-3-3 of José Mourinho's Chelsea, the design differed, but the idea was similarly effective. We reverted to our usual 4-4-1-1, ordering two midfielders to sit deep, wide midfielders to track back to assist full-backs, and Gerrard deployed behind striker Milan Baroš. Gerrard was perfect in that role, hassling Chelsea's deep midfielder Claude Makélélé. With Makélélé unsettled, Chelsea were never able to control the pace over two legs despite dominating possession, while they lived in fear of our captain's ability to score or create anywhere within 30 yards of goal.

We knew we were only going to get through those three matches with clean sheets. Mission accomplished. Benítez had outwitted Capello and Mourinho. Liverpool's chairman Moores had his own description for Rafa: 'Our Special One'.

Everyone at Anfield presumed we would attempt to overcome Milan with the formula that had given us our shot at glory. It was the same in Milan, where manager Carlo Ancelotti asked Crespo – on loan from Chelsea – to provide a detailed report on our strengths and weaknesses.

'By the final I knew everything about you,' Crespo told me. 'After you beat Chelsea, Carlo said to me, "You know Liverpool very well. Please follow them and give me a document so I can explain to the team how Liverpool play." I studied and wrote everything about you and your team. That was my preparation. I watched a game against Arsenal at Highbury, the game after your semi-final when you lost 3-1. It was a big defeat. I thought if we take care of our identity, stick to our idea, we could play a great final. The way I thought you could score was maybe a corner and Hyypiä header, or maybe something amazing from Stevie G or Luis García. I gave the document to Ancelotti. I do not know if he used it or not!'

I spent the build-up similarly assessing Milan. The scout report in my head identified multiple threats in Ancelotti's side, although because of the way they set up, two players worried me most: Pirlo and Kaká.

Milan had evolved since their classic eighties/nineties line-up of Sacchi's 4-4-2 and were now playing a 4-1-2-1-2 diamond. They were a *Who's Who* of European football legends, packed with existing and future

World Cup and Champions League winners. Seven of their line-up had been victorious in a European Cup final penalty shoot-out against Juventus two years earlier. Pirlo was the modern playmaker controlling the tempo with his incisive and varied passing rather than outmuscling midfield opponents to win possession. That was the job of his midfield allies Gennaro Gattuso and Clarence Seedorf. Our number 10 was critical as a first line of defence as much as a creative measure. We needed someone with energy and awareness to shadow Pirlo and make the maestro's evening uncomfortable. Thirty yards ahead, Milan had World Cup winner and future World Player of the Year Kaká, arguably the best around in that position at the time. I thought it inconceivable we would line up without an orthodox defensive midfielder to patrol the zone in which Kaká operated behind Milan's strikers. Fortunately, this was Didi Hamann's forte.

My curiosity grew before the game when Gerrard confided in me that Benítez had told him he was going to start with Harry Kewell. Even though our supporters had lost faith in Kewell because of his injury record, whenever he was available Benítez was tempted to use him. I partially understood that because Harry was so gifted in possession and would offer more attacking threat than others. If he played on his favoured left wing, maybe he could trouble the great but ageing Brazilian right-back Cafu.

That was not my worry.

'Where are you going to play?' I asked Gerrard, trying to figure out who was making way.

The captain was central midfield, so Kewell would play as the number 10 rather than on the left. That alarmed me. Filling the gaps, I realized that if Gerrard was falling back into central midfield, and Alonso was a guaranteed starter, Hamann was out.

Who was going to look after Kaká? Who was going to push up against Pirlo? Kewell did not possess the experience, fitness or defensive awareness to do the same job on Pirlo as Gerrard had on Makélélé. Harry was a provider or goalscorer, not someone to repel attacks at source.

Gerrard had mixed feelings. 'I was delighted I was playing in the middle,' he said. 'My concern before the team was picked is that I could have been on the right of midfield because of Didi and Alonso. They would have been my first two picks for sure. I wasn't really fussed whether I was off-the-front or centre-midfield.' Closer to kick-off, he too had nagging doubts. 'I thought we could have picked a "safer" team,' he said. 'No way in the world would I have left Didi out because of the instant security he provided. From a personal point of view – knowing when you go forward you do not have to worry what is behind. Didi was such a comfort blanket.'

I was shocked and worried. Why change what had worked against Chelsea? Aside from that, Hamann was used to playing in prestigious games, not least the World Cup final in 2002. Invaluable experience.

I said nothing to Didi. We had trained as usual, with Rafa alternating personnel in the 4-4-1-1, keeping everyone guessing about the starters. Even on the coach to the stadium, Didi presumed he was in. I avoided conversation.

'I'm glad you didn't tell me,' he said. 'I would rather not know. Your thoughts might be somewhere else. I was thinking about the game. What's gonna happen? What are we going to do? It would have been detrimental to my preparation and performance if the manager had told me. I did not know I was not playing until he said Kewell's name in the dressing room. I was disappointed, yes, but then you've got to get in the right mindset, as hard as it was, because I fully expected to play and I didn't see it coming.'

No one did. All these years on, I had to ask Rafa: what were you thinking?

'I decided I did not want to go into the game only to defend,' he explained. 'By the final I thought we could play with more confidence. We were playing well after beating Chelsea, and I had confidence that we could play, pass the ball and get forward. That is why I wanted Stevie and Xabi as the two in the middle because of their quality on the ball, and I knew Stevie could attack and defend. With Harry, although the fans were always saying he was injured, when you analysed his game he had such quality on the ball. He was good in the air, a good dribbler, a good shot. So we wanted to use him between the lines to trouble the AC Milan defence. We knew he could do something.'

Whatever the justification, it could not have gone worse. I am not being wise after the event. What happened in the first half was the sum of my fears. Pirlo and Kaká ran the game and made most of us look out of our depth.

My most critical observation is this: we did not look or play like a Rafa Benítez team.

'The biggest problem was the defensive midfielder,' Rafa acknowledged. 'We were not so accustomed to playing a team with Milan's diamond formation, and with Kaká free it was a system that we found it difficult to adapt to. Kaká was between the lines, Stevie going forward, Xabi not the quickest, and the centre-backs could not go against him because you had to look after Milan's two strikers.

'Sometimes you have to say the other team is really good. They have a way of playing you cannot control at that moment.'

There was another prominent factor in our terrible start. No matter what team or formation a coach chooses, he cannot legislate for players being overcome by the occasion. You can react in two ways ahead of a Champions League final, puffing out your chest and feeling you belong, or looking into the eyes of a star-studded opponent, strolling past the glittering European Cup and thinking, 'Should I really be here?' Self-doubts need immediate expulsion. Allowed to fester, they consume you.

That is what happened to Traoré in the game's opening moments. I noticed his anxiety in the tunnel as I glanced down the line at my teammates. Everyone was nervous. Most of us felt ready. Djimi looked terrified.

His edginess showed itself immediately. Receiving the ball at left-back from Gerrard straight from kick-off, he passed down the line and gave the ball to Gattuso. Then he made the mistake of chasing his own misplaced pass rather than staying in his position. Having made it back to left-back, he fouled Kaká near the corner flag.

Thirty seconds had been played, the props from the opening ceremony were still being cleared, and Liverpool were about to go one down.

Milan's free-kick leading to the quickest goal in European Cup final history is peculiar. Pirlo was a set-piece expert, and in normal circumstances the taker in that position will try to deliver the ball where it is most difficult to deal with, between the goalkeeper and line of defenders so that one of the attackers can attack the ball aerially. Instead, Pirlo kicked low to the edge of our penalty area. If it was anyone else you would say it was poor, possibly even mishit.

Not Pirlo. This had to be pre-planned.

He turned his body and struck the ball in such a way it is obvious he did not want to put too much elevation and power on what was a pass more than a cross, sending it in Maldini's direction. Rather than join the cluster of bodies waiting near the 6-yard box, Maldini had deliberately hung back outside the penalty area. With our defence taken by surprise by this unorthodox set-play, Maldini eased in unmarked and beat Dudek with a right-footed volley – his first touch of the game.

Fifty seconds on the clock.

Game plan ripped up? Not yet.

For thirty minutes we seemed reasonably competitive, and the immediate response to going behind was to force Milan keeper Dida into a save from Hyypiä's header, and a terrific volley from John Arne Riise, which looked goal-bound until striking defender Jaap Stam. These encouraging signs meant that when Kewell suffered a recurrence of a groin injury on 18 minutes (hobbling for another five until he was subbed), rather than call Hamann, Benítez remained ambitious and turned to another creative midfielder, Vladimir Šmicer.

Our first change of system did not help us tactically, altering to a 4-2-3-1 rather than addressing the Pirlo and Kaká conundrum about to be spectacularly exposed.

We were working our way out of defence into midfield fairly well.

Passing options ran out in the attacking third. When Kewell was on, García and Riise had nowhere to go when receiving in wide areas, crowded out by the full-backs Cafu and Maldini and covering midfielders Gattuso and Seedorf. Kewell played too high up the pitch, so what was supposed to be 4-4-1-1 was more like 4-4-2 and there was no link between midfield and attack. Once Kewell was off, Šmicer played on the right and García in a more central role, but Baroš was isolated. I counted five occasions when Riise had the ball on the wing, able to deliver with his trusted left foot. Each time, Baroš was the only attacker in the penalty area, a mismatch against Stam and Alessandro Nesta.

That meant that even during our reassuring moments in possession, the tactical malfunction was evident. And as is often the case when a side is unbalanced, Milan were becoming more dangerous whenever we attacked. Our shortcomings were laid bare every time we gave the ball away. With each breakdown in their half, Pirlo could collect, look ahead and see Kaká in space between our defence and midfield. Hyypiä and I were constantly running backwards as the Brazilian waited to pick his pass.

What made us even more susceptible is the quality of the Milan strikers' movement. Our defensive line underwent a relentless examination, making it essential none of us were out of synch. If one of myself, Hyypiä, Steve Finnan or Traoré were a yard back from the others, we were in trouble. Whenever Kaká cruised forward and we stepped up to try to play Crespo and Shevchenko offside, we were praying for a linesman's flag.

At 1-0, there were a couple of times when Kaká played the strikers through and we were lucky to escape. There would have been at least two close first-half video assistant referee (VAR) calls in the modern era. As the warning signs became more frequent, I was howling for greater protection. It was only a matter of time before Milan got it right.

Milan's second on 39 minutes came from such a counter-attack, García still appealing for a penalty after Nesta fell on the ball with his hand. Pirlo took out three of our players with a 6-yard ball to Kaká. He was away, balletically drifting through the gears, choosing his option.

I had never played against Kaká before. I obviously knew he was good. Only when sharing the pitch with him did I realize how extraordinary he was. He kept showcasing his ability to receive the ball back to goal, control, spin and waltz at our defence. He had a rhythmic running style, a player of such grace and balance he could hurt you with his dribbling or passing.

'Against a "normal" player, if they turned or spun away I could probably recover, or at least have a good chance of recovering,' Gerrard explained. 'But the speed Kaká used to travel with the ball – it was like he ran faster with the ball than without it. It reminded me of when I'd first come up against Steve McManaman when I was very young and training with the first team.'

The only way to stop Kaká was to make sure he never received enough possession. With Pirlo dominating midfield, we were failing, taking our punishment twice in five minutes before half-time.

For Milan's second, Kaká picked out Shevchenko running beyond Traoré on our left, and what was either a deliberate, perfectly placed cross or a scuffed shot dropped to Crespo, who clinically beat Dudek at the far post.

Now I was frantic for half-time so that we could reshape.

'I said to Pako [Ayestarán, the assistant manager], be ready because we will change to five at the back,' said Rafa. 'As soon as I speak to the players, take Didi to warm up.'

The pain was not over. Milan's third after 44 minutes demonstrated what we were up against, a goal worthy of any final created by a superstar ready to leave his indelible mark. This time it was Gerrard's loose pass falling to Pirlo deep in Milan's half, but what followed was sheer footballing brutality. Pirlo exchanged a pass with Cafu, then slid another of those short, swift, penetrative dispatches to Kaká. What the Brazilian did was mesmerizing, turning Gerrard with his first step and in the next striking a slide-rule 50-yard pass between our centre-backs. I saw it coming but was powerless, my outstretched right leg serving only to magnify the visual magnificence of the supply to Crespo.

In that split second, the Argentinian realized that only an equally audacious finish was worthy of such an assist. Without breaking stride, he clipped beyond Dudek. Suffice to say, I appreciate its beauty more now than I did then.

'Maybe it is one of my greatest goals,' said Crespo. 'I scored a goal similar to this against Fiorentina in the league, but this was better being in the final. At that moment, I felt so good it was like anything was possible. Really, I thought I could do anything. I felt confident, free and really in good shape. If I needed to dribble, if I needed to shoot, if someone asked for the ball so they could score, I thought I could do it. I was so ready for that match. I prepared for it like it was the World Cup final and the last game of my life, eating well and only drinking water for days. Mentally and physically I was never fitter. Now I was in this amazing team, with these amazing players. Just look at the names. Wow. Since being a boy in Argentina, seeing Marco van Basten score two in the Champions League final for Milan, I had dreamed of this.'

We were being bullied and taunted. Not physically, and not in a provocatively arrogant way. They were just far better. It happens. Had I been in my co-commentator's chair, I would have been applauding.

The UK's broadcasters understandably reached the same conclusion. 'Milan are playing football from out of this world – nobody could live with this,' said ITV commentator Clive Tyldesley. 'Game well and truly over,' said Sky's Andy Gray, a statement many Liverpool fans took particular relish informing me about in the days that followed. You can't blame Gray. I thought the same when I was out there. We were all guests at the Kaká and Pirlo show, Milan giving one of the greatest of all European Cup final performances.

What did Gerrard think?

'Fucking hell,' he said. 'I actually felt individually and collectively inferior to them. It was a feeling like we weren't on Milan's level, personally and as a team. They were out of our reach. I was a bit scared, to be honest. I knew this could get worse. Usually you think maybe we could try x, y and z, but there was no positivity in my mind. I remember Xabi and me having conversations, saying, "What can we do? We just can't get any control." The pitch just felt so big and it felt like we were both lost in there. Whatever we did, I knew Rafa had to do something.'

There is one question I have been asked thousands of times since 2005: what really happened at half-time? The greatest games can create the biggest fictions. Few have been documented and romanticized more than the fifteen-minute interval in the Atatürk Stadium.

There is a charming idea that we huddled and listened attentively as Benítez delivered a Churchillian address, pumping our blood to inspire the mother of all cup final fightbacks. Rafa was measured, not rousing. No one considered a comeback. If the referee had walked into the dressing room and asked if we wanted to halt the game and take a 3-0 defeat, plenty would have shaken hands. The only way to make this better was to stop it getting worse.

Right-back Finnan was arguing with the club physio Dave Galley about whether he was fit to continue. He pleaded to stay on, but Rafa explained he could not take the risk. After struggling to recover from his tough start, Traoré had been told to 'take a shower' – the polite code for being subbed. Now he was re-tying his bootlaces and being given a change of position. Hamann was already warming up outside, preparing for the second half. Major problem. Another eleven were about to join him. Substitute Djibril Cissé, kitted out and ready for his introduction, had to put his tracksuit back on.

Rafa was as shocked as all of us, but calm amid carnage. Out came the tactics board for a reshuffle: three centre-halves, two sitting midfielders, Gerrard and García as roaming number 10s behind Baroš. This was the system we had used so effectively in Turin, Hamann and Gerrard naturally giving it a significant upgrade.

Given that Milan's formation under former Juve manager Ancelotti was not so dissimilar to Juve's under former Milan manager Capello, I have always thought that Rafa had this plan B if circumstances demanded it. He was not panicked when restructuring.

'Yes, maybe in the back of my mind was the Juventus game,' Rafa confirmed. 'It was a change I often made when I was in Spain. Against Barcelona we would play five at the back because of the width of the Nou Camp. You needed to cover your full-backs against their wingers. At 3-0 down you need to find some solution, and this was all about managing the gaps in the middle. Didi was a specialist in the position.

'I knew I had to give something to the players. At 2-0, I was writing some words. Then we conceded another. I was thinking about how I can motivate the players in English. My English is not great now, so imagine at that time! I was worried about making a mistake with my language. Sometimes in those days I would say to Stevie "Be careful with the player on the wine" when I meant to say "on the wing"!

'There were two key decisions. First, five at the back. Then to switch the substitution so Finnan, not Traoré, was changed.' The priority was gaining control – making it more of a fight – not to engineer a complete recovery. 'My message was we had worked so hard to be here and now we had nothing to lose. For the next twenty minutes we just wanted everyone to try their best. Then, if there was nothing, maybe we would have to try to reduce the damage. The main thing is get a goal and see what happens in the reaction of the teams.'

Beyond the players' tunnel you could hear the faint sound of 'You'll Never Walk Alone'. Our club anthem was not being sung as it had been an hour earlier, or as it is before every Liverpool home game. This was slower, gentler; as if we were attending a requiem.

I felt utterly helpless. We were being outclassed by a technically superior opponent, stripped of hope. Given Milan's greater quality I knew there was a possibility we would be beaten before kick-off, but I'd thought nothing would demean the achievement of reaching the final. The prospect of an embarrassing scoreline changed that. Even the prestige of defying the odds and getting so far was being snatched from us.

My mind was not only on closing the seemingly unbridgeable gulf in class. I was thinking of my family and friends who had made the trip to Turkey, and how I would struggle to look them in the eye upon our return to Merseyside. I would be tormented by this tainted memory, each reminiscence about one-sided finals, every quiz about memorable defeats, and all casual references to this Liverpool team accompanied by a laughter soundtrack. We would never shed the burden.

I specifically recall being aware that Milan had beaten Steaua Bucharest and Barcelona 4-0 in previous finals, and how their hunger to eclipse that meant there was no prospect of mercy. Some later suggested that Milan's players had already started celebrating.

'No, impossible – impossible,' Crespo told me, the hurt of those false claims still raw. 'In a dressing room with Maldini, Pirlo, Stam, Seedorf, Nesta, everyone? No way. Nobody was even thinking of that. Nobody approached the second half like it was 3-0. The message was clear. We start again like it is 0-0.'

Milan were too experienced, too professional to think any other way. They were as bloodthirsty as ever.

Although I understand the obsession and theatrical licence taken with some of the half-time flashbacks, there is no need for the behind-closed-doors fantasies. The facts in open view are dramatic enough. 'What happened to Liverpool in the first half?' has always struck me as more appropriate and verifiable. 'What the hell happened to AC Milan in the second?' even more so. As the saying now goes at Anfield, cometh the hour, cometh Hamann.

When Milan kept pickpocketing our midfield and adding to their goal tally, Didi was not so sure he would be the designated saviour. 'The first thing I thought when Rafa told me to get ready was, "Thank fuck for that, I am coming on,"' he said. 'Then I thought, "What the fuck am I going to do? We are 3-0 down!" Usually, unless you are an attacking substitute, the further you go behind the less chance you've got of getting on. As the goals were going in, I never thought about coming on. When the third one went in I thought, "That's it." I was just empty. We were up against a better team but never gave ourselves a chance to win. When we got into the dressing room, Rafa didn't say anything to me. He told the lads to have a drink and we'll make a change, telling everyone I was coming on for Djimi. So I went through where I would be at the set-pieces and then went outside with Pako.'

While we readied to drag ourselves through the remainder of our ordeal, Hamann felt more emboldened. 'The longer I was warming up, the more I thought, "You know what? Fuck it. If we get the first one I'm pretty sure we will get another one." The fans were still singing. Not with a full voice, I did not think, but in a way that was saying "it's OK, we're going to support you whatever happens". It was a strange feeling, but every final we had played had turned into a dogfight in which we always came out on top. Obviously we were a long way from that, but I did know even the best team might react if they conceded. What I was really focused on was making sure Milan did not score again. Don't concede, get the next goal, see what happens. That was all we could think about, really.'

Milan anticipated Rafa's reaction, tentatively imagining Hamann's introduction was a preventative measure against further punishment. 'When Benítez put Hamann in the middle and let Steve Gerrard free it was a great substitution, but I think he put on Hamann to cover the defence to stop losing another two or three goals,' said Crespo. 'You had more order, more equilibrium in your team. Then, something happened . . .'

Initially, positive signs were modest, but Didi's presence changed the pattern. Because Gerrard pushed up against Pirlo, there were several occasions at the start of the second half when full-backs Maldini and Cafu were unable to locate their playmaker. This forced a pause and a reassessment, by which time they were closed down. In the first half, Milan's full-backs had space to ease into our half unchallenged. Now they looked to Gattuso and Seedorf and saw wide centre-backs and wing-backs covering, making forward passing options riskier.

Ninety seconds after the interval there was a tactically significant sequence. Maldini was forced to ignore an easy 6-yard inside pass to Pirlo because Gerrard was there. When Maldini looked up there was no choice but to hit long, hopefully, awkwardly and wastefully, down the left with his right foot. Hyypiä cleared. Kaká tried to collect. Who was there to pick up the loose ball? Hamann.

Within five minutes of the second half, three successful tackles by Alonso, Gerrard and Hamann on Gattuso, Seedorf and Pirlo were one more than our midfielders had managed against the Milan trio in the whole first half. We had not been able to get near them for forty-five minutes. Now we could hunt in a pack, so even when Kaká turned away from his man in his own half and began one of his forward dances – as he did when skilling Alonso in the 48th minute – Hamann was in his eyeline. Kaká elected to pass short to Seedorf. End of move.

The other rudimentary difference is we stopped suffering for individual mistakes. We made two in two minutes and escaped. Dudek fumbled a 49th-minute cross and it luckily bounced to safety. Next, Traoré miscontrolled, allowing Crespo to pounce, Milan's break ending with Kaká winning a free-kick after Hyypiä's foul on the edge of our penalty area. This time Dudek made an excellent save from Shevchenko.

'People do not talk so much about that one,' said Dudek. 'When I saved it I thought, "At least I have done something in this game." If that goes in? No way back.'

Then came six minutes which for Liverpool supporters echo in eternity.

Inevitably, the starting pistol for what is referred to as the 'Miracle of Istanbul' – three goals between minutes 54 and 60 – was fired by Gerrard. After Riise intercepted a wayward Maldini delivery to the edge of our penalty area, Gerrard clipped a pass which Pirlo would have been proud of to send our wide man scurrying down the left. By the time Riise (or 'Ginger' as we call him) checked his run 40 yards up the pitch, his next move was back to Gerrard. Stevie passed inside to Alonso and instantly scampered towards the Milan penalty area – something he would not have been free to do earlier. As Gerrard took his position, Alonso swapped possession with Hamann and then fed it back to Riise, now another 10 yards up the pitch. Four players worked the situation brilliantly with seven passes.

Before our reshuffle, whenever Riise was in this position to cross he had only Baroš to aim for. This time, Nesta was marking Baroš, Stam was on García, and Gerrard was alone on the edge of the area, 5 yards ahead of Pirlo, Gattuso and Seedorf who were ball-watching, unaware of the threat.

Riise's first attempt to cross was blocked by Cafu so Gerrard had to check his run by the penalty spot. That should have meant the chance to pick out Gerrard was gone because Stam had time to get close and make a challenge. It also made it more difficult for Stevie to use his forward momentum to get pace and power on any header.

What Gerrard did with the successful second cross, stretching to make meaningful contact and beat Dida, is so difficult to do. Stam, knowing he was too far from Gerrard and having failed to react, sought a scapegoat. He looked accusingly at Maldini. Gerrard looked to the Liverpool fans at the far end of the stadium. 'My initial reaction was a bit of relief,' he said. 'I asked for more from the fans out of emotion. It was an "at least we've scored one for you" type of thing. Then it quickly swung into a bit of hope.'

The tone of the UK commentators was suddenly cautiously optimistic. 'Hello, hello,' Tyldesley said. 'A grain of doubt in Milan's minds. Hold on. This could be some ride. You never know with Liverpool.'

Our confidence swelled, while Milan momentarily lost focus, continually squandering possession from kick-off. We had it back within eleven seconds of their restart, although there are a couple of details in the build-up to Šmicer's second, just two minutes after Gerrard's header, which underline how fate smiled on us. First, we put together a crisp eleven-pass move which was halted by the linesman's flag against García. For some reason Spanish referee Manuel Mejuto González either did not see it or encouraged the game to go on. It is a ridiculous decision since Milan were defending the edge of their box and had no advantage, forcing Seedorf to hastily clear upfield straight to Traoré.

We attacked again, Traoré finding Riise on the left. He won what would have been an innocuous throw-in off Gattuso – a non-threatening position but for what followed.

Not for the last time in Liverpool's Champions League history, here is where we must give thanks to UEFA's multi-ball system. Kaká had seen the ball bounce 40 yards out of play and, as would have been the case when using a single ball, presumed he had plenty of time as Riise retrieved it. The Brazilian took the opportunity to adjust his shin pad, unaware that an alert ball boy was hastily supplying Riise for the throw-in, assisting us in our desire to keep the game at 100mph. When Riise threw to Alonso, Kaká was a couple of yards away, bent over, fixing his socks. Had he not done this, the short throw to Xabi might not have been made. Kaká would have been there either threatening or making a challenge, or forcing Alonso into a pass which was less speedy and proactive.

As Alonso rapidly redirected the ball inside to Hamann, Kaká realized the game had moved on. He was too late.

Hamann had now guided the ball sideways to Šmicer.

Vladi's strike from 25 yards was more audacious than venomous and Dida was slow to react, possibly distracted by Baroš's positioning as it looks like the shot will deflect off him. Instead, the striker avoided contact and Dida's hand was not strong enough to keep the ball out.

These small details had huge ramifications.

Hope became belief.

'Every time I see Vladi's goal now I think, "How well did Baroš do?"' said Gerrard.

He contributed even more to the equalizer.

My first sense that something was changing came early in the second half when I realized how much space I had as the right-sided of three centre-halves. Our new system worked well against Milan's diamond because their wide midfielders, Gattuso and Seedorf, played narrow. There was no one within 15 yards of me whenever I took possession out wide. It gave me a chance to use the space and run forward those 15 yards and see what options opened up, knowing I had Hamann ready to cover me.

With Šmicer now a right wing-back, we exchanged passes in the 50th minute and I went on an underlapping run from centre-half, bypassing Seedorf. I attempted a give-and-go with Baroš, but his return ball was not in my path, so I ended up in a fifty-fifty tackle with Stam. That came to nothing, but it was encouraging that I could get so far up the pitch and beyond Milan's midfield. It needed a strong challenge from a centre-back to deny progress.

This was an important memory in the build-up to the equalizer on the hour mark.

Once more, Milan were careless from kick-off. We had it back within seven seconds and were on another charge. Fuelled by our fans making the Atatürk sound like Anfield, I felt a surge of conviction as if I was back on the school playground. I repeated my underlapping run from centre-half, made the same movement to combine with Šmicer and Baroš, and this time the striker's hold-up play allowed Gerrard to join in. Baroš's clever lay-off was perfectly weighted, enabling Gerrard to take the ball in his stride running at full pace into the penalty area and invite a mistimed challenge as Gattuso toiled to track his run.

'I knew who it was at my back and I knew he was going to have some kind of bite,' said Gerrard 'He was one of those players. He couldn't help himself. So you just delay . . . just delay . . . and then I just felt his touch on my leg and I was gone.'

While the supporters were ecstatic, I wanted more than a penalty. All I could think was 'Red card, red card!' It had to be. Gerrard had a goal-scoring opportunity. There is no way he would have missed. This was a professional foul. I pleaded with the official, impelling him to take firmer action. I knew Milan going down to ten men would change everything, regardless of whether we scored the pen. They would have had to take a striker off and ditch their diamond formation.

This was not a case of trying to get a player unduly sent off. I was remonstrating with the referee to get him to apply the rules correctly. There is a distinction between that and gamesmanship, conning an official to get an opponent into trouble. The more you see the replay of

Gattuso taking Stevie down when he has a goalscoring opportunity, the clearer it becomes that he should have been dismissed. In the new world of VAR, Milan would have been a man down.

Referee González showed yellow. Even though we were about to complete the most improbable comeback in European Cup final history, I was fuming.

Then I saw García try to pick up the ball and went berserk again. 'Fuck off, Luis,' I screamed. Alonso was the designated penalty-taker.

Alonso stepped up, scoring on the rebound, and then nearly had his neck broken by Baroš in the celebrations.

Hernán Crespo still finds those six minutes incomprehensible. 'The first goal, for Stevie G to score a header from that angle? Not normal,' he said. 'Then Šmicer from so far? No. Then a penalty is saved by Didi and the ball still lands back at the feet of Xabi Alonso to score again? No. There were goals we knew we could expect from Liverpool. Not those goals. They were strange goals. I thought, "This is not possible." How I remember it is, after your six minutes to make it 3-3 we started to play well again and make opportunities to score.'

If scoring three in six minutes was the first fairy tale, getting through the next sixty-one without conceding was its equal. Here is where my memory tricked me, and perhaps everyone else watching that night.

Gabriele Marcotti, the English-based journalist for Italy's *Corriere dello Sport* in 2005, sums up the general view of the game. 'The enduring narrative was out of 120 minutes, Milan were in control for 114,' he said. 'That is why there was so much disbelief. Those six minutes were a freak. Milan were in control and they started to play well again at 3-3. They were ahead, stumbled, and now off and running again. There was a sense they were still going to win.'

This is not just the Italian perspective. 'Those six minutes were pretty much the only six minutes you had all night,' recalled Tyldesley. 'You went from 0-3 to 3-3, but Milan dominated the rest of the match.'

That is how I recalled it, too. Until I rewatched the game.

Milan undoubtedly regained their composure and looked the more accomplished side again. What pleased me is that in the twenty-five minutes following our equalizer we were able to make the game more like a conventional, evenly contested final. To do that, every player in red had to be at 100 per cent technically and tactically – the polar opposite to the first half. For forty-five minutes we were nothing more than a punchbag. That was not the case after half-time. This was a proper fight now. At one stage our fans were even shouting 'Olé!' as we kept the ball, our midfield trio unrecognizable.

For all the talk of an illogical, irrational comeback, although the six-minute spell is obviously unique in a fixture of such stature and there is no disguising the freakishness of the timing and nature of our goals, from a tactical perspective, what happened in the second half in Istanbul is not so unbelievable or inexplicable. On the contrary, it is a vivid, albeit extreme example of a manager proactively influencing the characteristics of a game.

'Didi made the difference because he gave us balance,' said Rafa. 'Always in my teams I think about balance. People say your teams are always defending. I say, "No, what we have is balance." With balance you can defend well and attack, because you have organization. That makes you more difficult to play than anyone. How many times did we play teams when they said how tough it was to play us? Why? Because we were organized. It was not defensive. When we scored three goals in the second half in Istanbul, when we beat Real Madrid 4-0 two years later, or beating some teams 7-0, we were not defensive. The problem in the final at the beginning was we did not have that balance. In the second, we had balance. Milan had some chances with Shevchenko, but no, they did not have the same control.'

The contrast was not only in midfield. As one of the three centre-backs, Traoré was playing like a veteran, safe with his passing, timing his tackles and saving us with a goal-line clearance on 70 minutes to prevent Shevchenko restoring Milan's lead. When we reference heroism in a final we naturally focus on match-winning goals or saves, but Traoré's personal recovery from fragility to fearlessness made him one of the most unlikely and celebrated of Istanbul legends. It says so much about his personality that he shrugged off his difficult first half, at the end of which he was going to be subbed, to give the performance of his career.

Both teams could have won it in the last ten minutes. García was sent beyond Milan's defence with a sublime 50-yard pass from Gerrard. Had he controlled it, he had only Dida to beat.

Within forty seconds of that came my showdown with Crespo. For obvious reasons, that resonates with me more than it does with Hernán. 'I have never watched the match again,' he admitted. 'It is too hard for me to watch. I do remember trying to give Kaká that assist to score and he hit it over the bar. Straight after that I was substituted for Jon Dahl Tomasson.'

Unfortunately for us, the second wave of incessant Milan pressure had not yet begun. It didn't until the 86th minute, when Ancelotti introduced the versatile Brazilian Serginho on the left. The tactical switch went beyond personnel, Milan replicating our three-centre-back system, with Nesta flanked by Stam on the right and Maldini on the left. Cafu and Serginho were wide wing-backs, denying us the space we had enjoyed in those areas and putting more direct, defensive pressure on Riise and Šmicer, who had been able to focus more on attack than resistance throughout the second half.

My recollection was of this change coming earlier, probably because once Serginho was on the last few minutes of the ninety felt like an hour, and extra-time was the ultimate endurance test.

Serginho's prompt influence suggests Ancelotti should have acted sooner. In the first half the diamond cut us open, every Milan player contributing to their flawlessness. His dilemma after an hour must have been who to take off. Eventually, Ancelotti replaced Seedorf. Serginho's presence on Milan's left was a massive problem for me because Šmicer could not defend, and I could not get dragged wide and leave Shevchenko or Tomasson unoccupied. Everything we did started to look at full stretch again, my desperate tackle on Shevchenko on 87 minutes a sign of what was coming in extra-time.

Here is where Benítez made his next game-changing decision. He had seen enough of Serginho after four minutes, so at full time Gerrard was given his third position of the night, playing extra-time as our right wing-back, Šmicer moving further forward. This was an astute response.

'The difficult thing in football for a coach is making decisions during a game,' explained Benítez. 'You have a lot of people who help you before and after a game. You can organize training sessions, try to keep things dynamic and organize the team. I have always had good staff and a lot of analysts around to give information. But since being a young manager, the one thing I felt I did well was make decisions. Sometimes you change and it goes well. Sometimes it does not go so well. The key is you get more right. When the level between the teams is big, you can do nothing. When the level is similar, these substitutions and changes of system can make a massive difference. That is the difference between a normal manager, a good manager and a very good manager.'

Gerrard's duel with Serginho was critical to our survival. If Benítez had not reacted to Ancelotti's change, Milan would have won. I am sure of it.

'I understood why I was being moved there but I was getting a bit leggy,' said Gerrard. 'I knew Serginho was fast and skilful, so I was a little bit anxious. Once I knew I could match him, I settled.'

There were four crucial challenges by Gerrard on Serginho in those extra thirty minutes, preventing him from providing assists into the penalty area. When he did cross, he was forced to from deep. That was still almost enough to win the cup.

Serginho was the source of my first serious bout of cramp, after 110 minutes, forcing me to stretch to cut out his low cross. After a minute of treatment I was compelled into a replica interception from an almost identical delivery.

This was how I approached defending, always preferring to attack the ball no matter how accurate the delivery in that perilous corridor between the keeper and defenders. That is why I was vulnerable to scoring own-goals during my career. I am not embarrassed by that. That was the hazard of putting myself in danger to make a clearance, and 99 per cent of the time I could make the block, as I did in Istanbul, proving it was the right decision. I have seen plenty of centre-backs deliberately hold back a second so that they do not have to make that decision, allowing a speeding ball across the floor to glide across the 6-yard box in the hope the striker is not in a position to tap in. 'There is nothing you can do about a ball like that,' the commentators say. Yes, there is. You can throw your leg at it and forget about the risk of deflecting past your own keeper.

I could do nothing about the Serginho assist which nearly won Milan the final with the last meaningful act of extra-time, his perfect cross met by Shevchenko. Now it was Dudek's turn to become our saviour, his double save from the Ukrainian's bullet header and follow-up volley 3 yards from goal a signal that someone above was on our side.

Jerzy is sure someone was. 'I was reading the book of Karol Józef Wojtyła, Pope John Paul II, in the week before the final,' he explained. 'Coming from Poland, he was an idol to the Polish people. I had met him when I was with the national team and given him my goalkeeper shirt, because he too was a goalkeeper when he was young. He died fifty-three days before the final, so when I made that save from Shevchenko, I dedicated the save to him and named it "The Hand of Karol". Diego Maradona had his "Hand of God" and now I had the "Hand of the Pope".'

Dudek can be seen shaking his head in disbelief after making the block. 'It is because I knew it was the end of the game,' he said. 'When the ball was about to be delivered, I saw two strikers free and I was shouting at Sami [Hyypiä], but it was impossible to cover. I thought it was Tomasson who made the header. Only after the game did I know it was Shev. All I was trying to do with the rebound was make myself as big as possible. Shev hit it as hard as he could, so I just raised my hand and it deflected over. I thought, "Wow." That is the moment I wanted more than anything. Every sportsman hopes for that once in their career. A second when you can say, "Fuck, I did it. This is what I have waited all my life for." The first thing that happened next is Riise gave me a kiss!

'I said it is the bit of luck I needed. Then when I went to see my old goalkeeper coach in Holland, Pim Doesburg, he said to me, "No, remember all those years you practised. You worked five years for this. Remember all those times working on reflexes. This was not luck, it was intuition. A reaction." Maybe it was everything in one.'

For Milan, disbelief and anxiety now turned into despondency. 'When Dudek made the save from Shevchenko, I was sitting on the bench and I knew then this would not be our trophy,' said Crespo. 'With penalties, all I felt was a negative sensation.'

In Milan's previous three European Cup victories, in 2003, 1994 and 1990, they wore their all-white second kit and kicked off from left to right, from the perspective of the dugout. Maldini won the coin toss with Gerrard and switched ends to replicate that pattern, which is unusual in a cup final. Maybe he remembered those wins. Maybe he was thinking ahead. The penalties were taken at the end of the stadium where Milan's fans were situated.

Superstition lurks in cup finals. We were as delighted as the Italians with their choice because Liverpool won their previous four European Cups in all red against sides in all white. Having come from so far behind, we couldn't care less which end the penalties were taken.

My mind was preoccupied with memories of Liverpool's last European Cup final victory, in 1984, when Bruce Grobbelaar distracted the Roma takers with his wobbly legs routine, Bruno Conti and Francesco Graziani shooting over the crossbar. I gave Dudek a quickfire history lesson about Grobbelaar, urging him to try to get into the Milan players' heads. He had other priorities.

'Before the game I watched a hundred Milan penalties,' he told me. 'I watched the Milan penalties from the final with Juve in 2003 with the goalkeeper coach Ocho [José Ochotorena], and I had a book with all the names of their penalty-takers and which side they tried to score. The plan was when Ocho saw a player coming he would raise his right or left hand to signal where he would put it. I wanted to encourage whoever was coming forward to choose his favoured side.

'Then before the penalties you came and told me to put more pressure on them, saying do what Brucie did. I was just thinking, "Yes, Carra, but I have to remember what I had in my book!" I was also thinking, "This is the fucking Champions League final. I can't do Mickey Mouse things." I was not that kind of showman.'

As two years earlier, first up was Serginho.

'For the first pen I just raised my hand, shuffling a little to the left and to the right,' Dudek said. 'He tried exactly the same pen as two years earlier and hit it over the bar. I thought "OK, that went well" and played the mind games. Every time they came, I picked up the ball, handed it over and looked into their eyes. My confidence at that time was incredible. Even though Ocho was raising his hands, I was no longer looking.'

When Hamann and Cissé scored and Pirlo also missed, we were virtually at match point when Riise stepped up. Dida dived the same way, to his right, for every pen. This time he made a great save.

In our huddle on the halfway line, Gerrard was poised. Given the uncertainty around his future, his penalty had the potential to be his last kick for Liverpool. 'I was fifth up,' he said. 'Rafa asked me if I wanted one. I said, "Yeah, definitely." I left it to him which [one]. I was pleased it was the fifth. As it went on, I started to think, "It's definitely coming down to the last one." My heart was beating ten to the dozen, just telling myself to trust myself, stick to the process and all that. I didn't picture Shevchenko missing.'

Shevchenko was the match-winner in the Old Trafford shoot-out in 2003, confidently striking to Gianluigi Buffon's left. Sadly for him, his failed attempt to chip Dudek in Istanbul is as memorable.

'I wanted to stay on my feet as long as possible and I think Shev changed his mind as he moved to the ball,' said Dudek. 'I moved a little to the left and right, but did not want to go down too early. When I saved it, for the first second I did not know if that was the game over. It was only when I saw you and the other guys running towards me I realized. I was so focused on what I was doing during the penalties. In that moment, absolutely my life changed for ever.'

Into the second day of play at 12.29 a.m. on 26 May, my mum Paula Carragher's birthday, Liverpool were European champions again.

There is no better cure for cramp than the prospect of getting your hands on the European Cup. I was out of the blocks, breaking my 100m sprint record to reach Dudek, then dashing to our fans where I spotted family and friends for the first of hundreds of commemorative photographs. On the most iconic of them all, when Gerrard lifted the trophy, I was nowhere to be seen. The red ticker tape was released and the cramp caught up with me again, leaving me creased up on the podium. Instead of me standing alongside Gerrard, I see substitute Josemi on the skipper's arm.

No matter. In the immediate aftermath of a monumental victory, some players say the scale of the achievement has not yet sunk in. For me, it was instant. How could it not be? Three-nil down to that Milan team? We all knew this was a final like no other, and because it was the club's fifth European Cup, UEFA tradition declared we kept the trophy rather than handing it back after a year and swapping for a replica. Even the greatest Liverpool teams did not win like this.

'We left the dressing room two hours before and we were on the floor, we were beat,' said Hamann, who created one of the most enduring images of the evening by sharing a cigar with the Liverpool chairman. 'And then to sit in the same spot . . . I don't think there were any wild celebrations. It was just disbelief.'

'This is the most emotional final ever, no matter what is played in the future,' said Rafa. 'As a manager I am proud to be part of this team, this group and this success. Wherever I go, fans want to mention it.'

As we prepared to give the media our immediate thoughts about our contribution to football history, our former manager Houllier was near the dressing room with his brother Serge. I urged him in. Knowing how cynical football can be, I can tell you that lesser men would have been embittered by the experience of losing their job and missing out on the chance to lead the side into the Champions League. Houllier did not see our victory like that. He was more like a proud father thrilled with our success than an ex-coach seeking credit. This was not his Liverpool team any more, but he was right when he observed that it consisted largely of his players, only Xabi Alonso and Luis García among them whom he had not signed or managed. It felt right that his contribution be recognized, and as the years have passed I've never stopped feeling happy that we shared that moment.

In the Milan dressing room, where some of the players had not even bothered to collect their losers' medals, the post-mortem was under way. 'It was like a cemetery,' said Crespo. 'We all felt this season was a deception. We finished second in the league to Juventus and now we had lost the final. So, after some amazing performances, we did not reach our goals. That is difficult for any player. When everyone was going to the dressing room, I stopped and walked back to hide behind the photographers. I needed to see Steven Gerrard with the trophy. I needed it because I felt I was in some kind of dream. No, not a dream. A nightmare. I had to convince myself it happened. And yes, it did happen.

'On the coach – silence. Like someone had died. At the hotel and airport, not a beautiful scene. The fans waiting for us were angry. They shouted at Maldini. Really, at Maldini! It was bad. They said we did not play with heart or courage.

'We still had one game to play, a 1-1 draw against Udinese. Nobody wanted to.'

Crespo even considered the most extreme response of all. 'I really wanted to finish my career,' he said. 'I did not want to play any more. If you do everything to win that trophy and it is not enough, then football is impossible. For a week after, I never looked at my telephone. Step by step I recovered and rebuilt my career. It was really, really hard, but it helped me to leave Italy and return to Chelsea and start again.'

Nine of those who played in Istanbul would have their vengeance in Athens two years later, Milan beating us 2-1. I thought the teams more evenly matched going into that final, Benítez having built a stronger squad, but we could not find the same inspiration.

I know so much has already been written and said about Istanbul. In my 2008 autobiography I dedicated a chapter to it. I was still a player, then, the memories fresh. I doubted anything else in my career could eclipse it – especially the manner of the victory – but still hoped to add the Premier League.

People often ask me if my biggest regret is never winning the English title. Naturally I agree. But the more I consider it, the more I feel the tone of that question is wrong. My biggest regret is that through all of my Liverpool playing career we were never in a position where we should have won the Premier League. We were always outsiders defying rather than meeting realistic expectations, with a habit of finding a way to win even when the odds were stacked against us. We won the UEFA Cup 5-4 against Alavés despite suffering the heartache of a last-minute equalizer; scored twice in the last eight minutes to beat Arsenal 2-1 in the 2001 FA Cup final; and in the 2006 FA Cup final there were echoes of the Atatürk as Gerrard inspired a comeback from 2-0 down against West Ham United, Hamann again coming off the bench and the captain equalizing in the last minute before we won a penalty shoot-out after a 3-3 draw.

The character and mentality of our side were not unique to 2005. It was in the DNA of the team, and we made it synonymous with the Anfield era between 2001 and 2010. I love that.

'We did not have the quality of Manchester United, Barcelona and Bayern Munich,' said Didi Hamann, 'We had to work one hundred per cent right to the end for everything we got in ninety-nine out of a hundred games. Over thirty-eight games you can't do it. But in a one-off game? I don't think there was a more spirited team than us.'

I said earlier that without Houllier there would have been no Benítez, and without Benítez there would have been no Istanbul.

I would extend that.

Without Istanbul and its legacy, restoring our elite European status, I am not sure Liverpool would have caught the attention and imagination of Jürgen Klopp, with his passion for emotional football. He faced his own daunting Anfield revival project when he walked through those

Shankly Gates ten years later. No young manager on the outside looking in could have failed to be drawn to the passion of those European nights, lured to Anfield's possibilities.

I was part of a new generation fed up with hearing ex-players telling us how great Liverpool were in previous decades, every summer bringing another anniversary of a title or European win. 'I want to tell my kids my own stories,' I said in a TV interview before that final. 'Decades from now, I want to be able to talk about how I won the European Cup with Liverpool. I want to play my part in the greatest games.'

There are none greater than the 2005 Champions League final.

Job done.

MATCH DETAILS

Tuesday, 7 May 2019
2018/19 UEFA Champions League semi-final, second leg
– Anfield –

Attendance: 52,212   *Referee*: Cüneyt Çakir

LIVERPOOL 4 – 0 BARCELONA
(Liverpool win 4 – 3 on aggregate)

Origi *7, 79*
Wijnaldum *54, 56*

Liverpool	**Barcelona**
Manager: Jürgen Klopp	*Manager*: Ernesto Valverde

	Liverpool			Barcelona
GK *1*	Alisson Becker		GK *1*	Marc-André ter Stegen
RB *66*	Trent Alexander-Arnold		DF *20*	Sergi Roberto
CB *32*	Joël Matip ʏ c		DF *3*	Gerard Piqué
CB *4*	Virgil van Dijk		DF *15*	Clément Lenglet
LB *26*	Andrew Robertson ▼ *45*		DF *18*	Jordi Alba
DM *14*	Jordan Henderson (c)		MF *22*	Arturo Vidal ▼ *75*
CM *3*	Fabinho ʏ c		MF *5*	Sergio Busquets ʏ c
CM *7*	James Milner		MF *4*	Ivan Rakiti ʏ c ▼ *80*
RW *23*	Xherdan Shaqiri ▼ *90*		MF *7*	Philippe Coutinho ▼ *60*
LW *27*	Divock Origi ▼ *85*		FW *10*	Lionel Messi (c)
ST *10*	Sadio Mané		FW *9*	Luis Suárez

Substitutions

	Liverpool			Barcelona
CM *5*	Georginio Wijnaldum ▲ *45*		DF *2*	Nélson Semedo ▲ *60* ʏ c
LB *12*	Joe Gomez ▲ *85*		MF *8*	Arthur Melo ▲ *75*
FW *15*	Daniel Sturridge ▲ *90*		FW *14*	Malcom ▲ *80*

Wednesday, 24 April 1985

1984/85 European Cup Winners' Cup semi-final, second leg
– Goodison Park –

Attendance: 49,476   *Referee*: Erik Fredriksson

EVERTON 3 – 1 BAYERN MUNICH
(Everton win 3 – 1 on aggregate)

Sharp *48*	Hoeness *38*
Gray *73*	
Steven *86*	

Everton	Bayern Munich
Manager: Howard Kendall	*Manager*: Udo Lattek
GK *1* Neville Southall	GK *1* Jean-Marie Pfaff
CB *5* Derek Mountfield	DF *5* Klaus Augenthaler (c)
LB *3* Pat Van Den Hauwe	DF *3* Holger Willmer ▼ *66*
RB *2* Gary Stevens	DF *7* Hans Pflügler Y █ c
CB *4* Kevin Ratcliffe (c)	DF *4* Norbert Eder ▼ *73*
CM *10* Paul Bracewell	MF *2* Wolfgang Dremmler
RM *7* Trevor Steven	MF *10* Norbert Nachtweih
LM *11* Kevin Sheedy	MF *8* Lothar Matthäus
CM *6* Peter Reid	MF *6* Søren Lerby
CF *9* Andy Gray Y █ c	FW *11* Ludwig Kögl
CF *8* Graeme Sharp	FW *9* Dieter Hoeness

Substitutions

DF *13* Bertram Beierlorzer ▲ *66*
FW *15* Michael Rummenigge ▲ *73*

Friday, 26 May 1989

1988/89 Football League, First Division

– Anfield –

Attendance: 41,7835   *Referee*: David Hutchinson

LIVERPOOL 0 – 2 ARSENAL

Smith *52*

Thomas *90+1*

Liverpool	Arsenal
Manager: Kenny Dalglish	*Manager*: George Graham

GK *1*	Bruce Grobbelaar	GK *1*	John Lukic
CB *2*	Gary Ablett	SW *5*	David O'Leary
RB *4*	Steve Nicol	RB *2*	Lee Dixon
CB *6*	Alan Hansen	CB *6*	Tony Adams (c)
LB *3*	Steve Staunton	CB *10*	Steve Bould ▼ *76*
RM *7*	Sergio Busquets	LB *3*	Nigel Winterburn
CM *5*	Ronnie Whelan (c)	MF *4*	Michael Thomas
CM *11*	Steve McMahon	MF *7*	David Rocastle
LM *10*	John Barnes	MF *8*	Kevin Richardson
CF *8*	John Aldridge	MF *11*	Paul Merson ▼ *73*
CF *9*	Ian Rush ▼ *32*	CF *9*	Alan Smith

Substitutions

FW *14*	Peter Beardsley ▲ *32*	MF *14*	Martin Hayes ▲ *73*
		MF *12*	Perry Groves ▲ *76*

Saturday, 1 September 2001

2002 FIFA World Cup qualifier, Group 9

– Olympiastadion, Munich –

Attendance: 63,000   *Referee*: Pierluigi Collina

GERMANY 1 – 5 ENGLAND

Jancker *6*

Owen *12, 48, 66*

Gerrard *45+4*

Heskey *74*

Germany	England
Manager: Rudi Völler	*Manager*: Sven-Göran Eriksson

	Germany			England	
GK 1	Oliver Kahn (c)		GK 1	David Seaman	
CB 2	Christian Wörns ▼ 45		RB 2	Gary Neville	
LWB 3	Jörg Böhme		LB 3	Ashley Cole	
CB 4	Thomas Linke		CM 4	Steven Gerrard ▼ 78	
CB 5	Jens Nowotny		CB 5	Rio Ferdinand	
CM 6	Dietmar Hamann Y c		CB 6	Sol Campbell	
RWB 7	Marko Rehmer		RM 7	David Beckham (c)	
CM 8	Michael Ballack ▼ 65		CM 8	Paul Scholes ▼ 83	
CF 9	Carsten Jancker		CF 9	Emile Heskey Y c	
AM 10	Sebastian Deisler		CF 10	Michael Owen	
CF 11	Oliver Neuville ▼ 78		LM 11	Nicky Barmby ▼ 64	

	Substitutions			*Substitutions*	
MF 14	Gerald Asamoah ▲ 45		MF 16	Steve McManaman ▲ 64	
FW 18	Miroslav Klose ▲ 65		MF 14	Owen ▲ 78	
DF 15	Sebastian Kehl ▲ 78		DF 15	Jamie Carragher ▲ 83	

Tuesday, 18 June 1996
1996 UEFA European Championship, Group A
– Wembley Stadium –

Attendance: 76,798   *Referee*: Gerd Grabher

ENGLAND 4 – 1 HOLLAND

Shearer *23* (pen), *57*   Kluivert *78*
Sheringham *51, 62*

England	Holland
Manager: Terry Venables	*Manager*: Guus Hiddink

		England				Holland
GK	1	David Seaman		GK	1	Edwin van der Sar
RB	2	Gary Neville		RB	2	Michael Reiziger
CB	5	Tony Adams (c)		CB	3	Danny Blind (c) Y c
CB	6	Gareth Southgate Y c		LB	15	Winston Bogarde
LB	3	Stuart Pearce		RM	6	Ronald de Boer ▼ 73
RM	11	Darren Anderton		CM	4	Clarence Seedorf
CM	4	Paul Ince Y c ▼ 68		CM	12	Aron Winter Y c
CM	8	Paul Gascoigne		LM	14	Richard Witschge ▼ 46
LM	17	Steve McManaman		RF	17	Jordi Cruyff
CF	10	Teddy Sheringham Y c ▼ 77		CF	10	Dennis Bergkamp Y c
CF	9	Alan Shearer ▼ 76		LF	11	Peter Hoekstra ▼ 72

		Substitutions				Substitutions
MF	7	David Platt ▲ 68		DF	18	Johan de Kock ▲ 46
MF	14	Nicky Barmby ▲ 76		FW	9	Patrick Kluivert ▲ 72
FW	21	Robbie Fowler ▲ 77		MF	20	Phillip Cocu ▲ 73

Saturday, 20 May 1989

1989 FA Cup final

– Wembley Stadium –

Attendance: 82,800   *Referee*: Joe Worrall

LIVERPOOL 3 – 2 EVERTON

Aldridge *4*   McCall *90, 102*

Rush *95, 104*

Liverpool	Everton
Manager: Kenny Dalglish	*Manager*: Colin Harvey

GK 1	Bruce Grobbelaar		GK 1	Neville Southall	
CB 2	Gary Ablett		RB 2	Neil McDonald	
LB 3	Steve Staunton ▼ 90		LB 3	Pat Van Den Hauwe	
RB 4	Steve Nicol		CB 4	Kevin Ratcliffe (c)	
CM 5	Ronnie Whelan (c)		CB 5	Dave Watson	
CB 6	Alan Hansen		CM 6	Paul Bracewell ▼ 59	
CF 7	Peter Beardsley		RM 7	Pat Nevin	
CF 8	John Aldridge ▼ 73		CM 8	Trevor Steven	
RM 9	Ray Houghton		CF 9	Graeme Sharp	
LM 10	John Barnes		CF 10	Tony Cottee	
CM 11	Steve McMahon		LM 11	Kevin Sheedy ▼ 78	

Substitutions	Substitutions
FW 14 Ian Rush ▲ 73	MF 14 Stuart McCall ▲ 59
DF 12 Barry Venison ▲ 90	MF 12 Ian Wilson ▲ 78

Wednesday, 26 May 1999

1999 UEFA Champions League final

— Nou Camp, Barcelona —

Attendance: 90,245   *Referee*: Pierluigi Collina

MANCHESTER UNITED 2 – 1 BAYERN MUNICH

Sheringham *90+1*	Basler *6*
Solskjaer *90+3*	

Manchester United	Bayern Munich
Manager: Alex Ferguson	*Manager*: Ottmar Hitzfeld

	Manchester United		Bayern Munich
GK 1	Peter Schmeichel (c)	*GK 1*	Oliver Kahn (c)
RB 2	Gary Neville	*SW 10*	Lothar Matthäus ▼ *80*
CB 5	Ronny Johnsen	*RB 2*	Markus Babbel
CB 6	Jaap Stam	*CB 25*	Thomas Linke
LB 3	Denis Irwin	*CB 4*	Samuel Kuffour
RM 11	Ryan Giggs	*LB 18*	Michael Tarnat
CM 7	David Beckham	*CM 11*	Stefan Effenberg Y c
CM 8	Nicky Butt	*CM 16*	Jens Jeremies
LM 15	Jesper Blomqvist ▼ *67*	*RW 14*	Mario Basler ▼ *87*
CF 19	Dwight Yorke	*CF 19*	Carsten Jancker
CF 9	Andy Cole ▼ *81*	*LW 21*	Alexander Zickler ▼ *71*

	Substitutions		*Substitutions*
FW 10	Teddy Sheringham ▲ *67*	*MF 7*	Mehmet Scholl ▲ *71*
FW 20	Ole Gunnar Solskjaer ▲ *81*	*MF 17*	Thorsten Fink ▲ *80*
		MF 20	Hasan Salihamidžić ▲ *87*

Wednesday, 3 April 1996

1995/96 FA Premier League

– Anfield –

Attendance: 40,702   *Referee*: Mike Reed

LIVERPOOL 4 – 3 NEWCASTLE UNITED

Fowler 2, 55	Ferdinand 10
Collymore 68, 90+2	Ginola 14
	Asprilla 57

Liverpool	Newcastle United
Manager: Roy Evans	*Manager*: Kevin Keegan

	Liverpool			Newcastle United
GK 1	David James		GK 1	Pavel Srníček
CB 5	Mark Wright ▼ 45		RB 19	Steve Watson
CB 12	John Scales		CB 6	Steve Howey ▼ 82
CB 25	Neil Ruddock		CB 27	Philippe Albert
RM 4	Jason McAteer		LB 3	John Beresford
CM 15	Jamie Redknapp		RM 8	Peter Beardsley Y C
CM 10	John Barnes (c)		CM 22	David Batty Y C
LM 2	Rob Jones ▼ 85		CM 7	Robert Lee (c)
AM 17	Steve McManaman		LM 14	David Ginola
CF 8	Stan Collymore		CF 11	Faustino Asprilla
CF 23	Robbie Fowler		CF 9	Les Ferdinand Y C

	Substitutions			**Substitutions**
DF 22	Steve Harkness ▲ 45		DF 4	Darren Peacock ▲ 82
FW 9	Ian Rush ▲ 85			

Sunday, 13 May 2012
2011/12 FA Premier League
– The Etihad Stadium –

Attendance: 48,000   *Referee*: Mike Dean

MANCHESTER CITY 3 – 2 QUEENS PARK RANGERS

Zabaleta *39*	Cissé *48*
Džeko *90+2*	Mackie *66*
Agüero *90+4*	

Manchester City	**Queens Park Rangers**
Manager: Roberto Mancini	*Manager*: Mark Hughes

GK	25	Joe Hart	GK	1	Paddy Kenny
RB	5	Pablo Zabaleta	RB	42	Nedum Onuoha
DF	4	Vincent Kompany (c)	DF	35	Anton Ferdinand
DF	6	Joleon Lescott	DF	3	Clint Hill
LB	22	Gaël Clichy	LB	34	Taye Taiwo
AM	19	Samir Nasri	RW/CM	32	Shaun Wright-Phillips
CM	42	Yaya Touré ▼ 44	CM	17	Joey Barton (c) R ▮ c
MF	18	Gareth Barry ▼ 69	CM	4	Shaun Derry
MF	21	David Villa	RM	12	Jamie Mackie
FW	32	Carlos Tevez ▼ 75	FW	23	Djibril Cissé ▼ 59
FW	16	Sergio Agüero Y ▮ c	CF	52	Bobby Zamora ▼ 76

Substitutions	**Substitutions**

CM	34	Nigel de Jong ▲ 44	LM	13	Armand Traoré ▼ 59
FW	10	Edin Džeko ▲ 69	FW	10	Jay Bothroyd ▲ 76 Y ▮ c
FW	45	Mario Balotelli ▲ 75			

Saturday, 28 May 2011
2011 UEFA Champions League final
– Wembley Stadium –

Attendance: 87,695   *Referee*: Viktor Kassai

BARCELONA 3 – 1 MANCHESTER UNITED

Pedro 27   Rooney 34
Messi 54
Villa 69

Barcelona	Manchester United
Manager: Pep Guardiola	*Manager*: Sir Alex Ferguson

	Barcelona			Manchester United
GK 1	Victor Valdéz ʏ c	GK 1	Edwin van der Sar
RB 2	Dani Alvez ʏ c ▼ 88	RB 20	Fábio ▼ 69
CB 14	Javier Mascherano	CB 5	Rio Ferdinand
CB 3	Gerard Piqué	CB 15	Nemanja Vidic (c)
LB 22	Eric Abedal	LD 3	Patrice Evra
DM 16	Sergio Busquets	RM 25	Antonio Valencia ʏ c
CM 6	Xavi (c)	CM 16	Michael Carrick ʏ c ▼ 77
CM 8	Andrés Iniesta	CM 11	Ryan Giggs
RF 7	David Villa ▼ 86	LM 13	Park Ji-sung
CF 10	Lionel Messi	SS 10	Wayne Rooney
LF 17	Pedro ▼ 90+2	CF 14	Javier Hernández

	Substitutions		Substitutions
MF 15	Seydou Keita ▲ 86	MF 17	Nani ▲ 69
DF 5	Carles Puyol ▲ 88	MF 18	Paul Scholes ▲ 77
MF 20	Ibrahim Afellay ▲ 90+2		

Wednesday, 25 May 2005

2005 UEFA Champions League final

– Atatürk Olympic Stadium, Istanbul –

Attendance: 69,000   *Referee*: Manuel Mejuto González

AC MILAN 3 – 3 LIVERPOOL

Maldini *1*	Gerrard *54*
Crespo *39, 44*	Šmicer *56*
	Alonso *60*

Penalties

Serginho ✘	Hamann ✔
Pirlo ✘	Cissé ✔
Tomasson ✔	Riise ✘
Kaká ✔	Šmicer ✔
Shevchenko ✘	

Liverpool won 3 – 2 on penalties

AC Milan	**Liverpool**
Manager: Carlo Ancelotti	*Manager*: Rafael Benítez
GK *1* Dida	GK *1* Jerzy Dudek
RB *2* Cafu	RB *3* Steve Finnan ▼ *46*
CB *31* Jaap Stam	CB *23* Jamie Carragher ʏ▮c
CB *13* Alessandro Nesta	CB *4* Sami Hyypiä
LB *3* Paolo Maldini (c)	LB *21* Djimi Traoré
DM *21* Andrea Pirlo	DM *14* Xabi Alonso
RM *8* Gennaro Gattuso ▼ *112*	RM *10* Luis García
LM *20* Clarence Seedorf ▼ *86*	CM *8* Steven Gerrard (c)
AM *22* Kaká	LM *6* John Arne Riise
CF *7* Andriy Shevchenko	AM *7* Harry Kewell ▼ *23*
CF *11* Hernán Crespo ▼ *85*	CF *5* Milan Baroš ʏ▮c *85*
Substitutions	***Substitutions***
FW *15* Jon Dahl Tomasson ▲ *85*	FW *11* Vladimir Šmicer ▲ *23*
MF *27* Serginho ▲ *86*	MF *16* Dietmar Hamann ▲ *46*
MF *10* Rui Costa ▲ *112*	FW *9* Djibril Cissé ▲ *85*

ACKNOWLEDGEMENTS

Special thanks to all the players, managers, executives, TV producers, match officials, commentators and journalists who agreed to be interviewed, to share their memories, or to provide background material for these great games. I am grateful to John Aldridge, Markus Babbel, Geoff Banwell, John Barnes, Joey Barton, David Beckham, Oakley Cannonier, Stan Collymore, Michael Cox, Hernán Crespo, Adam Crozier, Ronald de Boer, Jerzy Dudek, Trevor East, Les Ferdinand, Robbie Fowler, Steven Gerrard, George Graham, Dietmar Hamann, Martin Hardy, Jordan Henderson, Xavi Hernández, Dieter Hoeness, Graham Hunter, Paul Joyce, Jürgen Klopp, Vincent Kompany, Amy Lawrence, Gabriele Marcotti, Brian Marwood, Javier Mascherano, Matt McCann, Simon Mullock, Gary Neville, Michael Owen, Kevin Ratcliffe, Peter Reid, Wayne Rooney, Ian Rush, Graeme Sharp, Teddy Sheringham, Geoff Shreeves, Alan Smith, Michael Thomas, Clive Tyldesley, Martin Tyler and Tom Werner.

Thanks to literary agent James Wills from Watson, Little, and the Transworld team, including Henry Vines and copy-editor Daniel Balado.

Scott Melvin, Jack Shreeves and Rio Clarke from Buzz16 Productions provided invaluable research across all eleven fixtures.

Many thanks to Chris Bascombe of the *Daily* and *Sunday Telegraph* for working with me on this project and putting my thoughts and analysis into words. Chris would like to thank his wife Paula, for her proofreading expertise, and his ten-year-old son Alistair, for enthusiastically checking the number of successful Fabinho tackles in the Liverpool v. Barcelona match!

And finally, thank you to my wife, Nicola, and daughter, Mia, for putting up with me watching even more football over the last few months, and my son, James, for spotting the moment when AC Milan went to three at the back in Istanbul!

ABOUT THE AUTHOR

Jamie Carragher was born on 28 January 1978 and after making his way through Liverpool's youth ranks made his debut for the first team aged eighteen. He played over seven hundred games for Liverpool, the second-most of any player in the club's history, winning the Champions League as well as ten other major trophies. He also made thirty-eight appearances for England.

Since retirement, Jamie has gone on to become one of the country's top football pundits and analysts. He was voted 'Pundit of the Year' by the Football Supporters' Association in 2016, 2017 and 2019, and was part of the Sky Sports team that won the RTS Award for Best Sports Programme for *Monday Night Football*. He is the host of the number one podcast *The Greatest Game with Jamie Carragher* and is a columnist for the *Daily Telegraph*.

ENGLAND 4
HOLLAND 1
1996

LIVERPOOL 3
EVERTON 2
1989